12-95

SUBJECT, TH

CON

CW01476099

Subject, Thought, and Context

EDITED BY

PHILIP PETTIT

AND

JOHN McDOWELL

CLARENDON PRESS · OXFORD
1986

Oxford University Press, Walton Street, Oxford OX2 6DP
Oxford New York Toronto
Delhi Bombay Calcutta Madras Karachi
Petaling Jaya Singapore Hong Kong Tokyo
Nairobi Dar es Salaam Cape Town
Melbourne Auckland
and associated companies in
Beirut Berlin Ibadan Nicosia

Oxford is a trade mark of Oxford University Press

Published in the United States
by Oxford University Press, New York
© *in this collection Oxford University Press 1986*

British Library Cataloguing in Publication Data
Subject, thought, and context.
1. Mind and body   2. Intellect
I. Pettit, Philip   II. McDowell, John
128'.2   BF161
ISBN 0-19-824736-2
ISBN 0-19-824944-6 Pbk

Library of Congress Cataloging in Publication Data
Subject, thought, and context.
Includes index.
1. Thought and thinking.   2. Knowledge, Theory of.
I. Pettit, Philip, 1945–   .   II. McDowell, John Henry.
B105.T54S82 1986   121   86-8783
ISBN 0-19-824736-2
ISBN 0-19-824944-6 (pbk.)

Set by Eta Services (Typesetters) Ltd, Beccles, Suffolk
Printed in Great Britain
at the University Press, Oxford
by David Stanford
Printer to the University

CONTENTS

LIST OF CONTRIBUTORS

PHILIP PETTIT is a Professor in the Research School of Social Sciences at the Australian National University, Canberra.

GREGORY MCCULLOCH is a Lecturer in Philosophy at the University of Leicester.

JENNIFER HORNSBY is a Fellow of Corpus Christi College, Oxford.

TYLER BURGE is a Professor of Philosophy at the University of California, Los Angeles.

JOHN MCDOWELL is a Fellow of University College, Oxford.

DAVID WIGGINS is a Fellow of University College, Oxford.

CHRISTOPHER PEACOCKE is Professor of Philosophy at King's College, London.

CRISPIN WRIGHT is Professor of Logic and Metaphysics at the University of St. Andrews.

JONATHAN LEAR is a Professor of Philosophy at Yale University.

INTRODUCTION

1. The contributors to this volume were asked to touch on some aspect or other of a problem area which has been much fought over in recent philosophy of mind. In this Introduction we aim to sketch the general shape of the terrain. We do not presume to speak for our fellow contributors, nor do we confine ourselves to what we suppose they would all accept. Our hope is that a partisan overview may help readers to place and appreciate the essays which follow.

2. A landmark we can begin from is Hilary Putnam's question 'Are meanings in the head?'[1] The answer 'No' gives vivid expression to a thesis Putnam urges about natural-kind words: namely that their meaning, on an individual's lips, is such that each is true of the actual instances of the relevant kind, demarcated as it would be by the best scientific taxonomy, whether or not these are the instances that would be determined by the individual's own conception of the kind.[2] 'In the head' serves here as a shorthand tag for a familiar picture of psychological facts (in a strict sense) as facts about individuals which hold independently of their relation to the external world: that is, we may say, as narrow facts.[3] According to Putnam's thesis, someone's meaning what he does by a natural-kind word is partly determined by a scientifically ascertainable fact about the world he lives in. So it cannot be a psychological fact on that

---

[1] See 'The Meaning of "Meaning"', in Hilary Putnam, *Mind, Language and Reality* (CUP, Cambridge, 1975), 215–71.

[2] Besides 'The Meaning of "Meaning"', see also 'Is Semantics Possible?', *Mind, Language and Reality*, 139–52. Similar ideas were independently expressed, about the same time, by Saul Kripke: see the third lecture in his *Naming and Necessity* (Basil Blackwell, Oxford, 1980). The main point can be found in Leibniz: see Chapter 3 of David Wiggins, *Sameness and Substance* (Basil Blackwell, Oxford, 1980).

[3] Putnam's initial attempt to formulate the conception is at p. 220 of *Mind, Language and Reality*. It is not very felicitous: see, for example, p. 246 of Jerry A. Fodor, 'Methodological Solipsism considered as a Research Strategy in Cognitive Psychology', in his *Representations* (Harvester Press, Hassocks, 1981), 225–53; and, for the idea expressed here, p. 228, where Fodor rightly attributes the idea to Descartes.

familiar conception: 'Cut the pie any way you like, "meanings" just ain't in the *head*!'[4]

To emphasize the point, Putnam exploits what has since become a standard philosophical genre, the Twin Earth thought experiment. Consider a scientifically uneducated speaker of English: he uses 'water' to mean what he takes, correctly, to be a stuff with a specific nature, conspicuously present in a more or less pure form in various parts of the world—in fact *water*, which is (though he does not know it) H_2O. Now imagine that his environment had been different in this way: where his actual environment contains water, the imagined environment contains a stuff superficially indistinguishable from it but with a quite different chemical composition. Had this been so, what is 'in his head' would not have been relevantly different.[5] But he would not have meant by 'water' the stuff he actually means by it, namely water (that is, H_2O); he would have meant the different stuff envisaged in the counterfactual supposition. So his meaning what he does by 'water' cannot be a state of affairs 'in his head'.[6]

3. Putnam's conclusion puts pressure on that familiar conception of the psychological, because it seems right, intuitively, to classify meaning what one does by a word as a state of mind.[7] Now if we stand by that intuition, and accept Putnam's thesis, we have a choice between two ways of responding to the pressure.

---

[4] Putnam, *Mind, Language and Reality*, 227.

[5] It would be captious to worry about whether the alteration which the supposition effects can be restricted to the environment, in view of the large amount of water in our physical composition.

[6] In this first version of the thought experiment, we consider only the physical environment. Putnam's own view is more complex than this might suggest, as will emerge; but it is useful to approach the complexity by degrees. Note that we have stated the thought experiment in terms of a counterfactual supposition varying the environment of a given subject. Another version (for which the 'Twin Earth' label is indeed more appropriate) envisages a *Doppelgänger* elsewhere in the actual universe. The difference matters for some purposes, but it will not affect any point we want to make.

[7] The case is thus not immediately similar to that of factive states like knowledge. The idea that knowledge is not a pure mental state (since it embraces an external fact) is more immediately natural than the idea that meaning something by a word is not a pure mental state. Not that the former idea (which is often appealed to as a parallel to the first of the two responses distinguished in the text) is quite unproblematic; but we shall not go into that here.

According to the first, meaning what one does by a natural-kind word has been revealed to be composite. The state of affairs in question is partly constituted by a psychological state—in the narrow sense associated with the conception that has come under pressure—and partly by relations between the individual and the external world. Something's being the state of mind it is cannot be purely a matter of how things are 'in the head', if meaning what one does by a natural-kind word is an example. Still, meaning what one does by a natural-kind word can be a configuration 'in the head', which is appropriately characterized as that state of mind by virtue of its external relations. There are many variations on this theme, but we shall not go into detail.[8]

That first response protects a form of the conception that has come under pressure: it incorporates a narrow psychological fact in a composite picture of the problem cases. Some version of this is often represented as the only possible way of accommodating Putnam's thesis.[9] But there is, as we said, a choice. The alternative response takes Putnam's conclusion to call into question altogether the credentials of that conception of the psychological, even as affording only one component in a composite picture of the relevant states of mind. Need there be a psychological state of that kind even partly constituting one's meaning what one does by a natural-kind word? No doubt what is 'in the head' is causally relevant to states of mind. But must we suppose that it has any constitutive relevance to them?

4. It can be difficult even to make visible the possibility of responding in this second way. That indicates how dominant is the familiar conception of the psychological which is protected by the first response. The attraction of that conception shows itself in various ways, but all seem to derive ultimately from some such thought as this: only on the lines of the first response can one hope to bring the phenomena Putnam notes within the purview of an investigation of the mental that might count as scientific.

---

[8] For a good sample of the possibilities, see Andrew Woodfield (ed.), *Thought and Object* (Clarendon Press, Oxford, 1982).

[9] This seems to be Putnam's own view: see, for example, *Mind, Language and Reality*, 227, and *Reason, Truth and History* (CUP, Cambridge, 1981), 18.

Given the usual paradigms of science, whose status as such we do not here want to dispute, that thought is highly plausible.[10] But it merely pushes the question one stage further back. Why should we accept that we can establish the reality of states of mind only by accommodating our talk about them to the usual paradigms of science?[11] Some of our contributors discuss such questions, and their discussions provide material for a less sketchy picture of the way of thinking that obscures the possibility of the second response; but we shall take this no further here.

5. We can formulate Putnam's thesis as follows: one's meaning what one does by a natural-kind word, though intuitively a state of mind, is *world-involving*. This is because it partly depends on the actual scientifically discoverable nature of something in the external world. (This formulation is neutral between the two kinds of response we have distinguished.)

How can someone have got his mind around the nature in question, though ignorant perhaps of the science that demarcates it? An answer would point to ways in which exemplifications of the nature have figured in the subject's cognitive and practical dealings with the world.[12] If we had given such an answer in detail, we would be in a position to say: he means the word as a word for *that stuff*, or for members of *that species*.

These demonstrative expressions are suggestive; for quite similar sorts of cognitive and practical relations underlie the possibility of crediting subjects with propositional attitudes in whose contents particular objects figure under demonstrative modes of presentation (to use a Fregean phrase). An example is the state ascribed by 'Henry believes this pen is valuable', said when the pen in question is

[10] It can be overstated. Fodor, in 'Methodological Solipsism . . .', argues that even within the framework of the first response the possibility of a scientific psychology is restricted to what is intra-individual, on the basis of an assumption that, for example, salt can be law-instantiating only under descriptions like 'NaCl'. This unwarrantably ignores descriptions on the lines of 'the stuff that has been related to so and so in such and such ways'. See Gareth Evans's reply to Fodor, in *The Behavioral and Brain Sciences*, iii (1980); and Christopher Peacocke, 'Demonstrative Thought and Psychological Explanation', *Synthese*, xlix (1981), 187–217.

[11] Notice that this is not an incipient recommendation of instrumentalism. It is tendentious to assume that the issue of realism about mental states and events is the issue of whether they are amenable to realistically construable *scientific* theory.

[12] Not necessarily first-hand dealings; but we are still suppressing the social environment.

visible by speaker, audience, and Henry.[13] Such propositional attitudes seem to be world-involving, in a sense parallel to that in which
Putnam's cases are. This puts pressure in a parallel way on the conception of the psychological as independent of the external world.
And here likewise there is a choice between a parallel pair of responses.[14]

It seems plausible that it is this parallel Putnam is aiming at when
he proposes that natural-kind words are indexical.[15] In fact the proposal seems off target. The parallel was originally suggested by a
natural occurrence of demonstratives; but the idea that propositional attitudes can be world-involving by virtue of being directed at
particular objects has a plausibility that is not restricted to cases
where there would be overt indexicality in a verbal expression of a
propositional attitude's content.[16] And, on the other side, there
seems to be no good sense in which natural-kind words can be made
out to be indexical.[17] But a flaw in Putnam's attempt to capture it
should not undermine the parallel itself.

One unfortunate effect of the parallel, particularly if it is formulated in terms of indexicality, is to encourage a blindness to the possibility of the second line of response; this is because versions of the
first response are especially strongly entrenched for the case of

[13] There is a complication here: it might be suggested that 'this pen' in the envisaged circumstances cannot be associated by anyone other than Henry with the
mode of presentation under which the pen figures in Henry's belief, since no one else
quite shares Henry's point of view. But the notion of the same mode of presentation
need not be used like this. And even if it is, such a form of words, in context, is still
intelligible as indirectly indicating a mode of presentation under which the pen figures
in Henry's thinking—part of the content of his thought. It is quite wrong to say, with,
for example, Fodor, 'Cognitive Science and the Twin-Earth Problem', *Notre Dame
Journal of Formal Logic*, xxiii (1982), 98–118, at pp. 116–17 (n. 10), that indexical
expressions always occur transparently in the attribution of propositional attitudes.

[14] The first response will tend to favour the way of thinking about indexicality developed by David Kaplan, in his unpublished monograph 'Demonstratives'; for a useful survey of work in this tradition, see Nathan U. Salmon, *Reference and Essence*
(Basil Blackwell, Oxford, 1982). The other response will tend to find congenial the
approach of Gareth Evans, *The Varieties of Reference* (Clarendon Press, Oxford,
1982).

[15] Putnam, *Mind, Language and Reality*, 229–35.

[16] Another plausible case involves proper names in the specification of content,
with participation in a communal practice as what carries the subject's mind, so to
speak, to the object; see Kripke, *Naming and Necessity*. But this case cannot come
fully into view until we stop suppressing the importance of the social context.

[17] See, for example, Tyler Burge, 'Other Bodies', in Woodfield (ed.), *Thought and
Object*, 97–120, at 103–7.

propositional attitudes with demonstratively expressible contents. It may be worth mentioning one bad reason for this. An insufficiently discriminating use of the jargon '*de re*' induces a conflation of two quite different ideas: first, the idea that a propositional attitude with a demonstratively specifiable content is *de re*, in the sense that it is world-involving by virtue of being directed at a particular object; and, second, the idea that in the attribution of such a propositional attitude the demonstrative occurs outside the specification of content in the strictest sense (in the sort of way made explicit by forms like 'Henry believes, of this pen, that it is valuable'). The former idea leaves room for the second line of response; the latter is tailor-made for the first.[18]

6. What comes under pressure in the two ways we have mentioned is a conception of psychological facts as facts about individuals that hold independently of their relation to the external world. Now Putnam's suggestion is that there are two defects here: not only the discounting of the *physical* environment, on which we have been concentrating so far, but also the discounting of the *social* environment involved in conceiving psychological facts to be facts about individuals taken by themselves.[19]

It is in the latter connection that Putnam introduces what he calls 'the division of linguistic labor'.[20] In the case of natural-kind words, what this amounts to is that ordinary speakers intend that the extension of their words should be what experts would determine. That seems correct, and it is an instance of a general phenomenon that seems highly important. However, there is a difficult question, which

---

[18] The distinction cuts two ways: one cannot properly support the claim that a state of mind is object-involving in itself by appealing to the possibility of attributing it transparently, and some people may have wanted to do this. But clearing away this faulty argument does not impugn the object-involvingness of the relevant mental states. Notice that Burge endorses a version of the defusing sort of response, in the case of propositional attitudes with demonstratively expressible content: see p. 86 of 'Individualism and the Mental', in *Midwest Studies in Philosophy*, vol. IV (1979), 73–121; and p. 97 of 'Other Bodies'. The background of this is a framework imposed in Burge's 'Belief *De Re*', *Journal of Philosophy*, lxxiv (1977), 338–62; for a protest, see John McDowell, '*De Re* Senses', *Philosophical Quarterly*, xxxiv (1984), 283–94. The upshot is that the only 'grain of truth' Burge can find in Putnam's attempt to capture the parallel is a point about the introduction of natural-kind terms, and this misses the intuition about world-involvingness.

[19] See Putnam, *Mind, Language and Reality*, 271.

[20] Putnam, *Mind, Language and Reality*, 227–9.

this insight of Putnam's does not resolve, about how the roles of the social environment and the physical environment in individual psychology should be understood to be related.

This is a good point to introduce our second landmark: a series of articles by Tyler Burge, in which he focuses explicitly on the importance of the social environment for a proper understanding of an individual's mental states.[21] What Burge does is to give a new twist to the Twin Earth genre.

Suppose someone with a general competence in English would assent to many sentences containing 'arthritis' which, as used by him, would be true. This makes it reasonable to credit him with beliefs, and more generally propositional attitudes, in specifying whose content we would use 'arthritis'. Now suppose he comes to affirm 'My arthritis has spread to my thigh'. In fact arthritis affects only the joints, so his utterance betrays some sort of misunderstanding. Does that preclude attributing to him the false belief that his arthritis has spread to his thigh? Ordinary practice would suggest not.

But now imagine that our subject's world had been exactly like the one we began by placing him in (in effect ours) except that in the imagined world 'arthritis' is correctly used in the subject's community for any rheumatoid ailment, of joint or limb. Had this been so, what is 'in his head' would not have been different. But his claim 'My arthritis has spread to my thigh' would have expressed a belief that might be true. He would simply not have had beliefs whose contents could be correctly given in terms of the notion of *arthritis* (that is, a rheumatoid ailment of the joints). Under a counterfactual supposition that varies the actual situation only in respect of the subject's social environment, we see that the contents of his mental states would have been different. So social context is revealed as constitutive of content, not external to it.

7. Notice that Burge's case for this conclusion does not turn on any naturalness of the kind *arthritis*. In fact the classification effected by 'arthritis' is not particularly natural: the term is used for a family of disorders, and drawing the boundaries as we do seems no more a matter of cutting nature at its own articulations[22] than including

---

[21] See 'Individualism and the Mental', 'Other Bodies', and 'Two Thought Experiments Reviewed', *Notre Dame Journal of Formal Logic*, xxiii (1982), 284 93.

[22] Cf. Plato, *Phaedrus*, 265ᴇ (cited by Wiggins at p. 5 of *Sameness and Substance*).

other rheumatoid complaints (including some outside the joints) would be. In any case Burge's thought experiment works equally well with words that lack even the low-grade natural-kind status of 'arthritis' (his examples include 'sofa', 'brisket', 'contract', and 'red').[23] So the thought experiment does not depend on that insight of Putnam's (as we believe it to be) which one can express dramatically by saying that nature itself helps to determine what we mean by our words. But this independence can cause misunderstanding. By overbalancing the scales in favour of the social environment, we may lose hold of a genuine insight about the importance of the physical environment.[24]

Not that Burge ignores the physical environment. On the contrary, he expresses sympathy with Putnam's claims about it.[25] And there need not be any threat to Putnam's insight in holding, as Burge does, that the physical environment has its constitutive significance for individual psychology only as mediated by the social environment.[26] The risk of losing the insight comes from the specific way in which Burge recommends this thesis about mediation, by a thought experiment whose apparatus has nothing in particular to do with natural kinds.

It is inessential to Putnam's point about, say, 'water' that the chemical composition of the stuff has actually been discovered by experts. The thesis that the physical environment's role in individual psychology is mediated by the social environment comes to this: against the background (as before) of a story about an individual's cognitive and practical dealings with the stuff, we can say that what he means by the word is determined by its correct use in his community, and its correct use in his community is as a word for *that stuff*.[27] But the communal standards we thus gesture at—which determine that a stuff superficially indistinguishable from *that* stuff

---

[23] See 'Individualism and the Mental', 80–2.

[24] This may be connected with Burge's attitude to the case of propositional attitudes with demonstratively expressible contents: see n. 18 above.

[25] See 'Individualism and the Mental', 117, n. 2.

[26] See 'Other Bodies', 102.

[27] This formulation makes no concessions to those who ask, in sceptical response to one reading of Wittgenstein, 'Cannot the world help shape a subject's mind independently of any community?' See, for example, Simon Blackburn, 'The Individual Strikes Back', *Synthese*, lviii (1984), 281–301; cf. Wright's contribution to this volume.

(which is in fact H$_2$O) but chemically distinct from it would not count as *water*—need not reside anywhere, so to speak, except in the nature of the stuff itself. The standards need have no special anchorage in the minds and practices of members of the community who actually know the stuff's chemical structure. What is required is at most that there *could* be experts, and to say that is to say no more than that the stuff has a scientifically discoverable nature. Conversely, although it makes the point dramatic to consider cases in which an individual's own conception of a natural kind would (if allowed to bear on the matter) determine the wrong extension, that is inessential too. Even if knowledge of the chemical composition of water pervades the community, the point remains that the communal standards for the correct use of 'water' are partly dictated by the nature of the stuff itself, rather than wholly a matter for unconstrained communal convention.[28]

Burge's thought experiment, in contrast, turns essentially on divergences between individual misconceptions and communal standards of correctness. Apart from natural-kind cases, the idea that the world itself can serve as repository of the communal standards is not available: with 'sofa' or 'brisket' the communal standards have to be conceived as realized in the detailed practice (mistakes aside) of an actual subcommunity whose members count as experts. This carries over into the application of Burge's thought experiment to the natural-kind term 'water'.[29] In the general case there would be no substance to the idea that what makes someone an expert is that his classifying practice knowingly articulates nature at its own joints. The availability of that idea in the natural-kind case reveals the actual existence of experts as inessential there. But the generality of Burge's apparatus—its applicability to the natural-kind case and others alike—leaves it looking as if the actual existence of experts is what matters in the natural-kind case too.[30] To be sure, there is the difference that in the natural-kind case the relevant experts are

---

[28] Of course it is merely conventional that we use 'water' for that stuff rather than for something else or not at all; but it is not a matter of convention what stuffs there are. The points made in this paragraph suggest that there is a risk of misleadingness in making the claim about the social environment in terms of 'the division of linguistic labor'.

[29] 'Other Bodies', 100–1.

[30] At p. 119 (n.8) of 'Other Bodies', Burge notes that Putnam's case does not require actual experts, and that his thought experiment diverges in this respect.

scientists,[31] and that might be read as encapsulating the point about world-involvingness that makes the natural-kind case special. But if the point is pressed home, actual experts can, as we have seen, drop out in the natural-kind case, as they cannot in the others. Keeping all the cases on a par risks making it seem that the difference between the natural-kind case and the others is merely institutional or sociological (a matter of the professional category to which the relevant experts belong). It consequently risks obscuring the special point about world-involvingness that can be made in the natural-kind case.

8. Insistence that the social environment is partly constitutive of an individual's mental life is reminiscent of our third landmark: namely one reading of Wittgenstein's reflections on rule-following, and of one strand in his argument against the possibility of a private language.[32] In a cognate but at present mostly separate philosophical tradition, one must be struck by an echo of theses about the social constitution of the cognitive subject.

To mean something by a word, one must regard oneself as responsible to a norm. Wittgenstein himself extends his thoughts about rule-following from meaning to content-bearing states like wishes or expectations,[33] and that suggests a generalization on these lines: our dealings with content must be understood in terms of the idea that mental activity is undertaken under the aspect of allegiance to norms. Now the idea of allegiance to a norm is empty if no substance can be given to the distinction between obedience and the illusory appearance of obedience. And Wittgenstein's point, on one reading,

---

[31] See 'Other Bodies', 100.

[32] Recent exegesis of Wittgenstein in this vein takes off from Saul Kripke, *Wittgenstein on Rules and Private Language* (Basil Blackwell, Oxford, 1982). See also Christopher Peacocke, 'Rule-Following: the Nature of Wittgenstein's Arguments', in Steven Holtzman and Christopher Leich (eds.), *Wittgenstein: To Follow a Rule* (Routledge and Kegan Paul, London, 1981), 72–95; and John McDowell, 'Wittgenstein on Following a Rule', *Synthese*, lviii (1984), 325–63. On the relation between Burge and Wittgenstein, see Philip Pettit, 'Wittgenstein, Individualism and the Mental', in Paul Weingartner (ed.), *Epistemology and Philosophy of Science*, Proceedings of the Seventh International Wittgenstein Symposium (Hölder–Pichler–Tempsky, Vienna, 1983).

[33] See, for example, *Philosophical Investigations*, translated by G. E. M. Anscombe (Basil Blackwell, Oxford, 1953), I. 437.

is that we can give substance to that distinction only by understanding individual obedience or disobedience in a communal context. In the different philosophical idiom we alluded to above: the individual cognitive (or, generally, psychological) subject must be seen as constituted by its relation to a community.[34]

Burge's thought experiment turns essentially on our willingness to credit subjects with propositional attitudes whose contents they imperfectly understand.[35] The Wittgensteinian considerations—whatever exactly they are—seem clearly in the spirit of Burge's approach,[36] but they have no such limitation. This may make room for a strengthening of Burge's attack on individualism about the mental.

As things stand, it can seem that a fundamentally individualistic conception of individual psychology might accommodate Burge's point, on these lines. Considered in themselves, the states and events in an individual's mental life can be characterized in a way congenial to individualism, in terms of their position in a 'functional' structure—a network of intra-individual causal potentialities. The interest of communal languages is this: a structure of rational connections between publicly interpreted sentences can model, with tolerable adequacy, the structure of actual and possible causal relations in terms of which mental phenomena are to be, ultimately individualistically, understood.[37] What Burge shows, on this view, is only this: though a communal language of which an individual's mastery is at various points defective can model the structure of his individual psychology, the model, which is extrinsic and in principle dispensable, will—not surprisingly—be less than a perfect fit.[38]

---

[34] These remarks are in any case no more than a programme for an exegesis. But there is a risk of its seeming clear in advance that nothing useful could result from the programme, if we do not stress that the topic is meant to be restricted to personal mental states, not the sub-personal states fruitfully postulated in cognitive psychology (which precisely do not need a subject). For this distinction, see D. C. Dennett, *Content and Consciousness* (Routledge and Kegan Paul, London, 1969), Chapter 4.

[35] See 'Individualism and the Mental', 79, 83.

[36] See 'Individualism and the Mental', 115, where 'responsibility to communal conventions' strikes the note of allegiance to the norms in force in one's community.

[37] For positions on these lines, see Brian Loar, *Mind and Meaning* (CUP, Cambridge, 1981); and Andrew Woodfield, 'On Specifying the Contents of Thoughts', in Woodfield (ed.), *Thought and Object*, 259–97.

[38] See Woodfield, 'On Specifying the Contents of Thoughts', 292, 296–7 (n. 11).

Burge's thought experiment poses a challenge to individualism, and this position responds in a way that is analogous to the first—the less radical—of the two lines of response we distinguished to considerations like Putnam's. According to that line of response, a world-involving state of mind is constituted by a world-independent circumstance (a configuration 'in the head') together with facts about its relation to the physical environment. Somewhat similarly here, a belief-ascription with the content of the belief given in a language the subject speaks is seen as rendered true by a compound circumstance: on the one hand, a state of affairs whose intrinsic nature is in principle intelligible individualistically; and, on the other, the fact that the content-sentence's role in a communal language largely constitutive of the subject's social environment is a close enough reflection of the intra-individual functional role of the state in question. If one takes this view, one will not find much substance in the idea that the cognitive subject is socially constituted.

This purported defusing of the threat Burge poses to individualism trades on the appearance that his point can be confined to some merely local mismatches between the causal structure of an individual's psychology and the rational structure of a communal language. The Wittgensteinian form of the point gives no such appearance, and this affords clearer scope for a scepticism about the defusing move. The defusing idea is that rational relations within a communal language form a structure constitutive of the contents that can figure in a composite total picture of an individual's psychological organization; and that we are to arrive at the individualistic core of the total picture by abstracting the sheer structure from an account of this network of rational relations, and by looking for a network of causal relations between intra-individual items that nearly enough exemplifies that abstracted structure. But scepticism about this seems well placed: in a weak form, because the idea of a normative structure sufficiently rich to reflect (even approximately) the structure of a person's psychological organization, and abstracted from rational relations within an interpreted language, is merely programmatic; more strongly, because there is an a priori argument that the normative interconnections necessary to make intelligible the presence of content in our full picture of mental life *could* not be reflected in the structure of a network of functional roles characterized in non-content-involving terms. The a priori argument is from Donald

Davidson's article 'Mental Events', and what it alleges is a radical incommensurability, not just a likelihood of local mismatches.[39]

In exploiting the possession of propositional attitudes by subjects with an imperfect understanding of their contents, Burge's thought experiment challenges a picture of the mental as a realm of hard-edged facts available with a special directness to the subject's own scrutiny.[40] It seems right to be suspicious of this picture. But if the thought experiment is the sole material for the attack, it seems too easy to blunt the challenge on the lines we have described: the defusing move yields a position in which it must be accepted that no such picture fits the mental as a whole, but a place can be preserved for precisely such a picture as part of the composite truth about the mind.[41] The line of argument we have just mentioned, if carried through, would block this: it would compel a response to Burge's challenge analogous to the second—the more radical—of the two responses we distinguished to considerations like Putnam's.

9. How should we think about the relations between subject, context, and content?

Let content be what is specified in a 'that' clause in the attribution of, say, a belief or an intention. The considerations we have discussed indicate that the content of a person's mental state can be partly determined by his physical or social context. The crucial question is whether this should be accommodated in the more radical way or the less radical way.

The less radical way protects a conception of intra-individual psychology as theorizing about context-independent events and states, with context-dependent attributions of content understood as generated by amalgamating truths of intra-individual psychology with truths about context. In some versions, intra-individual psychology is supposed to be entitled to use a notion of context-independent

---

[39] Davidson's article is reprinted in his *Essays on Actions and Events* (Clarendon Press, Oxford, 1980), 207–25. Loar attacks Davidson's argument in *Mind and Meaning*; for a discussion of the issue, see John McDowell, 'Functionalism and Anomalous Monism', in Ernest LePore and Brian McLaughlin, (eds.), *The Philosophy of Donald Davidson: Perspectives on Actions and Events* (Basil Blackwell, Oxford, 1986).

[40] See 'Individualism and the Mental', 99–105.

[41] For a particularly clear example of a position on these lines, see Colin McGinn, 'The Structure of Content', in Woodfield (ed.), *Thought and Object*, 207–58; see especially pp. 253–5 (with an explicit mention of Burge at p. 254).

content ('narrow content') for its own purposes, so that the theory of content becomes stratified: 'broad content' in the full composite account of mental states, 'narrow content' in intra-individual psychology. But this is not universal.[42]

What about the more radical way? Recall the echo of theses about the social constitution of the cognitive subject. That suggests that we might formulate the objection to the less radical way on these lines: if we leave the *communal* environment, at any rate, out of consideration, with a view to focusing on the topic of intra-individual psychology, then our picture will contain nothing at all that is recognizable as a subject of mental states.[43] That casts suspicion on the label 'intra-individual psychology'; for there will be no obvious reason in that case to accept that the findings of such a discipline would have any constitutive relevance to the mind. From this standpoint, the postulation of 'narrow content' in some forms of the less radical response will look like a self-deceptive attempt to conceal the disappearance of the cognitive subject from the picture. There is scope for a similar charge of obliterating the cognitive subject against the less radical of the two ways of accommodating the content-determining role of *physical* context; but we shall not go into that here.

The difference between the two styles of response crystallizes around the notion of context. It is neutral ground that context partly determines (broad) content. The less radical response accommodates that by regarding the environment, social and physical, as straightforwardly external to a realm of context-free psychological facts. In the more radical response, in contrast, the notion of context undergoes a shift. We can no longer regard the social and physical environment as simply surrounding the psychological subject. Rather, we have to accept that contextual facts inextricably permeate the field of psychological investigation, even when what is under study is the psychological organization of an individual.

Though we find the radical style of response congenial, we would not claim to have done much more here than draw attention to its possibility. Even that is perhaps a sufficiently ambitious under-

---

[42] See McGinn, 'The Structure of Content'.

[43] This would undercut the possibility of putting Wittgenstein's point as Kripke does in *Wittgenstein on Rules and Private Language*, where there is supposed to be such a thing as how things are in the mind of an individual taken altogether by himself; it is just that such circumstances do not suffice for meaning or content.

taking. If the radical style of response is an option at all, it seems clear that the choice we have tried to describe is a fundamental issue for the philosophy of mind; but it is an issue that has gone unnoticed in much excellent recent work in the field.

CHAPTER 1

BROAD-MINDED EXPLANATION AND PSYCHOLOGY*

PHILIP PETTIT

1. Introduction: The Issue of Explanatory Dispensability

Broad-minded explanation is explanation which calls on beliefs, desires, and the like—in general, on intentional states—that are themselves broad or wide. The question I wish to raise in this paper is whether such explanation is ever psychologically indispensable; in particular, whether it is ever more than a stand-in for an account which only invokes narrow psychological states.

The broad–narrow divide is drawn at different places, depending on where the boundary is thought to fall between a person's 'core', as some at least will take it, and his context or surrounds. By some accounts the boundary falls at the surface of the body; by others it falls somewhere nearer the brain; by still others, it cannot be located in such physicalistic terms. We can leave open the issue between these accounts, however, defining the broad–narrow distinction as follows. A token or particular state is narrow if the presence of that type of state is guaranteed by the context-independent character of the subject; otherwise the state is broad.

This definition is meant to be neutral on the issue dividing dualists and materialists. For all that it says, the context-free character of the subject, or indeed the character of any part of the world, may be physical or non-physical. The idea is that, whatever the stuff out of which people are composed, their narrow states are those which supervene on how it is with the subjects, independently of the nature of their environment, while their broad states are those which

* © Philip Pettit 1986. I am indebted to a number of people for comments on earlier versions of this paper. In particular I must mention Jeremy Butterfield, Michael Devitt, Peter Forrest, Peter Godfrey-Smith, Frank Jackson, Mark Johnson, Graham Macdonald, John McDowell, Peter Menzies, David Papineau, Huw Price, Christie Slade, Jack Smart, Kim Sterelny, and Stephen Stich.

supervene on how it is both with the subjects and with their environment. The narrow states cannot cease to exist without a change in the appropriate context-free base; keep the base constant and they are bound to survive. By contrast, the broad states may cease to exist without any change in that inner space. A change of context, just on its own, can cause one of the states to disappear.

Under this account of the broad–narrow divide, any narrow type of state that I exemplify will be realized also in a *Doppelgänger*: that is, in someone who, though inhabiting a distinct and perhaps very different environment, is indistinguishable from me in context-independent character.[1] This is not true of every broad state: depending on the variation in context, it may or may not be replicated in my unearthly twin. We have on offer here a thought test for the 'spread' of a state. Given the state, consider whether it is replicated in all the subject's possible *Doppelgänger*. If it is, the state is narrow; if it is not, the state is broad.[2]

I am going to assume that intentional states at least include some broad states, and that broad intentional states figure in psychological explanation. The traditional paradigm of such a state is knowledge. If someone knows that *p*, when the truth of that proposition turns on things outside himself, then he is not in a narrow state. Where it was not the case that *p*, no one would know that *p*, for what is known must actually obtain.

Knowledge is broad because it requires context to be such that its content is true. Other intentional states such as belief and desire are less demanding in regard to truth, but may still involve requirements on the world which ensure that they are broad. Consider the belief that *p*, where the content or meaning expressed by the '*p*'-sentence is determined in part by how the world is: this may be because the sentence contains a proper name, a natural-kind term, a demonstrative,

---

[1] Twin Earth, under Hilary Putnam's original presentation of this sort of idea. See his 'The Meaning of "Meaning"', in his *Mind, Language and Reality* (CUP, Cambridge, 1975).

[2] This means, I accept, that for someone to believe that he is such and such is for him to token a broad state; his twin will token the different type of state that he, the twin, is such and such. See Harold Noonan, 'Russellian Thoughts and Methodological Solipsism', in Jeremy Butterfield (ed.), *Language, Mind and Logic* (CUP, Cambridge, forthcoming). I am consoled by John McDowell's observation that nevertheless the twins will each instantiate the state of believing oneself to be such and such.

or whatever. This belief will be broad because it will require the world to be such that its content remains the same, determining in particular the same truth condition: the same function from possible worlds to truth values.[3]

There are sources of breadth other than the facts just mentioned: viz. that the world determines the truth values of intentional contents, and that it sometimes determines even their truth conditions. One is the fact, alleged under some interpretations of Wittgenstein, that when an intentional state involves a rule-following disposition towards its content, then it requires that the community of the bearer be and remain of a certain character.[4] Another is the fact that if we assign a belief or whatever on the basis of what someone says, and if we overlook idiosyncrasies of understanding, construing his words in their standard community sense, then which belief we ascribe will depend in part on the practice of that community, in particular on how it uses those words.[5]

Back then to our question. Assuming that there are some broad intentional states, and that they figure in psychological explanation, are they ever indispensable in explanation? The question is crucial, since such indispensability is likely to be made a hallmark of genuinely mental intentional states. Broad intentional states may be of social or semantic importance, but, failing explanatory indispensability, they will not be counted in any sober inventory of the psychological realm.

They will be treated, in all likelihood, in the manner to which knowledge has become accustomed. The received analysis of knowing that *p* factors it into two components: on the one hand, believing that *p*; on the other, its being the case that *p* and that the belief that *p* is justified or whatever. This decomposition presents knowledge as a hybrid state, involving the psychological component of belief and a non-psychological environmental correlate. The belief component

---

[3] See Gareth Evans, *The Varieties of Reference* (Clarendon Press, Oxford, 1982). For a survey of the theories of reference involved see Nathan U. Salmon, *Reference and Essence* (Blackwell, Oxford, 1982).

[4] See my paper 'Wittgenstein, Individualism and the Mental', in Paul Weingartner (ed.), *Epistemology and Philosophy of Science*, Proceedings of the Seventh International Wittgenstein Symposium (Hölder–Pichler–Tempsky, Vienna, 1983).

[5] See Tyler Burge, 'Individualism and the Mental', *Midwest Studies in Philosophy*, Vol. IV (1979).

will do all the explanatory psychological work, on this account, and so knowledge will be denied a place among the furniture of the mind.

Intentional states figure in at least two sorts of psychological explanation: the explanation of action and the explanation of the appearance of other intentional states. In this paper I shall focus primarily on the explanation of action. I shall be arguing that while broad-minded explanation cannot be indispensable under the standard account of action-explanation, it is indispensable under an alternative and superior account. My claim is that if action-explanation invokes broad intentional states—as I am assuming it does—then it calls upon them indispensably. The force of the explanation is bound to be lost, if reference to those states is eliminated.

It would be possible for someone to concede my claim and then go on to say that this does not in itself establish the credentials of broad intentional states. What it shows, he will say, is that if our ordinary pattern of action-explanation is to be taken as a pointer to the nature of the mind, then broad intentional states have to be countenanced. But it also has to be demonstrated, he will add, that this pattern should be taken seriously: that it is not based, for example, on a misconception of the sorts of things that require psychological explanation.[6] I will not seek to provide such a demonstration in this paper. My argument is addressed to those who assume that the ordinary explanation of action is a fitting vantage point from which to plot the contours of the mind.

The argument is conducted as follows. In section 2 I set out three points of agreement between the standard account of action-explanation and the account which I shall be offering. In section 3 I characterize the standard account and in section 4 I show why it would force us to see broad-minded explanation as dispensable. In section 5 I present and provide support for my alternative to that account and in section 6 I explain why this, in contrast, gives no ground for thinking that we can dispense with broad explanatory states. Finally, in section 7 I give a brief characterization of the view of mental states implicit in my approach; in particular, I try to show where it differs from the orthodox functionalist one.

---

[6] Paul Churchland and Stephen Stich both take the view that ordinary action-explanation is misconceived. See Churchland, 'Eliminative Materialism and Propositional Attitudes', *Journal of Philosophy*, lxxvii (1971), and Stich, *From Folk Psychology to Cognitive Science* (MIT Press, Cambridge, Massachusetts, 1983).

2. Some Points of Agreement about Action-explanation

There are three important points of agreement between the standard account of action-explanation and the account which I shall be offering. These I need not defend in detail, precisely because they are agreed, if not on all sides, at least on both of the sides which we shall be examining.

The first is that action-explanation is reason-giving. The intentional states which it explicitly or implicitly ascribes to the agent give a reason for the action under its description as explanandum. Suppose the action is described as *A*-ing. The states invoked in the explanation constitute a reason for the person's *A*-ing if and only if they include a pro-attitude towards a certain sort of situation plus a belief that by *A*-ing the agent can bring about that situation.[7] I put on the car heater because (i) I wish to have a clear windscreen and (ii) I believe that putting on the heater will realize that goal. The pattern is familiar and uncontentious.

The second point of agreement between the different accounts is that action-explanation is cause-giving as well as reason-giving: specifically, that the complex of intentional states which gives a reason for the action also causes it to occur. If the agent's being in those states explains his action, then it is not enough that the states constitute a reason: despite their service in this regard, the action might be caused by something else. In order to have explanatory force, the complex of states must produce the behaviour as well.[8]

The third and final point of convergence is that action-explanation is pattern-giving, a pattern being a non-accidental regularity. This point is not often spelled out, but it is implicit in most accounts and is in any case persuasive.[9]

The idea is not that the explanation of action is guided by antecedently formulated principles, enunciating general regularities. It is only that the person who explains an action *A* by the presence of an

[7] This account is modelled on Donald Davidson's classic 1963 paper 'Actions, Reasons, and Causes', reprinted in his *Essays on Actions and Events* (Clarendon Press, Oxford, 1980). See in particular pp. 5 and 8–9.

[8] See Davidson, ibid., pp. 8–19. I ignore the further requirement that the intentional complex must produce the action in a non-deviant way.

[9] See Dagfinn Føllesdal, 'The Explanation of Action', in R. Hilpinen (ed.), *Rationality in Science* (Reidel, Dordrecht, 1980), 237: 'There must be some regularity, which we can at least roughly specify, that connects the reason with the action.'

intentional complex I must be able to argue for a pattern relating I-type profiles to A-type actions. The idea is meant to apply to any event-explanations. To explain an event E by a cause C one must be able to make out a general connection between C-type and E-type events. Or so the story goes.

Strictly, there are three strands to the story. The first is that for any causally related pair of events C and E, some relation such as the following must obtain: that the first necessitates the second, that it makes it more probable than not, or at least, excepting determination, that it makes it more probable than it would have been in an otherwise similar situation where the first had not occurred. Unless some such relation obtains between causes and effects, it is unclear why we concern ourselves so much with causes; in particular, it is unclear why we think of bringing about effects by bringing about their causes.

The second strand of the story is that a relation of the kind envisaged does not float free of the other general properties of the events and their situation. For whatever reason, we rule out the possibility that it should hold in only one of two otherwise similar set-ups. The relation is supervenient on other general properties. Keep those the same and it too must remain constant.

What is entailed by these two strands is that if someone causally explains E by C, then he commits himself to the truth of a universal principle. This principle is, at its weakest, that in any exactly similar situation the counterpart of C necessitates or in some sense probabilifies a counterpart of E. If this were all that held, however, we could not really say that causal explanation was pattern-giving. A pattern is given to us by an explanation only if it is picked out under an informative characterization and only if, so characterized, it is independently plausible. The pattern adumbrated here satisfies neither of these conditions.

The third strand of the story makes up the gap. It is agreed on all sides that when we explain an action, or indeed any event, we are in a position to offer an informatively characterized and independently plausible principle in support of the explanation. We can conceive of that principle as enunciating, or at least as providing evidence for, the general pattern entailed; in either case we can say that the pattern is given. The reason for saying that the principle may only provide evidence for the pattern is that the concepts used in the explanation, and therefore in the principle, may not be suitable for the precise formulation of the pattern.[10]

Notice that in envisaging the possibility that a principle may enunciate or just provide evidence for a pattern, we are conceiving of patterns in a distinctive sense. In this sense a pattern is something ontological, not a linguistic or epistemic entity like a principle or law or generalization. As a result it is a perfectly determinate, though not necessarily a deterministic sort of regularity; it is not subject to any vagueness or to any open-ended *ceteris paribus* clauses. Such imperfections may attend our efforts to express patterns but not the patterns themselves.[11]

The last strand of the pattern-giving story is borne out in our explanatory practice. For any event-explanation we offer, we can readily formulate a plausible principle linking the cause-type event to one of the effect-type. The stone broke the window, we say, and we go on easily to generalize about the effects on glass of stone-like objects thrown with a certain force.

If an explanation is to have its proper force, then cause and effect must be described so that we can generalize in this manner. Suppose we are told that the event which Johnny witnessed caused the branch to fall from the tree—or, even worse, that it caused the event which upset Aunt Mary. This does not explain, except in a purely empty way. It may give us grounds for believing that the event is intelligible, but, not suggesting a generalization, it does not serve the distinctive explanatory task of enabling us to find the event intelligible. The difference between finding an event intelligible and merely believing it so is immense. It is like the difference between finding a

[10] See Davidson, op. cit., p. 16, on the principle which most of us will offer in explaining the breakage of a window by a rock. 'A generalization like, "Windows are fragile, and fragile things tend to break when struck hard enough, other conditions being right" is not a predictive law in the rough—the predictive law, if we had it, would be quantitative and would use very different concepts. The generalization, like our generalizations about behaviour, serves a different function: it provides evidence for the existence of a causal law covering the case at hand.'

[11] Might a pattern resist the sort of formulation which we would describe as lawlike enunciation, and yet answer to a principle which provides evidence for it? Those who hold that causal explanations do not entail law-like connections would presumably say that it might. They could thereby endorse the points made in this section. For an example of someone who holds that causal explanation does not entail a law, see J. R. Searle, *Intentionality* (CUP, Cambridge, 1983), 120–1.

joke amusing and inferring that it is amusing from the reactions of others.

I conclude that event-explanation in general, and action-explanation in particular, must give a pattern as well as a reason and a cause. But what sort of pattern is provided in the action case? What type of principle is adumbrated in the explanatory invocation of intentional states? The way to get at the principle on offer in any explanation is to ask how we would generalize it to other cases and how we would modify those generalizations in response to various objections. As it happens, Paul Churchland has already gone through this exercise for the case of action-explanation.

His analysis goes as follows, where 'X' ranges over agents, 'O' over states of affairs, and 'A' over actions: for all X, all O, and all A, 'If (1) X wants O, and (2) X believes that A-ing is a way for him to bring about O under the circumstances, and (3) there is no action believed by X to be a way for him to bring about O, under the circumstances, which X judges to be as preferable to him as, or more preferable to him than, A-ing, and (4) X has no other want (or set of them) which, under the circumstances, overrides his want O, and (5) X knows how to A, and (6) X is able to A, then (7) X A-s.'[12]

I propose to accept this analysis, with one amendment. I would prefer to replace at least clause (4) with a simple *ceteris paribus* condition. The reason is that spelling out the clause as Churchland does suggests that we can independently determine that other things are equal. This is misleading. We can only tell *ex post* that a want is overridden. And in any case this is not the only story available to explain an agent's failure to do A under the circumstances described by the other clauses. We might want to say that the want was displaced by some other desire, where this does not have the same deliberative implications as saying that it was overridden. Or we might want to postulate the sort of breakdown often associated with weakness of will.

It is not a scandal that the principles on offer in action-explanations should be as open-textured as I am suggesting. The principles need not be taken to enunciate determinate patterns in nature, only to provide evidence of their existence. We should not be surprised to

[12] Paul Churchland, 'The Logical Character of Action-explanations', *Philosophical Review*, lxxix (1970), 221–2.

find that such principles cannot be explicated in detail; and this, no matter what view we take of action-explanation.

3. The Standard Account of Action-explanation

For all that has been said so far, we still have no story about why it is that mention of a cause, even if it provides evidence of a pattern, can have explanatory force: that is, can enable us to find the effect intelligible. We may agree that such mention of a cause is necessary for event-explanation. But why is it sufficient? The standard account provides the orthodox answer.

The story is that to find an event intelligible is to see it as a particular instance of how the world works generally. It is to recognize the event as unexceptional, as the routine operation of a recurrent process. Thus, so the account goes, to explain an event is to provide the materials for such accommodation to the singular. It is to regularize the event in question.[13]

Fully articulated, the predicate 'explains' has more than the two places required for the explanans p and the explanandum q. In order to specify an appropriate generalization, it must leave room for mention of the possibilities by contrast with which p is explanatory and q is explained: say, o and r respectively. And, more important for our present purposes, it also has to allow space for the assumptions against the background of which intelligibility is revealed: say, s. It is shorthand to say simply that p explains q. Properly speaking, we should say that p (rather than o) explains q (rather than r), given s.[14]

The standard account of explanation tells us something about the assumptions, s. On this account, what is assumed by way of background to event-explanation is that the world works to a causal order, embodying mechanical, if sometimes only probabilistic, patterns. The idea is that, given such a background, an event is rendered intelligible when we are shown that it is part of the dispensation assumed.

The standard account is not implausible, and it certainly holds of

---

[13] The view is sometimes known as the subsumption theory. See Christopher Peacocke, *Holistic Explanation* (Clarendon Press, Oxford, 1979), 154. I do not like that description, since it suggests that only in this form of explanation does a general principle play a role.

[14] See Bas C. Van Fraassen, *The Scientific Image* (Clarendon Press, Oxford, 1980), Chapter 5.

some event-explanations. It makes sense of two points admitted in the last section: that the explanation of an event mentions the cause, and that in the mode of mention it points us towards an independently plausible and informatively characterized pattern. This is precisely what we should expect if the point of the explanation is to display the event as an example of the mechanical order in things.

We saw in the last section that the principle deployed in an explanation may enunciate or, because of its conceptual limitations, may merely provide evidence of a pattern. This means that there will be two ways of regularizing an event: one, the proper way, by enunciating the pattern under which the event is subsumed; the other, the proleptic or anticipatory way, by merely providing evidence of its existence. Although it is less significant than proper explanation, notice that the proleptic sort is much more satisfactory than the empty account in which no principle is put on offer, as when we say that the event Johnny witnessed caused the branch to fall.

How does the standard account of explanation fare with action-explanation in particular? On the face of it, perfectly well. Folk psychology provides us with principles conforming to the belief–desire schema given in the last section. These can be taken as at least evidencing certain patterns in nature, thereby allowing proleptic regularization. When one of them is applied, as in the explanation of an action, then the instantiation of the antecedent—an intentional profile—is agreed to be the cause of the action explained. Thus we can coherently cast an action-explanation as an attempt to accommodate the action within a mechanical picture of the world, an attempt to regularize the action by displaying it as an instance of how the world works generally.[15]

---

[15] See for example J. A. Fodor, *Psychological Explanation* (Random House, New York, 1968), 45: 'our current account of causal explanations requires only that we demonstrate that a certain action occurs whenever specified conditions are satisfied'. Even Robert Cummins, who insists on the distinctive nature of psychological explanation, endorses such an account of action-explanation, and sees it as standard. See his *The Nature of Psychological Explanation* (MIT Press, Cambridge, Massachusetts, 1983), 14. In his view psychological explanation is distinctive so far as it follows a certain strategy for making sense, not of actions, but of capacities. The same is true of John Haugeland, 'The Nature and Plausibility of Cognitivism', *Brain and Behavioral Sciences*, ii (1978), 215–60. Some authors who endorse the regularizing account are cautious enough to insist that action-explanation involves regularization plus something else. See Colin McGinn, 'The Structure of Content', in Andrew Woodfield (ed.), *Thought and Object* (Clarendon Press, Oxford, 1982), 255, n. 3.

A striking feature of action-explanation is that the covering principles—those conforming to the belief–desire schema—are knowable a priori. One does not have to search around for inductive evidence to learn that if it is desirable that *p*, and if it happens that not *p*, and if one can ensure that *p* by *A*-ing, then other things being equal one ought to *A*. Equally, moving to the third person, one does not have to rely on inductive premisses to establish that if someone desires that *p*, believes that not *p*, and believes that by *A*-ing he can ensure that *p*, then *ceteris paribus* he *A*s. Such a principle gives expression to our conception of what it is to believe and desire things. Understand that conception and you will be in a position to see that the principle is true.

Is its a priori character a difficulty for the claim that the principle serves to regularize action? It is not a metaphysical difficulty, for sure. There is no reason why the principle on the basis of which an event is regularized and explained—even properly, let alone proleptically—should not be a priori. That it is a priori may mean just that it is so deeply embedded in our web of belief—and our way of speaking—that we cannot, at least as we are at present, envisage circumstances under which we would give it up. Why should principles that enjoy such an epistemic status be prohibited from serving in regularizing explanations?

Still, the a priori character of the principles may be thought to raise a methodological worry. With such principles, the failure of the consequent to follow cannot be allowed to disprove the law: it must be taken to show that the antecedent is not after all satisfied. This being so, it appears that the antecedent is not verifiable without verifying the consequent. And that would certainly be a problem; it would introduce a destructive circularity.

But the problem is overstated. It does not follow, from the fact that the falsity of the consequent would undermine the ascription of the antecedent, that the antecedent is not independently verifiable. We may have lots of independent evidence for ascribing the antecedent state: evidence related to the circumstances of the agent, his background training and skills, and his other actions and utterances.

If this gets rid of our first methodological worry, however, it leaves room for a second. The worry is that although the antecedent may be independently verifiable in a particular instance, we would not ascribe it in any instance unless we generally found that the consequent followed.[16] Consider a parallel. We may be able to judge in an individual instance that an object is fragile and a shock it receives severe, without being able to see whether the shock shatters the object. The antecedent of the following a priori principle is therefore independently verifiable: any fragile object which is submitted to a severe shock breaks. But we may still feel qualms about that principle, especially as a principle giving us an explanatory regularity. There is a conceptual connection between fragility and breaking which makes the principle suspiciously convenient.

The difficulty can be stated persuasively in the fragility case. The a priori covering principle, independently verifiable though its antecedent may be, does not have the same regularizing force as a principle which invokes the molecular structure of the object instead of its fragility. Molecular structure can be determined without reference to whether the object breaks under severe shocks, and there is nothing suspicious about the regularity which the principle invoking it reveals in the breakage. There is something shady in comparison about the regularization effected by the fragility principle.

But if the difficulty is clear in the fragility case, so is the resolution. The explanation by means of the a priori principle can be held to go proxy for an account in terms of molecular structure. Referring to fragility is referring to whatever intrinsic property it is—say, such and such a molecular structure—that causes things to shatter under certain pressures. Explaining by reference to fragility is not giving the ideal regularizing account, but only doing the best possible under ordinary conditions of ignorance: namely, indicating the form which the ideal account should take. Where the molecular structure account is a proper explanation, the fragility account is a proleptic one.

The person who defends the standard account of action-explanation can respond in similar fashion. The intentional profile invoked in action-explanation is subject to more result-independent conditions of ascription than the property of fragility. But if it is thought to be still suspiciously convenient, then the defender of the standard account can say that its explanatory force derives from the fact that it goes proxy for some intrinsic property of the agent. The picture is that the ideal principle to explain an action would invoke something like a neurophysiological state or complex of states, and

[16] This sort of difficulty is presented in Peacocke, *Holistic Explanation*, 147–55, as the failure to meet a certain 'conjunction restriction' on explanations.

that the intentional profile actually called upon stands to this as fragility relates to molecular structure.[17]

This supports our earlier suggestion that on the standard account of action-explanation, the principles will be taken to play a proleptically explanatory role, not a proper one. They will be seen as principles which merely provide evidence of the patterns in virtue of which the explanation works, not as principles that strictly enunciate those patterns: this, at least, if our concepts of pattern and principle are the ones deployed.[18]

Given this picture, it is natural to ask about the relation between belief–desire principles and the more fundamental laws which do enunciate the relevant patterns: this, assuming that the patterns can be formulated in law-like terms.[19] The principles obtain on the basis of those laws. But are they then reducible to them? Or do they obtain in virtue of those other laws, but in such a way that the laws cannot be used to define necessary and sufficient conditions for their truth? Are they merely supervenient, in other words, on those laws?

The supervenience story is the most common one in the recent literature, and it is usually elaborated as follows. Suppose that an agent instantiates a belief–desire principle, manifesting the intentional profile described in the antecedent and going on to display the behaviour mentioned in the consequent. The tokens of the two types of state in question—mental and behavioural—may also be capable of being typed differently—say, neurophysiologically; and if they are not susceptible to such typing themselves, they may be associated with a pair of token states that are. What happens on the supervenience picture is that in every instance where a belief–desire principle applies, it does so because of the satisfaction of another sort of law—say, a neurophysiological one—by the appropriate couple of token states; and the law on the basis of which it applies may vary more or less wildly from instance to instance.[20]

[17] See for example Fodor, *Psychological Explanation*, 34–6. For a comment, see D. M. Armstrong, 'Recent Work on the Relation of Mind and Brain', in *Contemporary Philosophy: A New Survey*, Vol. 4 (M. Nijhoff, The Hague, 1983), 56–7.

[18] Obviously one might take every principle to enunciate some pattern, allowing patterns to be more or less determinate. In that case, one would formulate the point of this paragraph differently.

[19] The assumption may be rejected. See n. 11.

[20] The supervenience picture is common to a variety of philosophies. It is developed in one way by Davidson's 'anomalous monism'—see 'Mental Events', reprinted in *Essays on Actions and Events*; and in another by certain functionalist theories—see Colin McGinn, *The Character of Mind* (OUP, Oxford, 1982), 33–6.

Enough has been said to show how the standard account of explanation can be fitted to action-explanation in particular. There remains one question. We saw in the last section that action-explanation is not only cause-giving and pattern-giving, but also reason-giving. What relevance can attach in the standard account to the fact that the intentional profile invoked in explanation of an action must be a reason as well as a cause? If the explanation of an action makes it intelligible just by displaying it as a regular event—an instance of how the world generally works—then the fact that the cause invoked is also a reason must be strictly irrelevant. It is the regularization of the action, and that alone, which illuminates the event. But something more must be said. The standard account will be seriously deficient unless it offers some story as to why action-explanation trades in reasons.

The defender of the standard account will probably run the following line. In explaining action our working procedure is to assume that people are more or less rational: this, both in the way they form their beliefs and desires—something we have not considered so far—and in the manner in which they act, given those intentional states. The assumption of rationality seems to be heuristically indispensable, offering us our only clues as to the causes of behaviour. But the fact of relying on such an assumption means that the causes we unearth in any instance necessarily appear also as reasons for the action explained. It is because they are reasons—and because they are reasonable attitudes to ascribe—that we identify them as causes, though it is because they are causes that they explain.[21]

This final twist puts the standard account in nice perspective. The explanation of action uses the assumption of rationality in the enterprise of representing behaviour as part of the causally ordered world. That it does so means that the causes it picks out are reasons,

---

[21] Some defenders of the standard account reject the assumption of rationality, even as a heuristic principle, and they will have to tell a different story. See for example Stephen Stich, 'On the Ascription of Content', in Woodfield (ed.), *Thought and Object*, 153–206. Of those who endorse it, only some make clear that the assumption is strictly heuristic: for example, Brian Loar, *Mind and Meaning* (CUP, Cambridge, 1981), 130–2. That action-explanation explains so far as it gives us a cause is explicit in Fodor, *Psychological Explanation*, 41: 'in the sense of causal explanation here at issue an event has been explained if we can show that sufficient conditions for its occurrence have been satisfied'. See too David Papineau, 'Representation and Explanation', forthcoming in *Philosophy of Science*.

and that the covering principles it mobilizes predict the effects which such reasons dictate. Still, the fact that the causes and principles have this rational aspect is not essential to the explanations in which they serve. Those explanations explain by displaying regularity; it is incidental that the regularity displayed is rational.

4. *The Standard Account makes Broad-minded Explanation Dispensable*

If the standard regularizing conception of action-explanation is adopted, then it follows, given some plausible supplementary premisses, that the broad-minded explanation of action is psychologically dispensable. I want to show why this is so, before exploring my alternative account of action-explanation.[22]

Suppose that we are presented with an explanation of an action in which the explanans involves a broad intentional state. That state requires something of the agent's milieu, and if the requirement were not fulfilled, then the state would not be available to provide an explanation; this, moreover, even if there were no corresponding change in the context-independent character of the agent. We can envisage the state as a piece of knowledge or a demonstrative thought, for example. The question is whether the explanation it supports is necessarily dispensable in favour of an explanation—specifically, a psychological explanation—which involves only narrow states.

There are strictly two cases to consider: one where the explanandum is narrow, the other where it is broad. I shall speak only to the

---

[22] The section which follows provides foundations for what normally passes by assumption or, at best, is briefly stated: see for example Jaegwon Kim, 'Psychophysical Supervenience', *Philosophical Studies*, xli (1982), 65. See also Michael Devitt, *Realism and Truth* (Princeton University Press, Princeton, 1984), Chapter 6, and Stephen Stich, *From Folk Psychology to Cognitive Science*, Chapter 8. A common form in which the assumption appears is that if the existence conditions for the cause mentioned in a cause-giving explanation include some which at another level of analysis can be seen to be causally inert, then the antecedent has been misidentified. This is often quoted as a reason for shrinking the psychological antecedents of action to narrow dimensions. Even Daniel Dennett, whose views on explanation are in many ways congenial to those expressed here, is moved by this. See 'Beyond Belief', in Woodfield (ed.), *Thought and Object*, 13 and 26. See also Colin McGinn, 'The Structure of Content', same volume, p. 208, and David Lewis, 'Belief *De Dicto* and *De Se*', *Philosophical Review*, lxxxviii (1979), 526.

second, since if broad-minded explanation is dispensable in this instance, it will certainly be dispensable in the first also. The broad intentional state in the case imagined I shall ascribe by the sentence '*Ia*', where *a* is the subject and '*I*' designates the property attributed. The broadly described action which serves as explanandum I ascribe by the corresponding sentence '*Aa*'.

I have to demonstrate that in any case like this, where the fact that *Ia* serves to regularize the fact that *Aa*, the explanation can be provided by mention only of narrow psychological facts. The argument which I have to offer is usefully set out in three stages.

Stage 1

Because it is broad, we can legitimately decompose the fact that *Ia* as follows: the agent is such that, world willing, *Ia*. We can decompose the fact that *Aa* in a similar mode: the agent acts so that, world willing, *Aa*. I assume that one and the same condition is involved on the world's side. Let us ascribe this in the sentence '*Cw*', where *w* is the world and '*C*' designates the property involved in the condition. On the one hand, then, we have: the agent is such that if *Cw*, then *Ia*—for short, *I*a*; on the other, the agent acts so that if *Cw*, then *Aa*—for short, *A*a*.

It will be useful to illustrate the sort of decomposition envisaged. If '*Ia*' stands for '*a* knows that *p*', then '*I*a*' is '*a* is such that, world willing, he knows that *p*'. And what is it for the world to be willing here? At the least, the world must be such that *p*. Whether other conditions must be fulfilled, and if so what, is matter for debate.

Another example. Suppose that '*Ia*' stands for '*a* wants this cup'. '*I*a*' will then be '*a* is such that, world willing, he wants this cup'. Here the world will be willing just in case it contains the very cup in question. '*I*a*' then comes to: '*a* is such that, given a world where this cup exists, he wants this cup'.

The illustration of '*Aa*' and '*A*a*' follows similar lines. Suppose that '*Aa*' is '*a* kicks a goal'. '*A*a*' will then be '*a* evinces such narrowly characterizable behaviour that, given a world where the consequences are as here, he kicks a goal'. Again, suppose that '*Aa*' is '*a* grasps this cup'. '*A*a*' will be '*a* evinces such narrowly characterizable behaviour that, given a world where this cup exists, *a* grasps this cup'.

In virtue of our decomposition, it may appear that we can always find a narrow-minded regularization to replace a broad-minded one:

this, assuming that the I^*-state can be regarded as a psychological state. Where we might have invoked the fact that Ia, we can apparently call upon the fact that I^*a and Cw. Since the I-state is broad, requiring that Cw, we know that necessarily it is the case that Ia if and only if I^*a and Cw.

But we should be cautious, for any number of parallel decompositions are also on offer. For example, we might have decomposed the I-state into an $I@$-state, where $I@a$ if and only if a is such that, if $1 + 1 = 2$, then Ia. Since $1 + 1 = 2$ in every possible world, we know that necessarily it is the case that Ia if and only if $I@a$ and $1 + 1 = 2$. If we are prepared to say that anything which the fact that Ia regularizes can be regularized by the fact that I^*a and Cw, we may be forced to add that it can also be regularized by the fact that $I@a$ and $1 + 1 = 2$.

Where we have decompositional alternatives of this sort, we have to decide which provides the best regularizing explanation. If we decide in favour of one of them, then we know that the type of state involved there is primary and that the states involved in the alternatives are gerrymandered out of it. The primary type of state is the true explanatory kind, as we might say; the other types are forgeries.

How ought we to decide between decompositional alternatives? If they are alternatives for a proper form of regularization, then we will select the one whose principle enunciates the pattern in nature in the theoretically most satisfactory way: the one whose principle counts as a law of nature, rather than a gerrymandered variation on the law. If the alternatives are rivals in proleptic regularization, then we will prefer that which seems, in the principle it deploys, to offer the most accurate picture of the sort of pattern in question; in other words, that which approximates most closely to the proper account that we envisage.

Have we been provided with enough evidence to think that any broad-minded explanation, proleptic as it is, can be replaced by a narrow-minded alternative; specifically, by a decompositional alternative? Surely not. For all that we know so far, the I^*-state may be just the gerrymandered conditionalization of the I-state on the fact that Cw. It may be that the best picture of the causal pattern at work is projected in the I-account, so that only the I-state is the true explanatory kind. In that case we would not want to say that the account could be replaced by an I^*-story, since there would not be any genuinely explanatory I^*-state.

This prospect is threatening in particular because, for all that has been said, the *I*-state may be purely relational; it may resemble the state of an object which consists in its lying to the right of another. The narrow state defined by conditionalizing such a purely relational property could not be described in any other way and would be wholly parasitic on the first. It would be as insubstantial as the state of an object's being such that, given an appropriately placed second object, it lies to the right of the second.

We need to close the possibility that the *I**-state is insubstantial. There is no hope of arguing that the *I**-account can replace the *I*-story unless we do so; at best it will seem to be a misleading reformulation of that story. The argument of stages 2 and 3 will close the possibility and will establish the explanatory credentials of the *I**-account.

The argument of stages 2 and 3 will seem to be unnecessary on the following assumption: that it can always be established by analysis or whatever that the *I**-state is the same token and of the same type as some salient context-independent state. Thus the state of being such that, world willing, one knows that *p* might be analysed as the state of believing under certain stimuli that *p*. Similarly the state of being such that, world willing, one wants this cup might be analysed as the state of wanting the cup which one believes is presented in such and such a way. I assume that such heroic attempts at analysis are not guaranteed of success.[23] That being so, we must try another tack if we are to be sure of finding, for any broadly explained action *A*, a narrow-minded way of regularizing the behaviour.

Stage 2

The following two propositions are irresistible:

(a) Every action is at least partly constituted by a change in the context-independent character of the agent, usually a manifest change describable as a piece of behaviour.

(b) Every such change is caused by a narrow state of the agent, a state requiring nothing of the environment.

The first thesis is entirely uncontroversial, since all that it rules out

---

[23] A guarantee might seem to be provided by the thought that there is always something it is like to instantiate an *I**-state, and that under that presentation it is always independently plausible to link the state with the appropriate behaviour. But the thought is scarcely persuasive. For an exploration of related matters, see Simon Blackburn, *Spreading the Word* (Clarendon Press, Oxford, 1984), Chapter 9.

is action at a distance of the sort that would involve no narrow change in the agent. The idea of such action is empirically outlandish and not even clearly coherent. Suppose a table moves in the vicinity of a number of agents. Assuming that it moves by human action, in virtue of what does it move by one person's agency and not another's? In virtue of nothing, apparently, if the action need not involve any narrow change in the agent.

The change in question will usually consist in a discernible movement of the body, describable—in narrow terms—as a piece of behaviour. The obvious exceptions are the changes involved in mental acts like deciding or concluding. Even when these are broadly characterized—as in someone's wishing a demonstratively presented colleague well—the changes will not be overt. In what follows, however, I shall speak for convenience as if the narrow change required for every action was a piece of behaviour.

The second thesis can be established as follows. A narrow piece of behaviour could not be the unmediated effect of some event or condition independent of the agent; otherwise the behaviour would not be of the agent's making: he would be the arena in which it took place, not its author. The narrow behaviour must be traceable to a state of the agent, a state which may itself be narrow or broad. If it is narrow, then the second thesis is uncontroversially substantiated. But what if it is broad?

The broad state cannot be purely relational, since then the behaviour could once again be cast as the unmediated effect of some external event or condition; it must involve some context-independent structure in the agent. That structure may be thought to combine with the environmental correlate in the production of the narrow behaviour or to produce it on its own, whether or not mediating external influence. But it is difficult even to conceive of how the combination picture would work. And so in this case too the second thesis is substantiated: the narrow behaviour is caused by a narrow state of the agent.

Our two theses put us in a position to identify a narrow replacement explanation—that is, regularizing explanation—for the broad-minded account which invokes the *I*-state. We know that the *I*-state and the *A*-action have each got narrow counterparts. Let us ascribe the narrow behaviour involved in the action by '*Ba*'. And let us ascribe the narrow state which produces this by '*Na*'. We may assume that if *Ba* and *Cw*, then *Aa*. But if *Na* and *Cw*, then *Ba* and *Cw*. So if

Na and *Cw*, then *Aa*. That means, I shall take it, that reference to the fact that *Na* and *Cw* can regularize the fact that *Aa*.[24] We have therefore found a narrow replacement explanation for our original *I*-account.

Have we yet secured our goal? Have we shown that under a regularizing conception of action-explanation, the broad-minded explanation of an action is always dispensable, at least in principle, in favour of a narrow-minded one? Not quite. The trouble is that for all we have been told, the *N*-state need not have any claims to be a psychological one; it might be purely neurophysiological, as the letter '*N*' was meant to suggest. We will reach our goal only at the end of stage 3.

Stage 3

The stages of our argument so far are complementary. Stage 1 gave us a narrow psychological state which we could not be sure was substantial. Stage 2 has given us a narrow substantial state which we cannot be sure is psychological. Happily, the two results can be married so as to produce the offspring we want.

Let us return to the case where the *I*-state helps explain the *A*-action. Our conceptual decomposition had given us, as narrow counterparts, on the one hand the *I**-state, on the other the *A**-action. What the theses of stage 2 tell us is that in any such case there are also two independently describable narrow counterparts. For the broadly characterized action we have the narrow piece of behaviour, ascribed by '*Ba*'. For the broad intentional state we have the narrow state which causes that narrow behaviour; this is ascribed by '*Na*'.

What is the relationship between '*Ba*' and '*A*a*', '*Na*' and '*I*a*'? I shall argue that it is as follows. If *Ba*, then *A*a*; but not vice versa. And if *Na*, then *I*a*; but not vice versa.

We may assume that if *Ba* and *Cw*, then *Aa*; but not that only if *Ba* and *Cw*, then *Aa*: after all, a piece of behaviour not satisfying the *B*-description might serve equally well to ensure that *Aa*. By contrast we know, not just that if, but also that only if, *A*a* and *Cw*, then *Aa*.

---

[24] I commit myself to the principle implicit here while discussing a different issue in Graham Macdonald and Philip Pettit, *Semantics and Social Science* (Routledge and Kegan Paul, London, 1981), 125–6.

It follows that if Ba, A^*a, since the fact that Ba ensures, given Cw, that Aa; and that ensures that A^*a. On the other hand it does not follow that if A^*a, Ba. It may be true that A^*a other than through its being the case that Ba.

A similar argument applies to 'Na' and 'I^*a'. We assume that if Na and Cw, then Ia; and we know that if and only if I^*a and Cw, then Ia. We can deduce that if Na, then I^*a; but not if I^*a, then Na.

The relationships characterized fit with the supervenience picture mentioned in the last section. The N-state that we have identified is one on which the I^*-state supervenes; it is a state such that the I^*-state cannot cease to obtain without its also ceasing to obtain. Similarly the B-behaviour is something on which the A^*-action supervenes. In each case we have a truth expressed in one terminology—that of 'N' and 'B'—which ensures a truth expressed in another—that of 'I^*' and 'A^*'.

These supervenience relationships are sufficient to resolve our stage 1 worry. We know that the I^*-state is not insubstantial, since it supervenes on the undoubtedly substantial N-state. This means that we can think of the explanation which invokes the fact that I^*a and Cw as revealing the antecedents of the A-action in a more illuminating way than the I-account. We can think of it as regularizing the action in terms of two factors rather than one, and as providing a better picture of the underlying causal pattern.

We have at last reached our goal. We can say that if action-explanation is regularizing in nature, then there will be a narrow-minded replacement available for any broad-minded story. This means that there will be little temptation to think of broad intentional states as genuinely mental. Unlike the narrow states, they will not be true explanatory kinds. It will be natural to cast them as hybrid states, straddling the psychological and the environmental. The elements of the hybrid I-state will answer to the fact that I^*a on the one side, and the fact that Cw on the other.[25]

One final note. On the supervenience picture developed in this section, it will make for economy if we think of the I^*-state and the N-state as one and the same token state, albeit tokens of different types.

---

[25] One might take the view that broad types of state serve important explanatory roles outside the province of action-explanation, and view them, for that reason, as genuine explanatory kinds. See Kim Sterelny, 'Is Semantics Necessary? Stephen Stich's Case Against Belief', forthcoming in *Australasian Journal of Philosophy*.

In particular, it will enable us to see how, short of overdetermination, we can describe both the I^*-state and the N-state as the cause of the A^*-behaviour. Such an identity hypothesis is generally assumed in the literature.

5. *The Alternative Account of Action-explanation*

I come now to my alternative, non-standard account of action-explanation. We know that all action-explanation gives us a reason, a cause, and a pattern. What we wish to understand is why mention of the reason or cause, in a manner which provides evidence of a pattern, is indeed explanatory, enabling us to find the effect intelligible. Specifially, we need a story about this which does not turn on the regularizing impact of the explanation.

On the regularizing account, explanation is marked by the role in which it casts the principle that it embodies. That principle is taken to enunciate, or at least provide evidence for, how the world as a matter of fact works. It is a given such that if the explanandum can be paired with a cause and the cause–effect pair subsumed under the principle, then the explanandum is intelligible.

This observation is the cue for envisaging an alternative. It might be the case that the principle represented a norm at which the world or some part of the world aimed, rather than just a datum about how it worked. In that case the explanandum would be made intelligible, not by being shown to exemplify the world's regular mode of operation, but by being depicted as something that had to happen if the world was to continue to satisfy the principle that represents its norm. We can speak here, in a slightly artificial usage, of normalizing explanation. The principle is a norm in the light of which the explanandum is required, rather than just a datum in the light of which it is regular.

Suppose that we are given an event E, a cause C, and a principle to the effect that if a C-type event occurs, then so does an E-type one: for short, if C, then E. We might formulate an explanation of E by citing the principle, citing the cause, and concluding: therefore E. But this formulation in itself leaves it unclear whether the force of the explanation is regularizing or normalizing. The regularizing thought is: if the principle generally obtains, and the antecedent is satisfied in this case, then the consequent is fulfilled too. The normalizing counterpart is: if the principle is generally to obtain, and the antecedent is satisfied in this case, then the consequent has to be fulfilled too. Either thought might be expressed in the original deductive formulation.[26]

We look everywhere for regularizing explanations, since we believe that the world generally works to uniform patterns. We will look for normalizing accounts only in domains where we think that selection or design or whatever has been effective in ensuring that the systems there satisfy this or that norm. We will think of the systems as being constructed in such a way that the rule of basic, brute pattern means that at a higher level of characterization the systems answer to the appropriate norms.

These assumptions mean that normalizing explanations can never be taken to deploy principles which enunciate, as distinct from providing evidence for, fundamental underlying patterns. We saw that regularizing explanation may be proper or proleptic, depending on whether the principle deployed plays one or other of these roles. There is no ground for drawing a similar distinction among normalizing accounts.

In order to elaborate the notion of normalizing explanation, it will be useful to construct an illustration. I apologize for the science-fictional character of the example I have chosen. It helps me to avoid the complications which all real-life cases raise.

The Martians, omniscient and beneficent, have made a gift to the university. They have put a set of robots to work in the gardens, promising to monitor and maintain their performance. We look on in awe. Here on a lawn is one of the metallic creatures, busily moving with a probe about the surface. There beneath a tree, scratching and scraping among the leaves, is another. What on earth are they doing?

The explanatory desire behind this question is a wish to be able to substantiate our conception of the robots as gardeners; we have sufficient faith in the ingenuity and good will of the Martians to think that it applies. We want to be able to see how their various behaviours—other than those we come to regard as mere noise—contribute to the gardening task. We will scan the behaviour, trying in each case to view the initiative as a gardening response to a situation of need: in particular, a situation which it is plausible to think that the robot registers in some way. We will rotate the situation and

---

[26] Here I am grateful to the letter if not the spirit of some remarks in T. L. S. Sprigge, 'Final Causes', *Aristotelian Society Supplementary Volume* xlv (1971), 161. See also Andrew Woodfield, *Teleology* (CUP, Cambridge, 1976), 84 and 91.

behaviour beneath our gaze, looking for descriptions 'S' and '*Gx*' such that the following principle is undeniable: if a system registers that *S*, and is bent on gardening, then, other things being equal, it *G*s.

We can easily envisage illustrations of this exercise. We ponder about the robot on the lawn until we conjecture that it registers that the grass is matted and, being a gardener, acts so as to aerate the roots. Again we puzzle over the creature beneath the tree until we realize that it probably registers that the leaves are decomposing and, in fulfilment of its gardening project, is doing what it can to rake them up.

The exercise is an example of normalizing explanation. Our conception of the gardener gives us a vague cluster of norms such that we expect any gardening agent to satisfy the antecedents of some, and, when it does, generally to satisfy the consequents too: generally rather than universally, because we can leave room for various blocks and imperfections, even ones we don't fully understand. We substantiate that conception when we see various robotic behaviours as occurring in order that such norms should be fulfilled.

The difference between regularizing and normalizing explanation comes in the assumptions against the background of which the explanation is offered. In the example on hand the assumption under which explanation is pursued is not just the regularizing thought that there must be some principles to which the domain of robots works. It is the stronger assumption that there are certain gardening principles to which, or at least to some of which, it must work in particular.

Suppose that we have a successful explanation of an event *E*—say, a piece of behaviour—by reference to an antecedent *C*—a registering of a situation of horticultural need. The idea is that we know more than the regularizing principle that if *C*, then *E*. We also know that it is because *E* is necessary for the satisfaction of that law—call it '*L*'—that it occurs. The assumptions are, on the one hand, *L*; on the other, if it is the case that if *L* then *E*, then *E*: this is another way of saying that if *E* is necessary for the satisfaction of the law, then it occurs.

The relation between these assumptions needs further clarification. The straight *L*-assumption is: if *C* then *E*. The other is that if it is the case that if *L* then *E*, then *E*. The consequent is the same in each case, so let us compare the antecedents. In the one case we have simply *C*; in the other, if *L* then *E*, or, more fully spelled out: if it is the case that if *C* then *E*, then *E*. The first antecedent ensures the truth of the second, as can readily be checked. And so the first, less complex assumption entails the truth of the other one.

But this seems to raise a problem. For it means, doesn't it, that whenever someone is possessed of an assumption sufficient for a regularizing explanation, he can also lay hands on an assumption sufficient for a normalizing one?

Normalizing explanation is defined so that this problem does not arise. The ground on which the normalizing assumption is believed cannot just be that the regularizing assumption holds. One must have a reason for thinking that if *E* is necessary for *L* then *E* occurs, over and beyond the knowledge that *L* obtains. This stipulation is not arbitrary, for it is fulfilled in the robotic example and in parallel cases. Given the preconception that the robots are gardeners, and given that *L* is a gardening norm whose antecedent they fulfil, we have a deep-seated reason for thinking that if *E* is necessary in a particular case for *L*—this, because the antecedent *C* obtains—then *E* occurs.

Generalizing our example, it seems that we are in a position to seek normalizing explanations whenever the following conditions hold. First, there is a more or less well-demarcated domain of explanatory concern, involving systems like the robots. Secondly, the systems in that domain are designed or selected or whatever so as more or less perfectly to fit a certain conception. And thirdly, we understand the conception sufficiently to be able to spell out norms at least some of which must apply to beings that fit the conception.

The most obvious case where these conditions are satisfied is with artefacts of a certain complexity. Given a chess-playing computer program, a pocket calculator, or even a central heating system, it is clear that there is room and need for normalizing explanation. The explanation will substantiate our preconception of the system, relating its behaviours to antecedent conditions in a manner which shows those behaviours to be the sort of thing required of a system of that kind.[27]

The conditions are also satisfied, I believe, in other circumstances. Take the case where we know that certain selectional pressures have

[27] The case of the chess-playing program will recall Daniel Dennett's notion of the Intentional stance. See his classic paper 'Intentional Systems', reprinted in *Brainstorms* (Harvester Press, Hassocks, 1978). The normalizing stance is a closely related idea.

governed the emergence of a species. With some skill and imagination, we may be able to work out a corresponding conception of the survivors, identifying norms which we think they must instantiate: norms such as those relating needs to efforts at fulfilment. This underpins a familiar sort of ethological normalization. The exercise is duplicated at another level of biology, when we concentrate on the selection of sub-systems and identify norms that we think these in turn must fulfil: say, the norms that require to be satisfied by a digestive system of a certain kind. At each level we elaborate a conception of the system in question, and we substantiate it in the identification of appropriate patterns of cause and effect.

Normalizing explanation should not be an entirely unfamiliar category. It is an instance of a widely endorsed conception of teleological explanation. According to that conception, an event E is teleologically explained as the means to a goal G if it is caused to occur by the circumstance of an E-type event's being necessary for the goal.[28] The conception fits our case, where the circumstance of an E-type event's being necessary for the obtaining of the C–E principle—a circumstance which is independently describable just as the occurrence of a C-type event—causes E to occur also.

So much by way of elucidating the notion of normalizing explanation. There are two further tasks for this section. First, I must show that action-explanation can be cast as an instance of normalization; and then, I must provide an argument that it ought to be seen in this way.

The three conditions sufficient for normalizing explanation are fulfilled in the action case. To begin with, we can certainly demarcate the class of human agents more or less adequately. We may have doubts about how far to include the immature and the demented, but in general we are quite clear about whether we are dealing with a proper human agent.

Secondly, we have reason to think that human agents will exhibit such actions, and indeed attitudes, as conform to a certain conception of what a normal person is. Every society requires as a condition of full membership that those who belong to it think and act in a manner which can be squared with such a conception, however

---

[28] This conception can be traced in Charles Taylor, *The Explanation of Behaviour* (Routledge and Kegan Paul, London, 1964); Larry Wright, *Teleological Explanation* (University of California Press, London, 1976); and G. A. Cohen, *Karl Marx's Theory of History* (Clarendon Press, Oxford, 1978).

loose. Social training is a process of moulding children so that they come to fit that ideal.

On this picture, training plays the role that design plays with an artefact like the chess-playing program or indeed the horticultural robot. To invoke it in this way, however, is not necessarily to endorse any sort of social relativism. We may still expect to be able to develop our conception of the human agent so as to encompass other cultures. One ground for that expectation is that no social shaping could produce agents who lived up to the local conception of the normal person unless evolution and biology provided appropriate predispositions. Those predispositions are the common inheritance of all members of the species, and suggest the possibility of intercultural accessibility.[29]

Thirdly, not only does social training ensure that people will fit a certain conception of the normal agent; it also enables each one of us to spell out norms which we expect such an agent to honour. He will satisfy the antecedents of a good many of the norms, and when he does so he will generally satisfy the consequents too. These norms include principles about the attitudes which people will form in the light of certain data or stimuli, and principles about the actions which they will choose in view of those attitudes. The principles fitting the belief–desire schema are normative expectations of precisely this kind; specifically, they are expectations governing the appearance of actions.

The fulfilment of our three conditions means that we can depict action-explanation as normalizing in nature. Under the picture on offer, we approach people in explanation with the presumption that the things they do—as distinct from reflexes, jerks, and the like—are prompted by beliefs and desires in such a way that they satisfy the appropriate principles. We presume that in general they are behaviourally rational, as indeed we make the presumption, in dealing with the formation of their beliefs and desires, that they are attitudinally so.[30]

This picture of action-explanation suggests that the exercise is

---

[29] For an a priori argument in favour of intercultural accessibility see Donald Davidson, 'On the Very Idea of a Conceptual Scheme', reprinted in *Inquiries into Truth and Interpretation* (Clarendon Press, Oxford, 1984).

[30] I have tried to characterize the distinction—and connection—between behavioural and attitudinal rationality in Macdonald and Pettit, *Semantics and Social Science*, 58–61.

rather like that which we imagined in dealing with our horticultural robots. It is an attempt to find such a characterization of people's doings as will enable us to substantiate our conception of them as more or less rational. This conception is more general in scope than that which we deployed with the robots, but it plays the same role. There we assumed that given the ends of a gardener, the robots were more or less rational subjects; we focused on action, but the assumption was also relevant to their attitudes, in particular to their dispositions to register and infer. Here we assume that given the rather more varied ends of the human being, ordinary agents are also more or less rational. Normalization in both cases comes to rationalization.

We have been considering the question whether action-explanation can be depicted as an instance of normalization, and, given that it can, the next issue is whether it ought to be cast in this way. Before we go to that question, however, there is an objection which must be turned aside. This is that on the normalizing picture, people are represented as selecting their actions in order to satisfy belief–desire principles, and that such a representation is not true to the phenomenology of deliberation.

The objection forces us to recognize that whereas the robots may have no conscious life, people certainly do. They don't act blindly in a manner that happens to sustain belief–desire principles. They act for reasons, and for reasons of which they can usually offer an account. The normalizing picture must be shown to fit with these facts about their subjectivity.

The claim is that no fit is available. It is suggested that under the normalizing picture, we must imagine the agent considering the sort of norms invoked in explanation and then acting so as generally to satisfy them. He would note the explanatory assumption that if someone believes this and desires that, then he acts in such and such a manner; he would recognize that he fulfils the antecedent of that assumption; and he would act so as to make the assumption true. Clearly, this is an absurd image of practical reasoning.

Happily, the image is not an essential part of the normalizing picture. It comes of a confusion between the third-person, explanatory version of a rational norm and its first-person, deliberative reading. Distinguish these and the objection is undermined.

The explanatory version of a belief–desire principle is roughly: X

desires that p, believes that not p, and . . . , so he does such and such. The deliberative version, since it is appropriate to X's own point of view, is rather of the form: it is desirable that p, it happens that not p, and . . . , so such and such needs doing. To say from the explanatory angle that X acts so as to satisfy the norm in question is to suggest that the deliberative version of the norm constrained him, consciously or unconsciously, not that the explanatory version did so. In its deliberative aspect, the fact that the norm applied constitutes a plausible reason for acting, and so the phenomenology of deliberation is preserved.

Let us agree that action-explanation, just as it can coherently be cast as regularizing in nature, can also be depicted as normalizing. The question to which we must now turn is whether it ought to be taken in this way. Assuming that one or the other account is the correct one, is there any evidence to suggest that action-explanation is better depicted as normalizing? I believe that there is.

The evidence I have in mind is the fact, already noted, that the principles engaged in action-explanation are a priori in character. It is not unthinkable that a priori principles should serve in a regularizing form of explanation. But if action-explanation is of the regularizing sort, the fact that the principles are a priori remains unexplained. By contrast, it becomes readily intelligible under a normalizing view of that explanation.

On the normalizing picture, the principles of action-explanation, relating beliefs and desires to behaviour, are norms which express our conception of the normal human agent. They are like the principles in which we might formulate our conception of a chess-playing program, or pocket calculator, or central heating system. Understand what it is to be a normal agent and it will be undeniable, for each of these propositions, that anyone who satisfies the antecedent will, other things being equal, satisfy the consequent too. That is to say, the principles will be a priori knowable.

That the principles are a priori does not mean that it is a priori that every normal agent satisfies the antecedents of all; nor that it is a priori that every noise and movement of every normal agent is subsumed by some principle; nor, above all, that every agent is normal. As we approach an agent with a view to substantiating our conception of the competent person, we must be prepared to find that he is not normal; that only in some of his responses does the conception fit; and that it fits only so far as he satisfies the antecedents of a limited number of principles.

Neither does the fact that belief–desire principles are a priori mean that it is easy to apply them to actions. It is not as if we can postulate any old rationalizing set of attitudes for every piece of behaviour we want to explain. We will have to meet independent constraints on the ascription of attitudes, since the attitudes themselves will have to be more or less rationally explicable. And we will have to ascribe such attitudes as serve over time in relatively constant patterns of explanation.

That the principles are a priori means only that we hold on to them as fixed points when we embark on the explanation of action. We keep them out of the reach of questioning as we search around, subject to other constraints, for the principle which each action can be best seen as exemplifying. The principles are never themselves at risk of revision or rejection. They serve as standards with which every action has to be squared, not as generalizations which any action is likely to confound.[31]

To sum up then, the normalizing picture of action-explanation makes sense of the fact that belief–desire principles are a priori knowable, whereas that fact remains unexplained on the regularizing account. I conclude that not only can we see action-explanation as normalizing; if we are to reflect all the relevant facts, then we ought to see it in this way.

This completes the main business of the section, but before passing on I want to return to a crucial point of contrast between the two accounts of action-explanation. We saw that on the regularizing account, the intentional profile may command attention so far as it is a reason for the action—the assumption of rationality is a heuristic device—but it explains the action so far as it is a cause; specifically, so far as it is a cause which displays a regular connection with the effect. What we now have to see is that while the profile remains a cause of the action, the normalizing account has it explain as well

---

[31] That the principles of action-explanation operate like a priori standards I argue in Macdonald and Pettit, op. cit., pp. 93–101. For a critique see J. E. Tiles, 'Pettit on Revising our Understanding of Individuals', *Analysis*, xliii (1983), 189–93. I try to respond to that critique in 'A Priori Principles and Action-Explanation', *Analysis* (forthcoming).

as command attention in its role as reason; and, correspondingly, that it has the assumption of rationality play a constitutive as well as a heuristic part.

It should be clear that on the normalizing conception of action-explanation, the intentional profile remains a cause. The original argument still carries: namely that unless the attitudes involved were causally responsible for the appearance of the action, then they could not be invoked to explain it. At the weakest, the attitudes must have made the action more likely than it would have been in an otherwise identical situation where they were absent.[32]

But if the intentional profile is a cause of the action under the normalizing conception, it is not just because it has this status—or the status of a cause displaying a regular connection with the effect— that it explains. In order to explain it must point us, not to any old regularizing principle, but specifically to one on which the agent is targeted: a principle of a kind that he is constructed to satisfy. It does this so far as it is a reason. As a reason it points us to a belief–desire principle of a kind suited to figure in rationalizing explanation. It is clear, therefore, that the intentional profile has to be a reason, not just to attract notice, but also to explain.

Another way of putting this point is to say that under the normalizing conception, the assumption of rationality plays a constitutive as well as a heuristic role. To explain an action is to show that in the light of the agent's intentional states it was required by a norm, in particular by a principle of behavioural rationality. But this means that to explain an action is to show that in the light of those states it was the rational thing to do. Seeing an action as rational, then, is no longer just a way of coming to find the regularly connected causes that make it intelligible. It is what making the action intelligible consists in.

On the regularizing picture, action-explanation is a form of cause-giving explanation that may happen also to give us a reason. On the normalizing image, it is a kind of reason-giving explanation which

---

[32] The pattern of cause and effect is not enunciated by the normalizing principle; the principle merely provides evidence of its existence. It will be enunciated, if it can be enunciated, by a very different sort of law. The law will not be hedged by an open *ceteris paribus* clause and, if the principle relates broad phenomena, then the law will distinguish the context-independent and environmental components in antecedent and consequent.

happens, albeit not just incidentally, to give us a cause. The contrast between the two conceptions is nearly complete.[33]

6. *The Alternative Account does not make Broad-minded Explanation Dispensable*

If action-explanation were of the regularizing kind then broad states, as we have seen, would not strictly be needed in psychology. Broad-minded explanation would be in principle dispensable. We now know that action-explanation is normalizing in character, not regularizing. The question, then, is whether this saves broad states from the redundancy to which they are condemned under the other dispensation. I shall argue that it does.

We know that for any broad state ascribed by '*Ia*', there are an indefinite number of decompositional alternatives. We identified the I^*-state of being such that, if Cw, then Ia; and the $I@$-state of being such that, if $1 + 1 = 2$, then Ia. These alternatives are designed so that they can apparently be invoked to explain anything which the fact that Ia explains: instead of this fact, we would call upon the fact that I^*a and Cw, or the fact that $I@a$ and $1 + 1 = 2$, or whatever.

In discussing regularizing explanation, we agreed that with such alternatives only one type of state can be regarded as the true explanatory kind; the others must be seen as gerrymandered entities. Which state is to be preferred? In general, the type that is called upon in the explanation that best reflects nature's mechanical patterns. This line of thought led us to give preference, in any case of the

[33] It will be obvious from these remarks how close I am in spirit to those who have argued, incorrectly as it may be, that reasons are not causes. The tradition in question is characterized—and criticized—in Macdonald and Pettit, op. cit., pp. 80–93. I also find much that is congenial in the writings of Donald Davidson and Daniel Dennett on action-explanation, though I remain unsure in the case of each as to how far they resist the regularizing model. See Davidson, 'Actions, Reasons, and Causes', and 'Mental Events', and Dennett, 'Intentional Systems'. See also John McDowell, 'Physicalism and Primitive Denotation: Field on Tarski', *Erkenntnis*, xiii (1978). Many recent writers recognize that a cause-giving explanation need not be causal in the regularizing sense. See for example Christopher Peacocke, 'Demonstrative Thought and Psychological Explanation', *Synthese*, xlix (1981), 213, and Peter Achinstein, *The Nature of Explanation* (Clarendon Press, Oxford, 1983), Chapter 6. John McDowell emphasizes the point in 'Functionalism and Anomalous Monism', in Ernest LePore and Brian McLaughlin (eds.), *The Philosophy of Donald Davidson: Perspectives on Actions and Events* (Blackwell, Oxford, 1986); he thinks it is implicit in Davidson.

sort envisaged, to the *I**-state rather than the *I*-state, or indeed the *I*@-state. The regularization which best seemed to mirror the pattern that a proper explanation would enunciate was that which called upon the fact that *I**a and *Cw*.

Turning now to normalizing explanation, we have to see whether the same result falls out. We assume that the point of calling on the fact that *Ia*, or on any alleged alternative, is to normalize the corresponding behaviour. Well then, the first question is whether the old criterion of explanation-preference still applies, for if it does, then it will again give the plaudits to the *I**-state. I shall argue that it does not apply, and then I shall take up the further question of what substitute criterion is relevant in adjudicating between alternative normalizing accounts.

The guiding interest of regularizing explanation is to present the event explained as an unsurprising moment in the causal unfolding of the natural world. If there are two versions of such an explanation and one gives us a better picture of the mechanics involved, then it is inevitable that we shall prefer this account. The same does not hold of normalizing explanation, because its guiding interest is quite different.

Its goal is to present the event explained as something which was required of the relevant system, given a certain conception of that system; specifically, given a conception motivated by our beliefs about its design or selection or whatever. Suppose that we have two versions of such an explanation, and that one has the merit, perhaps at some cost in other regards, of answering more precisely to the mechanical structure underlying the system's performance. Will we favour this alternative?

Not necessarily. The alleged merit is quite extrinsic to the normalizing drive, for it does not mean that the event explained is any the more readily seen as normative for the system. It will not motivate a choice of the marked alternative, though it might serve to break a tie. And certainly it will not weigh against any cost that is intrinsic to the normalizing goal.

The point is best made by returning again to our gardening robots. As we survey the robots and wonder about them, we can clearly distinguish between two different explanatory desires. On the one hand we will want a normalizing account of their behaviour which shows in what respects they are gardeners. On the other, at least if we have any curiosity, we will want to understand how they work mechanically: how they are constructed so that, exploiting the laws of nature, they succeed in sustaining their gardening profile. This is a desire for a certain sort of regularizing explanation.

Suppose now that we pursue the normalizing goal, and that, in explaining a particular piece of behaviour, we have to choose between two decompositional alternatives. Why is that robot scraping among those leaves? Because it registers that those leaves are decomposing and, being a gardener, does what it can to rake them up. Alternatively: because it is such that, world willing, it registers that those leaves are decomposing and, being a gardener—better perhaps, a gardener*—it acts so that, world willing, it does what it can to rake them up; and the world is willing, so it does what it can to rake them up. Of these roughly formulated alternatives, let us agree that the second more accurately reflects the mechanics involved. Ought we necessarily to endorse it, then?

Certainly not. The preference for such a parasitic alternative must strike us as bizarre. It will seem to spring from a confusion between the two different explanatory goals that we distinguished. When we are normalizing, why should we worry about the regularizing account that will be required once we turn our minds to the other task? The two tasks can be pursued separately. Running them together only introduces a further risk: namely that we will subject one or both to irrelevant criteria of achievement.

I conclude that the criterion of explanation-choice that operates with regularizing accounts ought not to be allowed to govern the selection of one normalizing story over another. Specifically, it ought not to be allowed to determine the judgement between decompositional alternatives. This result is important, for it means that the argument developed in section 4 is irrelevant, given that action-explanation is normalizing rather than regularizing. The argument gives us reason to prefer an I^*-account to an I-account if the aim is to regularize action, but not if the aim is to normalize it.

We turn now to the second question advertised. Given some decompositional alternatives for the normalization of an event, how ought we to judge between them? If the criterion invoked for judging between regularizing alternatives does not apply, then what yardstick takes its place?

The appropriate criterion is identified by reference to the guiding interest of normalization. The goal in normalizing an event is to substantiate a motivated conception of the system that occasions it.

Well then, if we are presented with decompositional alternatives, we will naturally prefer that which substantiates the conception most straightforwardly.

Let us return to the robot case, where we are choosing between different accounts of why the robot scrapes among the leaves. We already have two alternatives on hand: the *I*-account, as we may call it, and the *I**-account. We may add an *I@*-story as a third alternative. This would account for the event by reference to the fact that the robot is such that, if $1 + 1 = 2$, then he believes that those leaves are decomposing, and $1 + 1 = 2$. Of these accounts it is clear that the *I*-explanation substantiates the gardener conception of the robots most straightforwardly, and that we would naturally prefer this to the alternatives.

To resort to shorthand, our conception gives us immediate reason to think that if *Ia* then, other things being equal, *Aa*: if the robot registers that those leaves are decomposing, then it does what it can to rake them up. It gives us reason only indirectly to think that if *I@a* and $1 + 1 = 2$ then *Aa*, for in order to see this we must do some ratiocination. And equally it offers us only an indirect reason for believing that if *I*a* and *Cw* then *Aa*. The *I*-account is salient to someone who employs the conception, the others are not.

The reason why the *I*-account has this different status is that our conception of a gardening robot has a broad character. It offers us the prospect of a system which achieves a certain environmental equilibrium: in various conditions defined in terms of the system's surrounds, appropriate equilibrating responses are forthcoming. Given that conception, it is not surprising that the antecedents of the norms it embodies are broad states of the system, and indeed states which can be identified without recourse to the fact that $1 + 1 = 2$.

The fact that the system satisfies a norm with a broad antecedent and broad consequent means that it must be constructed so that when the corresponding context-independent condition is realized, it evinces a suitable context-independent response. But this does nothing to motivate a preference for the *I**-account over the *I*-account. Our focus in deploying the gardener conception of the robot is not on the isolated system. It is on the system considered in environmental integration.

We were dealing with the question which criterion ought to govern the decision between decompositional alternatives for normalizing an event. We have seen that the judgement has to be made on the basis of which candidate answers most directly to the conception deployed in the normalization. With this criterion in hand, let us now ask how the decision must go between broad-minded and narrow-minded accounts of human behaviour.

What is true of the gardening robot is true also of the human agent. To return to our original example, suppose that '*Ia*' stands for '*a* wants this cup' and '*Aa*' for '*a* grasps this cup'. Our ordinary broad conception of agents allows us to see directly that in appropriate circumstances the intentional state requires the action. But this is not so for the connection between the corresponding I^*-state and the action. Some inference is required to see that if the agent is such that, world willing, he wants this cup, and the world is willing, then he grasps this cup. The principle does not fall so directly out of the conception.

I conclude that if action-explanation is normalizing, as I have argued that it is, then the judgement between such decompositional alternatives as the *I*-account and the I^*-account goes the other way from how it would if action-explanation were regularizing in character. This means that in such cases we should regard the *I*-type of state as the true explanatory kind and the I^*-type as something gerrymandered out of it. More particularly, it means that we must regard the broad-minded explanation as indispensable. We may be able to reformulate a normalization that calls upon the fact that *Ia* so that it invokes the fact that I^*a and *Cw*. But the reformulation is misleading, since it misdirects us about the explanatory kind involved. And certainly it does not provide us with a replacement for the original account.

The considerations marshalled so far in this section concern normalization in general. I believe that they are sufficient to show that if broad intentional states are invoked to normalize action, then we may regard them as genuinely mental states, not mere hybrids. But there is also a special argument that can be made for that result, and I would like to conclude the section by mentioning this.[34]

The special argument is best presented as a response to a special objection. The objection is that, whatever of normalizing concerns in general, our interest in psychological explanation is in providing an

---

[34] The argument connects closely with Gregory McCulloch's paper in this volume.

account of how things get organized within the head, or at least within the hide, of the subject. We may operate with a broad conception of the normal agent, but nevertheless, so the line goes, we aspire to a story about context-independent connections. That being the direction of our interest, the lesson drawn is that we should see every broad-minded normalization as an account that goes proxy, in the absence of a better understanding, for a purely narrow-minded story. We should view every *I*-account as a story that is better expressed in the form of an *I**-explanation, and we should take the *I**-state as the true explanatory kind.

This objection foists a cognitive psychological ambition on folk psychology, as it is called. The cognitive psychologist, on at least one reading of his strategy, argues as follows. He admits, or at least may admit, that on the broadest and ultimate front the human agent is an environmentally integrated system requiring broad-minded normalization. But he argues that on a nearer and narrower front each agent must be a system designed to satisfy corresponding context-independent norms. The cognitive psychologist seeks to work out a conception of such a narrow system, and perhaps of narrower and narrower sub-systems, with a view ultimately to seeing how neurophysiology supports it. The objection suggests that this is the enterprise in which we folk psychologists are already unwittingly engaged, and that for that reason our broad-minded normalizations should be seen as our best attempts to get at hide-bound connections.

I have nothing against the idea of cognitive psychology. On the contrary, I believe that the top-down strategy just sketched is entirely plausible. What it promises, in my view, is the possibility of normalizing human performance at lower and lower levels. Leaving the broad-minded conception of the agent behind, the cognitive psychologist tries to work out a conception of the sort of narrow system—and ultimately systems—that would subserve the broader complex, and he then seeks to substantiate that conception in the identification of functional elements such as those responsible for information processing, information storage, information retrieval, and the like. The fact that the agent can be submitted to successively lower levels of normalization is in no way inconsistent with my claim that the topmost level, namely that of broad-minded explanation, is not dispensable in favour of narrower accounts. It remains indispensable, because it is alone in substantiating its particular conception of the human person.[35]

What is inconsistent with my claim, however, and it is the core of the objection presented, is the view that folk psychology is a vulgar version of the scientific enterprise: that it is really proto-cognitive psychology. Admit that view and the broad-minded character of ordinary action-explanation will seem to be of no consequence. It will be explained away as a product of the rough and ready nature of folk concepts.

As against this objection, we might argue that the depiction of ordinary action-explanation as proto-science is extremely uncompelling. I prefer to rely, however, on what I have described as my special argument for the indispensability of broad-minded explanation. The argument is that the conception of the human agent deployed and substantiated in such explanation is of outstanding intrinsic merit, and that the exercise cannot be seen, therefore, as something that goes proxy for a context-independent level of normalization: that is, for the deployment and substantiation of a distinct narrow conception of the person.

In order to motivate this thesis, let us go back once more to our robotic gardeners. For all that we have postulated so far, they are blind reasoners: creatures which, without engaging in any deliberation, let alone in any process of review and criticism, manage to act in a rationalizable fashion. Imagine now that not only do they conform to gardening norms: they do so by understanding those norms and, being committed to their implementation, by monitoring themselves and one another for their degree of norm-fulfilling success.

Even under the less complicated picture of the robots, it is plausible that we should want to substantiate the gardener conception of them, whether or not this is a first step in exploring their cognitive psyche; after all, their ultimate telos is to be gardeners. But under the picture now projected, we have reason multiplied to be attached to the substantiation of this broad explanatory conception. It is only by deploying that conception that we can hope to be able to understand the robots as they understand themselves and one another. It is only by substantiating that conception that we can participate with them in a shared understanding of what they do and why they do it.

---

[35] This means that I can endorse the substance of what William G. Lycan describes as homuncular functionalism. See his 'Toward a Homuncular Theory of Believing', *Cognition and Brain Theory*, iv (1981).

The lesson of the robotic parable is obvious. The norms to which each of us feels himself bound, the norms that we invoke in deliberation and review, are those associated with the broad-minded conception. Equally the norms to which we expect one another to be faithful are principles which involve environmental requirements. When any one of us, therefore, plays psychologist with his fellows, he will have reason to take broad-minded explanation seriously. He may have a particular commitment to developing cognitive psychology, but, even so, he cannot think that ordinary action-explanation is uninteresting.

The fact is that only by deploying and substantiating the broad conception of agents can any one of us hope to be able to understand his subjects as they understand themselves. It is only by cleaving to the broad-minded way that he can aspire to psychological understanding, as we might say, of a participant character. Such an understanding is obviously attractive in its own right, being a condition of interpersonal contact. But it also must appeal for instrumental reasons. It is essential, for example, if someone wishes to influence his fellows in the distinctively human manner, making it clear where the actions they evince or the attitudes they form are based on oversights and mistakes.

In the main part of this section we saw that the criteria relevant to normalizing explanation would suggest that the true explanatory kinds invoked in action-accounting are the broad I-states, not their I^*-surrogates. The special objection which we have been considering concedes that the argument offered may work in parallel cases but claims that it fails in the psychological one. The reason alleged is that the broad conception deployed in action-explanation is of no intrinsic interest, serving only to adumbrate the narrow conception which would suit a cognitive psychology. The special argument rebuts this charge, for it shows that on the contrary the broad conception is essential to the achievement of participant psychological understanding.

In conclusion, a comment on terminology. It is common nowadays to counterpoint the notions of folk psychology and scientific, in particular cognitive, psychology. I think that the contrast is misleading, for the category of folk psychology is too mixed a bag. It includes not only our deeply embedded ideas about how action should be explained, but also every currently fashionable story about the nature of dreams, or memory, or drives, or whatever. The special argument which we have just considered suggests that we ought to replace the contrast by one which sets participant psychology on the one side, observer psychology on the other. Participant psychology is what we practise when we seek to rationalize human actions—and of course attitudes—displaying them as the product of a greater or lesser fidelity to appropriate norms. Observer psychology is everything else. It probably attains its highest form in cognitive psychology, but it also includes the shifting conjectures of less scientific folk. The contrast between folk and scientific psychology was drawn on grounds of precision. The contrast between participant and observer psychology is based on grounds of purpose.

7. Conclusion: The Standard and Alternative Views of Intentional States

The more or less standard, functionalist view of intentional states depicts them as causal roles or transitional susceptibilities. To instantiate such a role or susceptibility is to be such that, given certain inputs, and given other interlocking intentional states, certain outputs are ensured. To believe that p or q is to be such that, given evidence that not q, and given the appropriate logical beliefs or dispositions, one moves to the belief that p. To believe that p is to be such that, given the desire that not p, one acts so as to change the status quo. And so on.

There are many issues about the precise interpretation of functionalism. I shall ignore all but one. This is a question about how to identify an intentional state functionally when there are a number of functional candidates available.

Suppose that we have a broad functional state S, a state which is characterized in part by reference to broad inputs and broad outputs. To instantiate it is to be such that, among other things, if C and $\ldots$, then E, where C and E are events which require the world to be thus and so. Consider now the narrow functional state which S presupposes. This will be a state characterized solely in terms of narrow inputs and outputs; specifically, it will be a state such that fulfilment of it in a congenial environment ensures the instantiation of S. We can identify it as the state S^* of being such that, among other things, if C^* and $\ldots$, then E^*, where these events respectively guarantee C and E in a cooperative world.

Grant that there is an intentional state of the bearer with which S and S^* are associated. The question then is; which functional state is the intentional one? They are different states, having different existence conditions, so they cannot both be the intentional state. We must decide between possibilities like the following. (1) S is the intentional state, and S^* is merely a precondition of it. (2) S^* is the intentional state, and S is a hybrid construction out of it. (3) S is the intentional state, but its only psychologically significant component is S^*.

Within the functionalist literature the general preference is for a position like (2) or (3). The reasoning is that the intentional state is a causal role, and that the state which does causal work, so to speak, is S^* rather than S. The environmental condition which makes the difference between S and S^*, after all, is acknowledged on all sides to be causally inert.[36] If S^* is taken to be suitably intentional, (2) will seem attractive; if not, (3).

This reasoning might be paralleled by another argument. Suppose we take intentional states to be causal roles in the sense of causal–explanatory roles. To instantiate an intentional state, then, is to be such that, given certain inputs and certain collateral states, such and such outputs are causally explainable. Suppose further that we take causal explanation to be regularizing in character. It will then follow that position (2) or (3) is the most reasonable one. All that can be causally regularized by S can be regularized by S^*, so parsimony and indeed simplicity will suggest that we should identify the intentional state, or at least its psychologically significant component, with S^*.

So much for the orthodox answer to the question raised. I am now in a position to indicate the view of intentional states to which my approach naturally leads. It is distinguished by the fact of endorsing the first possibility mentioned, providing an unorthodox answer to our question.

I am happy to go along with the picture of intentional states as causal roles, so long as this means causal–explanatory roles. What I wish to insist on, however, is that the sort of causal—better perhaps, cause-giving—explanation which is relevant to the identification of those roles is the normalizing, in particular the rationalizing, variety. I have argued that intentional states explain by rationalizing, and I have assumed that they are themselves explained in a similar manner.

This is to say that intentional states are rationalizing roles rather

---

[36] See n. 18.

than—as in the explanatory version of standard functionalism—regularizing ones. They are profiles characterized by the fact that given such and such inputs and collateral states, they render certain outputs rationally necessary. Those outputs will include transitions to other intentional states as well as initiatives of action.

With this conception of intentional states, it is clear how we should approach the question whether the intentional state in our example is S or S^*. We must conceive of S and S^* as rationalizing roles, and we will want to know which plays the role corresponding to the rationalizing potential of the state under discussion. In all the examples imaginable, the answer will be the broad state S. This will be cast as the intentional state, and the narrow counterpart S^* will be seen as a precondition of it. That is to say, position (1) will command allegiance; the unorthodox answer will triumph.

On the view of intentional states to which I am committed, then, they are states that become salient and indeed visible only from the standpoint of rationalizing explanation. Adopt the assumption of rationality *vis à vis* agents and their intentional states are promptly highlighted. Shift stance to consider agents in a regularizing mode, or even at some lower level of normalization, and these profiles will vanish from sight. They are real attributes of people, but, like secondary properties, they manifest themselves only to observers who occupy a particular perspective: specifically, the perspective of a certain explanatory disposition. They are rational–explanatory kinds, and they become salient only from a rational–explanatory viewpoint.

The intentional states that we ascribe to ourselves and one another are the precipitates of our explanatory practice. Cast action-explanation and attitude-explanation as regularizing and those states will come out in the standard, functionalist mould. Cast it as rationalizing and they will take the shape that I have described. Here as before we see the importance of the issue about explanation. There is probably no deeper question to be found in the province of philosophical psychology.

CHAPTER 2

SCIENTISM, MIND, AND MEANING*

GREGORY McCULLOCH

Introduction

This paper falls into three parts. In the first I describe how the classical notion of meaning is intimately bound up with the nature of folk
psychology—the 'discipline' in terms of which we understand ourselves and each other as ordinary thinking (etc.) beings. I set out the
view that in giving an account of what folk psychology is one works
with some classical notion of meaning, by which I mean the reference-determining sort of meaning familiar from the work of Frege
and his more recent followers. In this sense, folk psychology and
classical meaning seem to stand or fall together, since it is hard to see
what other purpose classical meaning is needed for. The emphasis of
this first part is more on description than argument. I do not so
much defend the view that there is an essential link between folk psychology and classical meaning as describe a link which is, I believe,
generally accepted to exist. The business of supplying arguments
occurs mostly in Parts 2 and 3.

The second part deals with the status of folk psychology as an
account of what mental entities are really like. It is considered
reasonable to expect that, one day, it will be possible to give explanatory accounts of something like behaviour that operate exclusively
with predicates that are *solipsistic*, in a sense that I shall briefly
explain. But this raises the question of the relationship between the
discipline that would employ these predicates, and folk psychology

* © Gregory McCulloch 1986. I read an earlier version of this paper at the Univer-
sity of Nottingham in October 1983, and benefited greatly from the discussion that
followed. I am particularly grateful to Bob Kirk, Nick Measor, and especially Robert
Black. In Parts 2 and 3 I am indebted to the work of John McDowell: see especially
'Meaning, Communication, and Knowledge', in Zak van Straaten (ed.), *Philosophical
Subjects* (Clarendon Press, Oxford, 1980), and 'Anti-realism and the Epistemology of
Understanding', in H. Parret and J. Bouveresse (eds.), *Meaning and Understanding*
(De Gruyter, Berlin, 1981). Finally, various changes for the better have been
prompted by the responses of the editors to an earlier draft, and my thanks are due to
them for this.

as we now have it. Do they amount to the same thing? If they do not, in what sense, if any, would the new discipline—'superpsychology'—underwrite the obvious descriptive and explanatory powers of folk psychology? Given some sort of underwriting, would this amount to an honourable scientific elimination of folk psychology? If there is no such scientific elimination, then what? Should the folk discipline be rejected, at least in austere moments, at best kept on as a useful fiction? Or is it rather the case that folk psychology involves a somewhat independent, perfectly valid system of descriptive concepts? I consider, and accept, a well-known argument to the conclusion that superpsychology and folk psychology are distinct. Then I aim for the conclusion that folk psychology does involve an independent, perfectly valid system of descriptive concepts, in the strong sense that it facilitates an understanding of agents which is not available from the perspective of superpsychology and related disciplines. This conclusion is then defended in Part 3.

The topic of Parts 2 and 3 is familiar enough to students of the philosophies of mind and of science, and has an intrinsic interest of its own. But it is evident that assumed positions on it are intruding more and more into the philosophies of language and of logic. In particular, the classical conception of meaning is sometimes criticized or swept aside on the basis of what I hope to show are indefensible scientistic assumptions about the answers to my questions concerning the relationship between folk psychology and superpsychology. Thus the three parts of my paper are related as follows. Certain attacks on folk psychology which I discuss in Parts 2 and 3 are also attacks on classical meaning, given the conclusion of Part 1. If folk psychology and classical meaning stand or fall together, and folk psychology falls, then classical meaning falls. On the other hand, if I succeed in defending folk psychology against these attacks, then I thereby uphold classical meaning. I do not think that issues to do with mind or meaning can be discussed very fruitfully without such detailed cross-reference as this. But some may disagree: and it is certainly worth stressing that the main argument—that of Parts 2 and 3—is intended to appeal to a wide audience. Even one sceptical about the idea that classical meaning and folk psychology are related as I describe could still, other things being equal, find some interest in my examination of the relationship between folk psychology and superpsychology. This goes, too, for those who do not care overmuch about meaning.

1. Mind and Meaning

1. The nature of folk-psychological properties is described by the following principle (among others):[1]

(I) Beliefs are individuated by their contents.

My understanding of (I) is as follows. We can make folk-psychological predicates by inserting sentences into the second gap of frames like '—— believes that ——', as in, say, '—— believes that London is pretty'. Such a predicate is then ready for application to some suitable subject for some folk-psychological purpose; say, as part of an explanation of that subject's behaviour. Something about the inserted sentence makes the resulting predicate represent the folk-psychological property that it does, rather than some other. One account of this 'something'—the account that I take to be the classical or traditional one—is that it is the meaning, or proposition, or content, expressed by the inserted sentence: a meaning, or proposition, or content that is of a *reference-determining* kind. Reference is that property of a sentence or sentence-part relevant to, or responsible for, the expression's logical behaviour, according to the classical approach. And logic matters to belief because believers, as believers, are required to respect it, by and large, in thought and action. On this classical approach, a believer's respect for logical matters may be understood as springing from his grasp—however this may be characterized—of the logical properties and relations that are determined by the meanings of the words which are used to characterize the beliefs that are ascribed to him. A report like

(1) Ralph believes that London is pretty

says that Ralph has a certain belief: and which belief this is is decided, on the account I am describing, by the reference-determining meaning of the sentence 'London is pretty'. Hence the slogan (I).

I hope this is fairly uncontentious as a description of how classical meaning is supposed to link up with folk psychology. The former is

---

[1] Throughout I take beliefs, and their superpsychological counterparts, as typical test cases for the comparisons that interest me. I do not think that any of the substantive issues are affected in any special way by this.

an ingredient in a theoretical account of the properties posited by the latter. Detailed defence of this approach would be another matter; a matter I shall not pursue here, for my main purpose lies elsewhere. So I pass on now to an apparent truth about classical meaning:

(M) Meanings ain't in the head.[2]

Argument for this conclusion may start from the following considerations. One may try to characterize the meaning, as grasped by Ralph, of a sentence like 'London is pretty', in terms of local or 'solipsistic' facts about him—say the ideas before his mind, or the intensions he associates with the words used, or his (aseptically described)[3] dispositions to respond to (aseptically described) evidence. But then it often seems perfectly intelligible to imagine that Ralph could have a *Doppelgänger*—d-Ralph—who is as similar as you like to him in physical and solipsistic terms, and who is embedded in a qualitatively identical environment, and of whom the following hold:

(i) he grasps the same solipsistic meaning as Ralph, but
(ii) the sentence whose meaning is thus solipsistically characterized has a different truth-value, in d-Ralph's mouth, from the one it has in Ralph's.

Given the possibility of such a situation, it follows straight off that solipsistic meaning alone will not do the job for which classical meaning is required on the approach outlined above. The reason is obvious: such cases show that solipsistic meaning need not determine reference (which, for a sentence, is its truth-value). This sets up the requirement for the classical theorist to specify meaning, in terms other than solipsistic ones, in such a way that the truth-values of the used sentences should be determined to come out as they actually do. One suggestion here—and this is the idea I understand to be enshrined in (M)—is that the references of the words used are themselves, somehow, part of the meaning that the classical theorist must characterize. If, then, Ralph and d-Ralph happen to be thinking of

---

[2] See Hilary Putnam, *Mind, Language and Reality* (CUP, Cambridge, 1975), 223–7.

[3] The qualifications are there because only behavioural and evidential characterizations which allow, say, atom-for-atom replicas in distinct but qualitatively identical environments to *exhibit the same behaviour in response to the same evidence* will be of use to 'solipsistic' theories. Thus *getting on a train to London* would not be a suitable description of a piece of behaviour.

different objects (London and d-London), it follows that 'London is pretty' has a different meaning in the two cases, and that in Ralph's case this meaning contains London, whilst in d-Ralph's it contains d-London. Hence the slogan (M).[4]

Again, this is not intended to be too contentious, as I take myself merely to be describing a general development which classical theorists seem to have had forced upon them. As with (I), I offer no detailed defence of the resulting doctrine. Instead, I pass on to a thesis that follows from (I) and (M) as explained here, and which is central to my main topic:

(B) Beliefs ain't in the head.

If meanings individuate beliefs, and the specification of meanings involves extracranial items like London, then the individuation of beliefs also involves such items. One cannot think of beliefs in solipsistic terms, given (I), since one cannot so think of meanings, given (M). In particular, we have the result that whereas Ralph believes that London is pretty,

(2) d-Ralph believes that d-London is pretty,

and the non-identity of London and d-London is enough to ensure that (1) and (2) ascribe different beliefs to our *Doppelgänger*.

2. An argument which is highly relevant to my concerns starts from this point. Its essential thrust is that this result shows folk psychology, straight off, to be faulty as an explanatory theory of behaviour, and in need of replacement by a theory that individuates its states less finely. *Doppelgänger* like Ralph and d-Ralph, it is said, display striking similarities in (aseptically described) behaviour which one reasonably expects a proper explanatory account of these matters to capture, most straightforwardly by saying that they *instantiate the same psychological predicates*. Folk psychology fails here, given the view of it that I have outlined, so the idea is that its work should be done by superpsychology, a discipline that will introduce new

---

[4] Cf. Putnam, *Mind, Language and Reality*, chapt. 12; Saul Kripke, *Naming and Necessity* (Blackwell, Oxford, 1980); John McDowell, 'On the Sense and Reference of a Proper Name', *Mind*, lxxxvi (1977).

predicates capable of being instantiated by *Doppelgänger* who happen to be thinking about different things. Such a position is nicely characterized by the demand that *methodological solipsism* be adopted as the guiding principle in the search for explanatory psychological predicates.[5] And here the antipathy between this approach and folk psychology seems particularly apparent, given the non-solipsistic commitment that (M) and (B) enshrine. The *Doppelgänger* consideration, in short, seems to suggest that folk psychology doesn't really do its job properly, and should be replaced by superpsychology. This suggestion could be elaborated as follows.

Superpsychology will involve predicates, explanatory of behaviour, that could apply to believers of 'London is pretty' and their *Doppelgänger*, and explain the behaviour that folk-psychological reports like (1) and (2) can be used to explain. Parallel to (1) and (2) one would have the superpsychological reports

(3) Ralph is ???

and

(4) d-Ralph is ???,

and there would appear to be a significant gain in explanatory generality. Let us call our putative superpsychologist 'Bruce'. Then, roughly speaking, Bruce may want to claim that he would be in a position to do the job—the explanation, etc., of behaviour—that folk psychology now is used to do, but in a position to do it better. For instance, his theory would not have the allegedly counterintuitive results in *Doppelgänger* cases; and it may also, one may reasonably hope, do the explanatory job in a more precise and quantifiable way. Folk psychology, in this future situation, would appear to be strictly superfluous: useful, perhaps, for ordinary purposes and in relaxed moments, but strictly eliminable in the overall story of how things are. If so, then one who spends his time—as the classical theorist of meaning does, according to me—servicing the predicates and notions of folk psychology is in many respects simply wasting his time, and would be better to switch, as Bruce's friends have already done, to the more scientifically respectable activity of speculating about the probable nature of the predicates of superpsychol-

---

[5] Cf. Jerry A. Fodor, 'Methodological Solipsism considered as a Research Strategy in Cognitive Psychology', in his *Representations* (Harvester Press, Hassocks, 1981), 225–53.

ogy. This is the sort of challenge that I am addressing in this paper. And I take it that nothing less than a demonstration of the fact that Bruce will not be doing the job that folk psychologists now do will be a satisfactory reply. For it would surely be rather feeble to set much store by the hope that superpsychology will never exist.

3. Before proceeding directly to that business, however, some comments are in order if certain possible misunderstandings are to be avoided.

The first comment is about meaning. It is crucial to be clear that the classical view of meaning that I described above is not seriously at odds, as far as it goes, with the views of those who think that there is a common content in the minds of our *Doppelgänger* Ralph and d-Ralph which should be 'peeled off' the logic by an accurate characterization of their 'inner worlds'. Simon Blackburn—a proponent of this view—makes the point very clearly when he suggests that (1) might be analysed after the fashion

(1′) Ralph thinks that the ϕ is pretty, and his thought is about London.

This analysis acknowledges, in the spirit of (B), that beliefs are reference-involving (note the mention of London as the focus of the thinking), whilst leaving room for the peeled-off content (given by 'the ϕ') that Ralph would share with d-Ralph.[6] Given (B), of course, such a shared content would not exhaust the content of the *belief* reported in (1). But this is not really important, since one would have available the resources to characterize some type of state—say a 'notional' state[7]—jointly instantiated by Ralph and d-Ralph, and responsible for all the behavioural consonances. Notional states are not beliefs, given the logical properties that are associated with these latter states. But (if they exist) they will do honest, perhaps essential, explanatory work: and who wants to argue about a word?

Now one can be sceptical about the existence of notional states so construed, for instance by remaining unconvinced that the required peeled-off contents will always be forthcoming. But what I want to stress is that this is not a particularly weighty consideration in the

---

[6] See Simon Blackburn, 'Thought and Things', *Aristotelian Society Supplementary Volume*, liii (1979).

[7] See Daniel C. Dennett, 'Beyond Belief', in Andrew Woodfield (ed.), *Thought and Object* (Clarendon Press, Oxford, 1982), 1–95.

present context. The temptation to think that it is comes from a tendency to assimilate proposals like Blackburn's to the sort of decomposition that is suggested by Fodor's plea for methodological solipsism. This latter decomposition, which I mentioned above, and shall discuss in more detail below, relates to the apparent duality of the role played by folk-psychological ascriptions when these are understood in the way that I described in Section 1. On the one hand, such ascriptions explain bare behavioural functioning (in the wrong terms, if the *Doppelgänger*-related complaint is correct). On the other, they relate subjects to extracranial items such as London. Put at its most stark, Fodor's plea is that this dual role should be shared between two distinct disciplines, one of which will try to capture the consonances between *Doppelgänger* that a solipsistic account highlights, while the other will trace the connections between these superpsychological facts and extracranial matters.[8] As I shall explain below, I have no reasonable quarrel with this as a proposal for a pair of new disciplines, one of which I am calling superpsychology. Furthermore, I do not deny that (say) Blackburn's peeled-off contents, if available, would be usable to characterize the states of this behavioural discipline. But plainly, a rejection of *Blackburn's* proposal is no rejection of *Fodor's*, since it leaves open plenty of possibilities for specifying superpsychological states—say in terms of causal or functional role, or (aseptically described) dispositions to respond to (aseptically described) evidence, or any number of so far unimagined possibilities—that have no use for a notion of content at all (remember that superpsychology is only a twinkle in the eye).

One should thus turn a jaundiced eye on those who complain that classical theorists of meaning are barking up the wrong tree in virtue of their involvement with (M) and (B).[9] Such critics are inclined to think that there is an intolerable strain in the classical conception because its deliverances on beliefs appear to be incompatible with the aspirations of superpsychology. And, like Blackburn, they are inclined to propose variant conceptions of meaning that are designed to be free from this apparent disadvantage, for instance by

[8] Cf. Colin McGinn, 'The Structure of Content', in Woodfield (ed.), *Thought and Object*, 207–58.

[9] Cf. Gilbert Harman, 'Meaning and Semantics', in M. Munitz and P. Unger (eds.), *Semantics and Philosophy* (NYU Press, New York, 1974); Hartry Field, 'Mental Representation', *Erkenntnis*, xiii (1977); McGinn, 'The Structure of Content'.

being such that Ralph and d-Ralph would apprehend the same meanings. I complain against these theorists in so far as they consider themselves to have got at the real notion for which classical theorists only grope. Of course there can be no general complaint against attempts like Blackburn's to characterize a sort of content that would be useful to the superpsychologist. The sensible thing to do is wait and see if they succeed. Complaint is entirely in order, though, if those who make the attempt claim to be doing properly a job which the classical theorist has botched. One can only sustain this conclusion on the assumption that superpsychology is (in part, at least) what folk psychology should be, and that the latter has failed to live up to some reasonable theoretical requirement, and has transmitted this failure to the classical theorists. But why assume this? Well, this is my main theme, the topic of the arguments of Parts 2 and 3. And I am suggesting that this issue is likely to be obscured if one merely argues about the sort of thing meaning should be.[10]

4. My second comment concerns an alleged mysteriousness exhibited by beliefs when these are understood in the classical way that I have described. The mysteriousness may be brought out by the following thought. Given that beliefs are just causal agents relating to the production and explanation of behaviour, why do we assign

[10] Here is as good a place as any to mention Dummettian attacks on the Frege-inspired view of meaning. These attacks bear on the topics of this paper in a number of ways. One attack concerns the sort of reference that one may intelligibly characterize meaning in terms of. It must not, according to Dummett, wheel free of the recognitional capacities enjoyed by the apprehenders of these meanings, on pain of making the acquisition and manifestation of such apprehension appear as quite miraculous feats. I do not know how much this point affects principles like (M) and (B) as I understand them, and in so far as they apply to beliefs etc. about epistemically recoverable objects. I am inclined to think that it affects them not at all: but if I am wrong, then my defence of classical meaning here just will not face up to this attack. Other Dummettian themes are more obviously relevant. McGinn, in 'The Structure of Content', seems to see Dummettian strictures on classical meaning as somewhat misformulated demands for what I am calling a solipsistic account of behaviour. McGinn thinks that Dummett is right about the conceptual/behavioural aspect of (classical) meaning, but wrong about the referential. McDowell, in 'Anti-realism and the Epistemology of Understanding', in Parret and Bouveresse (eds.), *Meaning and Understanding* (De Gruyter, Berlin, 1981), argues that Dummett imposes unwarranted scientistic constraints on the theoretical account of folk psychology (I reformulate here in terms of my discussion below). Roughly, my arguments in Parts 2 and 3 may be seen as supporting McDowell's conclusion and rebutting McGinn's implication that Dummett is right about *part* of (classical) meaning.

them classical meaning—and hence relations with extracranial matters—when these relations are completely irrelevant to that causal
role? And this may look particularly awkward for the classical
theorist of meaning; perhaps by reinforcing the *Doppelgänger* complaint that there is something wrong with folk psychology, perhaps
by dumping on him an extra problem avoided by the lover of
superpsychology.

Now I do not wish to deny that there is an interesting question
here. For some reason, men developed as folk psychologists, and
one wants to know why, partly out of a general interest in natural
history, partly out of a particular interest in the nature of man. But it
seems to me to be wrong to press this question in the present context,
since one is then far too likely to prejudge the more important questions at issue. I shall say that the correct, relevant response is to reject the antecedent: beliefs *aren't* just causal agents in the production
and explanation of behaviour. Of course, I shall need to produce arguments and clarification if this view of belief is to figure in a case
against claims made on behalf of superpsychology. But by the same
token, the supporter of superpsychology cannot be allowed to help
himself to premises that effectively secure the issue for him. We
shall see that having an unprejudiced view of what is going on when
folk psychology is being used is very much at the heart of the matter.

5. Finally, we must briefly clarify certain differences between a folk-
psychological report like (1), and its superpsychological counterpart
(3).

As they stand, (1) is rather more informative and useful, containing information that relates both to Ralph's behaviour and to his
relations with the extracranial item London. (3), we can allow, contents itself merely with the behavioural part of the matter. But Bruce
need not be unduly concerned about this difference. For the obvious
reply is that folk psychology is a hybrid enterprise that incorporates
two strands better kept separate. These strands are the explanation
of behaviour and the plotting of relations between the agent and the
environment; the two roles that Fodor discerns.[11] (3) is only concerned with one of these tasks, admittedly. But that doesn't necessarily impugn superpsychology, or the scientific enterprise of which

---

[11] Cf. McGinn, 'The Structure of Content'.

it is a component. All Bruce will need to do is supplement his psychology with a geographical discipline that deals with the relations that hold between agents and their extracranial surroundings, so as to yield, where required, interdisciplinary reports such as

> (5) Ralph is ???, and this state is related in an appropriate way to London.[12]

Then, he can go on to say, it will be with *such* reports that he will be able to do the job now done by folk psychology, but with the explanatory advantages mentioned above.

With these comments out of the way, I can now turn to my main business.

2. The Manifest Mind

6. Let us imagine a situation in which Bruce is equipped with his interdisciplinary reports like (5), and enquire whether he will have thereby supplanted folk psychology, at least in principle even if not in practice. In this enquiry, it will be convenient to start by considering a recent discussion of a similar question conducted by Macdonald and Pettit.[13] These authors consider the case of one, such as Bruce hopes to be, in possession of a scientifically respectable theory of his fellow human beings. And they endorse two arguments designed to show that he would not be able to dispense altogether with his folk-psychological understanding of what is going on. Their scientist, in fact, is a superneurophysiologist: but that will not matter for my purposes. These arguments seem to me to suggest a powerful defence of folk psychology, but only in the context of a fairly lengthy account of what folk psychology is. The task of Part 2 is to provide that account, and to reinterpret Macdonald and Pettit's arguments in its light, thereby upholding folk psychology against the attack I have outlined. Then in Part 3 I consider, and try to disarm, certain replies that Bruce might attempt.

Macdonald and Pettit's first argument is as follows:

---

[12] It is far from obvious that Bruce would be able to help himself to the notion of 'appropriate relation'—that is, reference—without making an ineliminable (and, from his point of view, damning) appeal to folk-psychological notions. Presumably his best hope is the somewhat forlorn one that reference can be explained in causal terms; but I do not consider this matter in the present paper.

[13] Graham Macdonald and Philip Pettit, *Semantics and Social Science* (Routledge & Kegan Paul, London, 1981).

[A]ny account of a piece of speech or writing which failed to find any [classical] meaning in it . . . would miss the most important feature of the matter to be explained, eliminating the difference between that matter and a string of meaningless signs emitted to keep [Bruce] busy (p. 73).

Macdonald and Pettit appear to have two points in mind. The first is that in apparently ignoring the *intention* with which the speech or writing is produced, Bruce will be ignoring its most salient feature, missing something crucial in Ralph's performance. And the second point is that Bruce would also be robbing himself of a useful source of information. As Macdonald and Pettit say, 'for all [Bruce] knows, the events of which he is giving an account may be attempts by a fellow scientist to communicate some important findings or insights' (ibid.).

However, it is not immediately clear that Bruce—or Macdonald and Pettit's superneurophysiologist—need succumb to this. If either really is equipped with a full interdisciplinary report, then it seems open to him to reply, shortly, that this would contain all of the information intended by the subject, in virtue of its geographical component, which would trace the subject's states back to the relevant features of the environment to which they relate. Of course, this still leaves the point that something *about Ralph* will be lost when the switch is made from (say) (1) to (5)—a suspicion which I join Macdonald and Pettit in harbouring. But since the correctness or otherwise of this suspicion is the very point at issue, it is clear that rather more needs to be said if any progress is to be made. Let us turn to Macdonald and Pettit's second argument.

This argument is based on the familiar point that one such as Bruce must maintain a folk-psychological understanding of *himself* if his results are to be intelligible to him. Macdonald and Pettit say that Bruce would at least have to

see the words in which [he] expressed [his results] as meaningful. . . . This means that the consistently scientific thinker . . . would have to put himself out of the world to which he held that such science applied. He would have to see himself as a lone rational ego, uniquely fitted for explanation on the established orthodox lines (p. 73).

Now this may work against the superneurophysiologist, who would then, I suppose, face the awkward question 'What can be so special about *you*?'. But there is room for doubt over its effectiveness against Bruce. To see this, imagine him explaining Ralph with the interdisciplinary report (5). Part of the total world that Bruce is out to comprehend will be the fact that

> (6) Bruce believes that Ralph is ???, and that this state is appropriately related to London.

Macdonald and Pettit's point is that (6) is couched in folk-psychological terms. On the face of it, though, it seems that Bruce could replace (6) with

> (7) Bruce is ????, and this state is appropriately related to Ralph's being ???, and standing in the appropriate relation to London,

and thereby escape the argument. One relevant point here seems to depend on the nature of ????. The temptation is to suppose that (7) misses something, namely the awareness of the bit of information about Ralph and London that (6) ascribes to Bruce. For if ???? merely describes some internal causal propensity of Bruce's, and this is in turn related to Ralph's states and his relation to London, then the grasp of the bit of scientific information that Bruce seemed to have acquired has disappeared. But this will perhaps only be so if ???? is not content-specifying. If it is—and who knows what the future may hold?—Bruce could claim that this bit of content captures the 'inner' component of the original, while the remainder of (7) specifies clearly the rest, which was confused in (6).[14]

As with the first argument, it seems fair to say that no very decisive point in favour of folk psychology has been forthcoming. What we have amounts to little more than suggestions: that Bruce misses something about Ralph when he stops seeing him in folk-psychological terms; and that Bruce anyway cannot dispense with seeing himself in these terms. What I propose to do is to vindicate the nerve of these suggestions by developing them within a suitably detailed account of the nature of the folk-psychological enterprise.

---

[14] It is rather hard to move forward on this. There will be, after all, (will there not?)

> (8) Bruce believes that Bruce is ????, and that this state is appropriately related to Ralph's being ???, and standing in the appropriate relation to London—

and it may be that Macdonald and Pettit's argument could get a grip because of the threat of a regress. Frankly, I find this thought rather baffling: anyway I pursue a different line (but see section 10).

7. First we need some distinctions. One can adopt a *descriptive stance* (DS) towards a set of phenomena (a system). In adopting a DS one typically makes predications of the system, and also subsumes it, via such predications, under appropriate generalizations, thereby generating new predications. Following and adapting Dennett,[15] we may distinguish three types of DS relevant to the present issue. Thus one may describe (etc.) something in *physical* terms, say by using the vocabulary of a suitable fragment of physical science. Or one can adopt a *design* DS and view the system as functioning, when all is well, in accordance with some abstract blueprint or design specification that describes the output and other functions of the system elicited by certain specified inputs. Such a blueprint will be more or less independent of physical descriptions, in the sense that it can be variously 'realized' in systems that are different when viewed from a physical DS. And there is the *Intentional* DS, in adopting which one describes (etc.) the system in folk-psychological terms—as having beliefs, desires, intentions, and so on. There are other types of DS (for example, moral, aesthetic) and many things to be said about, for instance, the suitability of and interrelations between the different DSs one may adopt in different cases. Some of these issues will come up in due course, but for the moment the basic point seems clear enough to require just one further comment. As I am here construing them, DSs are highly idealized, in the sense that adopting a DS is an essentially passive affair, involving only observation and extrapolation therefrom.

A more active note is sounded by what I shall call an *intervention strategy* (IS). As the name says, to adopt one of these is essentially to act upon a system to produce or prevent change in it. Again our three-way distinction is possible. Thus one can intervene physically with a system in a great variety of ways; or one can intervene at the design level by inputting in the appropriate way; or one can intervene Intentionally (say) by reasoning with the system.

There is an interesting asymmetry between these DSs and ISs regarding the interdependencies that exist between the levels. For instance, to adopt design or Intentional ISs will typically—if not necessarily—involve adopting a physical IS at the same time, since we do not often if ever come across systems that can be affected in any way but the physical. On the other hand, notoriously, adopting

[15] 'Mechanism and Responsibility', in Ted Honderich (ed.), *Essays on Freedom of Action* (Routledge and Kegan Paul, London, 1973).

design or Intentional DSs does not directly involve the adoption of a physical DS: trivially, because appropriate physical concepts need not be available; more interestingly, because there need be no direct conceptual links between the different levels of description. However, some parity with the dependency of design and Intentional ISs on physical ISs is restored by the doctrine of *supervenience*: the doctrine, roughly, that (a) design, Intentional, and (at least some) other descriptions apply to physical systems, and that (b) no change can be truly reported at the design, Intentional or other level unless there is a describable (in principle) physical change in the system.

Just as DSs are idealized by me as essentially passive, so I here think of ISs as blind, as mere unconceptualized proddings. But these two idealizations allow us to define something more realistic: a *pattern of engagement* (PE). A PE is a mixture of DSs and ISs with respect to some system(s). Description and intervention, ordinarily so called, are themselves probably best thought of as PEs, since description typically if not necessarily involves or presupposes selected interventions, and intervention usually—and perhaps necessarily, if it is deliberate—takes place against a background of descriptions and in the light of assumed ends. No doubt most of what passes for human existence can be seen as partially constituted by PEs as here defined, since it is hard to think of modes of being that do not involve acting on things conceived under some or other description. Obviously many human activities involve more than this, but the idea of the PE seems to capture something quite basic and ubiquitous.

Each PE comes complete with what I shall call *characteristic systems*. These are the things, considered from the point of view of the component DS, with respect to which it is appropriate to adopt the PE. Furthermore, one can speak of the *knowledgeable engagers* of a PE. A knowledgeable engager 'knows the ropes': he can understand and employ the conceptual apparatus of the DS, effect the legitimate interventions of the IS, and (where this is necessary) give an account of the characteristic ends that govern the PE. Knowledgeability, on this definition, thus involves the having of certain practical abilities, and merely being able to say how one might make the interventions (if, indeed, this is possible) will not count as being (fully) knowledgeable. I shall say, finally, that a knowledgeable engager *understands* the characteristic systems (in the manner appropriate to the PE), and exhibits this understanding when he knowledgeably engages. There is undoubtably ontological, metaphysical, and epistemological extravagance in all of this: and I shall deal with that at the appropriate time.

8. The immediate task is to compare superpsychology and folk psychology as PEs, in order to get a better idea of their characteristic systems and of the understanding of these that they afford. Only then will it be fruitful to raise the question whether the one could in principle replace the other. What Bruce has in mind is certainly a pure form of explanatory PE. The goal of the developers of superpsychology is the most comprehensive design DS available of systems like Ralph and d-Ralph. That is, given that these two exhibit the striking 'behavioural' similarities noted above, even though they are embedded in distinct environments (and even though they may have quite different physical constitutions), the aim is to find predicates like ??? which are (a) independent enough of the relevant physical ones to be true of our *Doppelgänger* and (b) such that having the associated property explains why a given input elicits the observed output. Attaining such an aim doubtless involves one or more ISs: for instance, all manner of inputs must be tried to determine the 'design-appropriate' ones; and detailed knowledge of underlying physical mechanisms would be useful, if not essential. Once attained, such a design DS could then be combined with various ISs in order to serve given ends or purposes (for example, a sort of use that requires proper functioning, or one that requires controlled malfunction, and so on). But we may presume that Bruce is primarily interested in getting the comprehensive DS for its own sake. And what we must compare is the PE of the putative enquirer, armed with this comprehensive DS and using it to explain this or that piece or stretch of behaviour on the part of some suitable system, and the PE of the typical folk psychologist. Would the former be making a better job of what the latter does?

As long as folk psychology is thought of as an essentially explanatory PE which requires the adoption of the Intentional stance, the answer 'yes' seems irresistible. In principle, at least, there will always be available the properly worked-out design stance that would serve the same purpose in a more scientific way, and the best defence of folk psychology that seems to be forthcoming is a pragmatic one. Sometimes, it can be said, the right 'blueprint' will not be to hand, or will be too voluminous, and explanatory and predictive purposes will then be better served by the adoption of the Intentional stance.[16] Now my aim is to do better than this. But the power of this pragmatic defence ought not to be underestimated. If the adoption of the Intentional stance really will always be *de facto* obligatory even when the emphasis is on 'scientific' prediction and control, then obviously there cannot be much wrong with the investigation into the nature of its predicates that the classical theorist of meaning, on my view of him, undertakes. Given that we are and must remain folk psychologists, what could be wrong with an enterprise that sets itself the task of describing certain aspects of the apparatus that we then employ? Perhaps some will find the Brucish craving for insight into the deep matters that are allegedly involved more exciting than the picturesque talk of 'grasping meanings' that the classical theorist is prone to use. But this is a matter of temperament, and there is no respectable argument here. We do 'grasp meanings' in the sense that our thinking and acting, by and large, is governed by the logical principles that meaning is used to explicate. Since the whole point of the pragmatic defence is that we cannot practically abstain from using an explanatory stance which characterizes agents in terms that are sensitive to these very matters, of course the attempt to describe them in systematic detail is respectable. It is something that is just there to be done.

However, this pragmatic defence can certainly be improved upon since, as I now intend to show in some detail, it is seriously wrong to think of folk psychology as an essentially explanatory PE of the type that superpsychology would be.

9. Naturally not all PEs are explanatory. Consider, for instance, the PE *treating another as a person*, which is an important element in morality. Whatever else is needed to characterize this particular PE, it does not seem right to speak of its characteristic end or purpose; and this alone marks it off clearly from explanatory PEs, which

---

[16] Stephen Schiffer, in section III of 'Truth and the Theory of Content', in Parret and Bouveresse (eds.), *Meaning and Understanding*, suggests that the assignment of classical meaning to (some) mental states may be practically very useful, if only because the geographical component of interdisciplinary reports may be otherwise unavailable because of straightforward epistemic limitations. But this is compatible with the view, which I take to be Schiffer's and which I am trying to rebut, that interdisciplinary reports could in principle replace folk-psychological ones. See also Dennett, 'Mechanism and Responsibility'.

characteristically aim for some ideal of descriptive adequacy. Of course, one *may* treat another as a person for some particular purpose, and it may be that some evolutionary or sociological explanation of why this PE exists is possible. But this does not show that each instance of its adoption is explicable in terms of the purposes it is intended to serve by the one who adopts it. And there seems no compelling reason why it should be possible to show this. Behaving decently is just something that some people sometimes do for its own sake, thankfully.

This PE can perhaps best be characterized in terms of the restrictions that govern its component DSs and ISs. Legitimate DSs, for instance, are mostly but perhaps not exclusively Intentional, and they also involve predications ('loyal', 'fair', etc.) that are not obviously an essential part of the explanatory apparatus of the Intentional stance. ISs are in turn even more likely to be Intentional, although again perhaps not exclusively so. But more than this, treating another as a person involves heavy restrictions on the ISs one may adopt, even on the Intentional level, since proper recognition of another's personhood just does involve a lot of non-interference, even if this is Intentional.[17]

What is folk psychology? Considered as an actual phenomenon, it is a PE, or (more accurately) a bundle of PEs. Let us first concentrate on *behaving as a folk psychologist*. One counts as engaging in this PE under a variety of conditions. One such is when adopting the (explanatory) Intentional stance towards some system(s)—when one explains and predicts in terms of beliefs, desires, intentions, and so on. One who treats another as a person is also a folk psychologist. As we have just seen, this may well involve Intentional explanation, but there is much more to it than this. Again, engaging in a conversation counts as behaving as a folk psychologist. This need have no moral component, and it is not obvious that any explanation has to be involved either, although one must (at least tacitly) view the other

---

[17] Dennett, 'Mechanism and Responsibility' 165 f., quite rightly points out that moral considerations are not automatically imported with the adoption of the Intentional stance. But his implication that seeing something as morally significant constitutes the adoption of a fourth level in the series *physical, design, Intentional* . . . is certainly mistaken, as the brief comments in the text indicate. Dennett's paper contains a valuable discussion of an issue quite closely related to the one in the present paper, although some distortion results from his failure to make distinctions that my apparatus of DSs, ISs, and PEs is intended to bring out. Most seriously, there is no indication of the extent to which providing explanations of behaviour is peripheral to the Intentional stance.

participant(s) under Intentional descriptions. And one could go on. The difficulty here is clearly that of finding some central or essential feature that characterizes folk psychology. Yet meaningful comparison with superpsychology surely requires this. Superpsychology, we have seen, is to be a design-explanatory PE. Folk psychology is never this, and (considered as an actual phenomenon) is not even always any kind of explanatory PE. So what is it? And is there any interesting sense of 'work' in which it does work which may or may not in principle be done better by superpsychology?

In effect, we are asking 'What is the mind?', given that minds are the characteristic systems of folk psychology. Now, one 'gets a grip' on characteristic systems, typically, just by engaging in the PEs, and knowledgeable engagers have the best grip of all. How do we typically get a grip on the mind?

Notoriously, there are two somewhat different ways. Each of us has a rather special acquaintance with certain aspects of one mind—his own—which is the source of various epistemic privileges. And beyond this, it is usual if not necessary for a mind to encounter others in the environment in which it finds itself. As we shall see, the ultimate force of my construal of Macdonald and Pettit's two arguments rests on this fact; the first argument exploits the 'third-person' view of mind, while the second exploits the 'first-person' view. But it is the interrelation between these two viewpoints which, I shall try to show, holds the key to our issue. By way of a preliminary, then, let us note the first distinctive feature of folk psychology. PEs as described by me so far have been markedly one-sided. That is, PEs are defined in terms of the notions *DS* and *IS*, and these two notions are defined as certain stances or attitudes that can be adopted towards what I called systems. The systems themselves were just left as brute phenomena, apt to be described and acted upon, set over against the adopter of this or that PE. In folk psychology, distinctively, things are not like this. Typical engagement in this PE (or bundle of PEs) is reciprocal, in the sense that the 'systems' which confront a given engager are themselves usually engagers in that very same PE with respect to the 'system' doing the original engaging, and all at the same time. Just think about how you conduct your daily business, and what the opportunities for being a folk psychologist are like, and you will see what I mean. Perhaps occasionally you explain why someone crossed the road in terms of his beliefs about and his pro-attitude towards something on the other side. Perhaps sometimes you cynically or in legitimate competition think of someone before you as something which can best be moved along by way of a certain Intentional intervention, and you act accordingly. But for the rest of the folk-psychological time, which is spent chatting, discussing, planning, loving, sharing experiences, and all the rest, things are not like this at all. Take, for instance, typical communication, which is certainly at the heart of things. In such an encounter each party adopts the folk-psychological stance inasmuch as each takes the other(s) to be fit and active subjects of folk-psychological predicates. Utterances are accepted as evincing beliefs, hopes, fears, desires, speculations, and so on. The things done by any other are seen as such in the light of some tacitly accepted story which can be told in terms of instantiated folk-psychological predicates. Because such stories are 'tacit'—whatever, exactly, that means—it is, perhaps, debatable whether they are correctly labelled 'theories'. But whatever the correct word, the communication that takes place in the light of these bodies of doctrine is certainly not the explanation of behaviour. What goes on is an essentially interactive product of centres of consciousness which are, in many respects, open to the view of each and all, complete with folk-psychological self-conception. This is *nothing like* what goes on when someone adopts the design-explanatory PE. Of course, someone may adopt any old explanatory PE with respect to a system which is simultaneously adopting that same PE with respect to him; and this may be discovered, and figure in an explanation of what the system is doing. But this is not the kind of reciprocity which communication (for instance) involves. The mutuality here is not something to be discovered and registered in a detached frame of mind. It is intrinsic to the very (folk-psychological) PE itself, and is accepted to be so by the engagers.

10. What I propose to do now is to develop these remarks into the beginnings of an appropriate reply to Bruce's challenge. To this end, I return to Macdonald and Pettit's two arguments, taking them in reverse order.

The second argument, recall, is to the effect that Bruce could not dispense altogether with folk psychology when undertaking his explanations, since he would at least have to maintain a folk-psychological understanding of himself. Put in my terms, this is the claim that one who adopts a design-explanatory PE with respect to some system will still be maintaining an Intentional, rather than a design, conception of himself. And the point seemed to bog down. The way out is as follows.

Consider the situation where someone is engaging in a PE with some system distinct from himself: a PE whose DS is articulated and explicit, in the sense that it is borne in mind by the engager and is what guides his interventions as such. Adopting a design DS certainly falls under this heading, along with all other explanatory PEs directed upon some distinct system. Although, by definition, such an engager is not an object of his engagement, he is still, in a sense, 'present' in his overall cognitive picture. He is there as the thing—mind, consciousness, whatever—that is engaging with the relevant system. This is not to say that the engager must work in the context of a wry, self-conscious picture of himself-the-engager going about his world-directed business; although it is possible to work in such a state of mind. It is, rather, to say that no matter how selflessly absorbed in its business the mind might be, it is still, implicitly, part of its own picture, taken for granted and unscrutinized. This may sound rather mystical: how is one 'present' in one's own other-directed explanations? However, this puzzlement derives, I think, from a completely unrealistic conception of what explanation, and other types of cognitive engagement, are like. This conception would have it that such things are or can be a purely passive and perhaps mechanical registration of and extrapolation from the phenomena before one: in other words, something like the idealized DS that I described above. But I doubt whether they are ever really like this. For instance, as I have remarked, explanation standardly involves a great deal of intervention with the system in question, which is why explanation is best thought of as a PE. Intervention requires action, and action requires some kind of implicit (at least) self-awareness, if not always then certainly in situations that exhibit the sort of complex structure that explanation involves. One has a set aim with respect to the phenomena, and actions are tailored accordingly. Even when intervention is not present, mere observation will almost certainly require action—manipulation of apparatus, changes of observational position, and so on. And even were all of this absent in some *recherché* case, self-conscious direction of attention, and reasoning about the phenomena, would still certainly be required in the type of case under consideration: and in this too the mind is 'present' to itself.

Self-presence is, of course, bound up with introspection. One's self-awareness when engaging in some complex PE may well be tacit, in the sense that one need not be having occurrent thoughts with the appropriate contents while so engaged. But such thoughts are producible on demand, say as a response to some question: and what facilitates the response is introspection. Moreover, our introspective view of ourselves is unregenerately folk-psychological; this is how we find ourselves, and no matter how our confidence in the accuracy of this picture may have been shaken, it does not go away. Macdonald and Pettit are suggesting, on my present interpretation, that it could not do so. This is not to suggest, of course, that one cannot take a 'third-personal' explanatory stance towards *oneself*: that would clearly be wrong. But it is to suggest that in so doing one would still be present in the tacit folk-psychological guise that is accessible to introspection. One would, in effect, enter one's whole story at least twice; as that upon which enquiry is directed, and as that which is directing the enquiry.

In some respects Macdonald and Pettit's claim, as here represented, is rather stronger than it needs to be. The suggestion is that our avowedly folk-psychological self-conception could not be dispensed with. To this it is tempting to reply that our mode of seeing ourselves could change given enough concentration and the right sort of education. And then it would be tempting to respond to this with the point that in so changing we should lose our grip on the very notions—explanation, understanding, enquiry, action—that define the Brucish project. The issues then become extremely dim. But these manoeuvres seem to me to be unnecessary. The real point at issue is whether or not folk psychology affords one access to a distinctive understanding of things that is not available from the design stance. Whether or not we could 'get by' without this understanding—whatever, if anything, that means—is a further question. Presumably, what we can 'get by' without is partly determined by what, if anything, we are aiming for. So the onus anyway is on Bruce to show that no respectable purposes would be compromised if (supposing this to be possible) our folk-psychological self-conceptions withered. (On the other hand, one must beware of a possibly trivializing defence which just builds the alleged purpose into the questioned activity). In any case, I want to postpone discussion of these difficult matters concerning the defence of folk psychology to Part 3, especially sections 16–18. For the moment, my aim is to describe as accurately as possible the extent to which folk psychology *differs* from superpsychology, regardless of the ultimate significance of this.[18]

To this end, we can at least say (a) that each of us has a distinctive first-personal view of himself; (b) that explanation and other types of cognitive engagement are conducted in the implicit light of this sort of self-conception; and (c) that this self-conception is folk-psychological. We can also therefore conclude that *behaving as a folk psychologist*—engaging in that PE with respect to another—is also guided by this sort of self-conception. Call this the *reflexive* property of folk psychology; those who treat others as folk-psychological entities see themselves that way too.

I think the reflexive property is essential to folk psychology as it exists. This follows from the fact that, as has already been remarked, central folk-psychological activity is reciprocal. In communication, for instance, each sees the other as an equal folk-psychological partner, and each accepts this. Whether or not it is possible to conceive of intellectual existence without communication, and so perhaps without a central element of folk psychology, it is obviously not possible to conceive of folk psychology without this. Yet I cannot engage with another in full-blooded folk-psychological interaction whilst being at the same time, if this is possible, alienated from my own folk-psychological self: for the alienation rules out the interaction. It would at best just seem to someone else that interaction was taking place. This still, of course, leaves it open to discussion whether anything ultimately important *goes missing* when interaction does: but I have postponed discussion of this. Folk psychology, dispensable or not, is centrally interactive and so essentially reflexive.

11. Macdonald and Pettit's first argument comes into its own now. The point seemed to be that something about Ralph would be missing from Bruce's interdisciplinary breakdown of him. And the difficulty was saying what this could be. The answer is: the equal partner with whom one engages in folk-psychological interaction. Folk psychology is typically *reflexive*, as we said. Well, it is *reflective* too. I engage in the folk-psychological PE with you and must simultaneously see myself in folk-psychological terms too: that is reflexivity.

---

[18] I am indebted to Robert Black here.

But I see myself, folk-psychologically, as a discrete self-aware centre of reflection, implicitly guided (much of the time) by its own intro-spectively available lights. And that is how I see *you* when I see you folk-psychologically: what goes for one goes for all. I see you as another one like me. That is reflectivity.

This may seem a little odd. But if so, I suggest that the cause could well be an implicit tendency still to think of folk psychology as a pre-dominantly *explanatory* enterprise, an inferior early model for superpsychology. Thus consider first Bruce's full explanatory break-down of Ralph. What is missing from this is the full folk-psycho-logical self-conception which Ralph, if he is a normal person, will have. This is not the trivial point that Ralph will have, for example, beliefs about Ralph-the-believer whose contents will resist Bruce's analysis. If we are allowing Bruce a full-scale interdisciplinary breakdown of Ralph's beliefs, then this must go even for Ralph's beliefs about himself. The point is, rather, that Ralph, like Bruce, is to himself a discrete centre of conscious awareness and activity, a unity that reflects upon itself and its surroundings. In Bruce's interdisciplinary story this unity finds no place, and Ralph becomes, so to speak, a dead phenomenon, a blank agency imprinted with causally efficacious traces of recoverable encounters with bits of its environment. The rest is missing.

I think that much the same happens whenever an *exclusively* explanatory stance is taken towards something, even if this stance is Intentional. To see something merely as an object of which certain aspects are to be explained just requires this sort of detachment. 'Treating another as an equal partner' in such an explanatory con-text then has to be taken as a metaphorical way of saying that cer-tain extrapolations are made from one's own case, considered in an explanatory light, to the other's. Thus if folk psychology is con-sidered as a merely explanatory PE, my point about reflectivity will seem odd, or trivial.

But we must remember that folk psychology is not a predomi-nantly explanatory PE, and that the 'extrapolation' involved in see-ing another as like oneself is not from oneself considered in an explanatory light. It is from oneself considered, in a first-person way, as an organizing, folk-psychological centre of awareness. To see *another* like *this* is to enter into a sort of cooperation. At the risk of sounding mystical again, we might say that interactors think of themselves as *we*; which is quite different from each thinking of himself as *I* confronted by something else. Consider, again, communication. Although sometimes this may take the form of two or more quasi-radical interpreters making their best efforts to scrute one another, this is not the standard case. Usually the direction of attention is outwards, from the collective point of view on some subject matter, towards that subject matter itself. To use an avowedly phenomenological mode, *we* collectively think and speak about *it*, directly. I do not split my attention between the subject matter, on the one hand, and another bit of environment—you—the manifest emissions of which can be treated, under my best analytical hypothesis, as being about that subject matter: and no more do you. This is definitely how it is from the standpoint of the folk-psychological PE when we jointly engage in it and communicate. We are the analogues of the manifest *I* of introspection, the implicit folk-psychological directors of an outwards-facing cognitive exercise.

It is, of course, an acknowledged fact that in viewing another from the Intentional stance some sort of spreading of oneself goes on. One sees the other as 'consistent, a believer of truths, and a lover of the good (all by one's own lights, it goes without saying)'[19]—such are the 'constraints' that govern the enterprise; without observing them, one cannot make the sense of others that makes it possible. But there is a danger of distortion here; and anyway, what I have been talking about is not just this. The distortion comes if one's attention remains fixed on 'interpretation', or the adoption of the Intentional stance, as an exclusively explanatory strategy that is governed by the aforementioned constraints. For this seems to involve the idea that one starts off with oneself as uncritically 'given', lights and all, then works out by a kind of analogy or anyway hypothetically to the case of other 'systems'. This is certainly empirically false as an account of how one gets into a folk-psychological community, almost certainly conceptually incoherent as a 'rational reconstruction' of what this involves, and of course the starting point of traditional and well-known problems concerning the intrinsic nature or even being of 'other' minds. Naturally I do not mean to suggest that these problems are entirely spurious. But if I am right about folk-psychological reciprocity, the emphasis is certainly wrong. From the present standpoint, radical interpretation and Intentional explanation generally

[19] Donald Davidson, 'Mental Events', in *Essays on Actions and Events* (Clarendon Press, Oxford, 1980), 222.

are at best (possibly idealized) offshoots of the folk-psychological PE. In the central examples of this PE, to repeat, one is neither alone nor detached nor interpreting nor explaining, but engaging reciprocally with other acknowledged folk-psychological entities. The 'spreading of oneself' is not something which one does as a prelude to explanation. Rather, that we each implicitly conceive of ourselves and each other as first persons, and in this sense all spread ourselves around, is just the way we find ourselves. What then goes on between us is something else entirely: think of how you put in the folk-psychological time.

12. Given all this, the original claim that I have taken off from—the claim that Bruce's full design-explanatory PE, if and when available, could in principle do what folk psychology now does, only better—is a long way off the mark. Behaving as a folk psychologist is not even the same sort of thing as engaging in a merely explanatory PE, so there just is no obvious dimension of comparison. Naturally there are certain replies and so on that Bruce can make to this, and we must consider these forthwith. But the position we shall start from is this. Typical folk psychologists interact with one another in a particular cooperative way, which presupposes that they each implicitly think of themselves and each other as manifest folk-psychological minds, capable of believing, desiring, intending, understanding, acting, and all the rest. In interacting with one another in this way they exhibit a distinct type of knowledgeability as engagers in a particular PE or bundle thereof. In so far as knowledgeability is a manifestation of a type of understanding (of the characteristic systems), engaging in this PE (or bundle of PEs) is a way of acquiring and manifesting a distinctive type of understanding of others: roughly, a sort of generalized case of the type of understanding of oneself that introspection affords. Switching to, say, a design stance involves engaging with and understanding the systems before one in a quite different way. Therefore the fully equipped Bruce could not do the job that the folk psychologist now does, only better. In viewing something from the Intentional point of view—or, more accurately, in participating with it in the (or a) folk-psychological PE—one is aware of aspects of it that are invisible from the design stance. These 'aspects' are precisely those which I attempted to characterize when speaking of the necessity to see another as one sees oneself, as a first

person, if one is to see him properly from the folk-psychological point of view.[20]

3. Scientism and Mind

13. It is plain that any Brucish response to the argument of Part 2 will be based on broadly metaphysical grounds. The principal apparent weakness in the position derives from my concession that, were the Intentional explanatory stance the whole of folk psychology, then Bruce could (in principle, *modulo* constraints imposed by the availability of information, the voluminousness of the design blueprint, and so on) fulfil his explanatory and predictive purposes without it. Since these will be, characteristically, the only purposes that he will consider to be relevant to the issue, is this not tantamount to giving him all he wants? Why should all the mystical description of the *manifest we* and so on be so much as of passing interest to him in this context? In more general terms, we may ask, what are these alleged folk-psychological 'aspects'? How can they really differ from those revealed by the superpsychologist's interdisciplinary breakdowns, when (it may be supposed) the final test of a view concerning what aspects and features something really has—the view's ability to predict and control the goings on to which these aspects may be relevant—is by my own admission neutral with respect to the two stances (subject to the stated qualifications)? If

---

[20] Oddly enough, Macdonald and Pettit briefly consider the interactive nature of folk psychology as being a possible basis for a reply to Bruce; but they let the point go. In their view, Bruce could satisfactorily reply by saying that interaction 'may simply be the result of tradition and training, and that that habit may yet prove capable of being broken'. Resistance to this on the grounds that interaction 'serves a distinctive interest' they allow Bruce to dismiss as follows:

He will say that the comment is made from a parochial and reactionary point of view and that the progress of knowledge ought not to be held back by an attachment to the satisfactions deriving from older schemes of thought (p. 72).

I find this rather puzzling. In the first place, they make it sound as though the object is to prevent Bruce and his friends from doing their research in superpsychology and so on, and to make them go around professionally participating instead. But it is no part of *my* project—nor really of Macdonald and Pettit's, as far as I can see—to deflect Bruce from his wholly proper search for new explanatory theories. The point is merely to stop him getting carried away by thinking that he is somehow working towards the whole truth of which folk psychologists have, at best, an imperfect and confused grasp. Moreover, why should Bruce be allowed to be so dismissive of the understanding that interaction affords? We shall see in Part 3 that there is no good reason for this.

folk-psychological 'aspects' do not issue in behavioural or other phenomena that would be in principle beyond Bruce's grasp, then what kind of aspects are these?

There is something in this to which I must certainly make concessions. My definition of a PE, and of the corresponding notion of knowledgeability and understanding with respect to the characteristic systems of that PE, is extremely liberal. Anything which incorporates distinctive predications that combine with appropriately matched interventions, and which constitutes an activity with enough structure for it to be possible for someone to be more or less proficient in it, counts as a PE on my definition. And anything which serves as the object of one of these activities falls, under the appropriate description(s), into the equally liberal ontological realm of characteristic systems. And a proficient (that is, knowledgeable) engager counts, in an equally liberal sense, as 'understanding' these systems as such. Now as a highly abstract manner of speaking this will perhaps be acknowledged to have its uses. But many will also want to stress that it is a *mere* manner of speaking: that given the serious metaphysical business of deciding (say) what there *really* or fundamentally is, and what genuine understanding of the nature of these things consists in—then, it will be stressed, PEs with their attendant characteristic systems and understanders are not on all fours, for all sorts of metaphysical and epistemological and other reasons. Despite the extreme difficulty of making this sort of claim watertight in particular cases, I should not want to dispute this. I should not want to say that there is *no* sufficiently deep and neutral conception of reality and how we confront it in terms of which PEs and so on can be graded with respect to their metaphysical sobriety, the genuineness of their claim to be sources of understanding of things. To take just one example that I have briefly mentioned already: the characteristic systems of the PE *treating another as a person* are considered, from the vantage point of this PE, to be *valuable*, and (on some construals) value is taken to be a real property of a thing, like its shape or colour (and of course these alternatives themselves may be objected to or embraced for different reasons). But this is a claim that is often contested on certain metaphysical and epistemological and psychological grounds. At least without a lot of further argument, it would cheapen my apparatus considerably if it were so understood as to make this dispute, and others like it, somehow spurious: and I have no wish for it to be understood in this way. So I shall have to work for my folk-psychological 'aspects'.

14. Bruce's standards of metaphysical sobriety are, I think, easy enough to discern: they take physical science as the touchstone. Indeed, it is fair to see his project as part of a characteristically 'scientific' synoptic or overall account of a world that can be seen in both the manifest and in the scientific image.[21] The manifest image is, roughly, the world of macroscopic objects and folk-psychological entities (persons) as seen by (enlightened) common sense, while the scientific image is the world as seen from the point of view of the physical sciences, whose main preoccupation is with the microscopic. The present topic is one of many long-standing philosophical perplexities concerning how these different images are to be reconciled—how, for instance, mind with its ordinary way of seeing things is to be represented as being part of a world that can be viewed scientifically. Conceiving of mental states as second-order, functional (say) properties of the physical matter that constitutes, for instance, the human body is perhaps the most satisfying reconciliation yet suggested, once it has been accepted that the world is *really* as it appears in the scientific image (or the best refinement thereof). But to accept this, the thought continues, just is to accept that the world is really, ultimately, as it appears to the most successful of those who adopt the explanatory stance towards it prescribed by Bruce. And one can hardly fail to accept that the scientific image is in this sense the primary one, on pain (at best) of committing oneself to unattractive instrumentalism with respect to science, or (at worst) of failing, indefensibly, to give it the metaphysical credit which it is due. Assuming the unsatisfactory nature of these responses, how could there be any room for participative 'understanding' and folk-psychological 'aspects'?

On the basis of thoughts such as these one can mount a strong, and a weaker, attack on folk psychology. The strong attack can only be resisted, I think, on the basis of a pretty fundamental rejection of the idea that there can be a scientific synopsis, given that *mind* is unquestionably one of the things that must show up in it, in some

---

[21] See Wilfrid Sellars, 'Philosophy and the Scientific Image of Man', in his *Science, Perception and Reality* (Routledge and Kegan Paul, London, 1963).

suitably scientific guise. This is the conclusion that I ultimately try to establish. But I try to do this without assuming things that Bruce, or one sympathetic to his general outlook, can reasonably dispute. So I proceed in stages, by way of a weaker 'reconciling' defence that corresponds to the weaker attack.

15. It is sometimes said that there is an intolerable clash between the scientific and manifest images: that no 'synopsis' is possible that could do justice to both. The respectable alternatives then presented are instrumentalism with respect to science, on the one hand, and *scientism* on the other. Scientism, as I understand it, is the view that the only genuine source of knowledge about the world and the things in it is that given by the developed physical sciences, and perhaps such disciplines as can be reduced to them, or successfully reinterpreted in their terms. I leave this characterization deliberately vague because, I shall suggest, no interesting refinement of it can be true. That is: I take it that the nature of the interactive folk-psychological PE is so unlike physical science in its methods, and in the type of 'understanding' to which it gives rise, that if it is accepted as genuine, scientism is wrong. Anyway, scientism is the one natural source of the strong attack on folk psychology that I mentioned above. Given that this 'mode of understanding' is so different from science and related enterprises, those of a scientistic bent will say, it is no real mode of understanding at all, and its 'characteristic systems'—or at least their folk-psychological 'aspects'—do not figure in the ultimate inventory of the universe.

This is reminiscent of the view that secondary qualities as we conceive them are not really qualities of things, but are qualities that we (erroneously) take them to have because of the action on us of quite different dispositional qualities really had by things. That is, minds like ours have a characteristic 'raw phenomenology'—things feel, taste, smell, etc., certain ways to them—and this largely perceptual phenomenology is bound up with a whole lot of concepts and discriminatory behaviour: thus things seem to us to *be* coloured, to smell certain ways, and so on. Or rather, they seem this way when viewed in the *manifest image*: this is how the world presents itself to common sense. But there is then an appearance of inconsistency with the scientific view of these same things, since on this view a particular instance of what common sense would call, say, redness comes out as a propensity to do certain things to certain sorts of light, roughly speaking. This apparent clash is resolved, by the scientism under consideration, by the claim that the deliverances of the manifest common-sense view are erroneous because contaminated. Our minds are so constituted that they register the presence of the relevant propensities by way of concepts formed with the aid of the raw phenomenology: and then the manifest image of the world mistakenly takes these mind-contaminated classifications to record faithfully the aspects of the real world to which they are responsive. As with colours and so on, so with folk-psychological 'aspects', which would be construed as Brucish properties liberally infected with the engager's interactive tendencies, and so with much else that appears in the manifest image: the strong scientism I have in mind would present the same 'error' theory.

I return to this sort of view later on, after considering something less extreme. For it is not obvious that a properly developed sense of respect for the scientific image necessitates so much repudiation. A less drastic view could allow, against this extreme scientism, and following suggestions developed by Dummett and McGinn,[22] that secondary qualities are real qualities of things, but of rather a special sort. They are special in the sense that they are only had by objects in so far as they are thought of from certain points of view (for example, those bound up with specific types of perceptual capacities with their attendant raw phenomenology); and that what it is to have one of these properties can only be specified by way of an ineliminable appeal to the relevant perceptual capacities, which appeal itself is couched in terms of the very concepts in virtue of which the discriminations in question are made. Secondary qualities are not, in short, qualities had by things *as they are in themselves*, or as considered from *no particular type of point of view*. This claim may be given bite, furthermore, by being joined to the claim that there *are* properties had by things as they are in themselves: perhaps (some of) the so-called primary qualities, certainly the geometrical and causal properties attributed to things by the mature sciences. And with this last flourish, of course, this view registers its proper respect for the scientific image.

What I have called the 'weak' attack on folk psychology is based on a parallel manoeuvre on the part of Bruce, which results in a view

---

[22] Michael Dummett, 'Common Sense and Physics', in Graham Macdonald (ed.), *Perception and Identity* (Macmillan, London, 1979); Colin McGinn, *The Subjective View* (Clarendon Press, Oxford, 1983).

that admits the reality of folk-psychological aspects but qualifies this in the same sort of way as the view just described qualifies that of secondary qualities. For surely it is always an intellectually defensible—if not obligatory—thing to do to seek out the properties that things have as they are themselves. Articulating a conception of the world in terms that are, as much as possible, independent of any particular point of view on them, just is a—perhaps the—natural culmination of responsible enquiry. Then the superpsychologist could claim that he is merely carrying out this sort of development with respect to *agents*. There is a budding scientist in each folk psychologist—witness the existence of Intentional explanations—and Bruce's new discipline will give him the account of how things are with, for instance, Ralph-in-himself, that this scientist craves. Coupled with geography, it will add further details about the links between this essential agent and his surroundings. Folk psychology not only mixes these facts in together in a most unscientific way, but also throws in some extra ones which are not, strictly speaking, facts about Ralph alone, but are facts about him which are ineliminably bound up with the participative points of view of the *enquirers*—the ascribers of folk-psychological aspects. Sure enough, these aspects are real, on the more liberal view envisaged, since (like secondary qualities) they give rise to unquestionably significant and systematic discriminations, and serve some explanatory purposes. But they are no more had by agents-as-they-are-in-themselves than secondary qualities are had by things-as-they-are-in-themselves. Their reality is, so to speak, qualified by being relativized to the (in this case) participative point of view. The unqualified reality is that discerned by the superpsychologist.

16. This, then, is the weak attack on folk psychology that I mentioned above. And it corresponds to the weak defence that I also there mentioned. For no very damning critique of the folk-psychological enterprise can be developed on these lines, and the classical theorist of meaning, also, is correspondingly vindicated. Those who concern themselves with the study of the conceptual resources of the folk discipline are exposed, if that is the right word, as dealers in something less than the absolute. According to this Brucish position, they are not full-blooded scientists. Rather, they have to be seen as concerned with the a priori quasi-logical (intensional) and logical

(extensional) principles that govern the structure of interactive appearance. But this is an intellectually respectable thing to do, and they would find themselves in good company. Since so much energy is expended in trying to achieve folk-psychological understanding of ourselves and each other, obviously an account of the resources that we utilize is of central intellectual significance. More than this, any attempt to delineate features of the manifest image is bound to be important and interesting just because that is the image in which we see the world in all but specialized contexts—however metaphysically revealing those contexts may be.

It is important that one cannot automatically defend any old PE in this way, thereby trivializing the defence in the objectionable way from which I distanced myself above. Value-laden PEs are again a useful example. Hume, for instance, explicitly compared values with secondary qualities: and there is a growing tendency to follow him in this (although Hume thereby dismissed values as illusions, in a scientistic spirit, whereas more recent views gesture in the direction of a defence of them along the lines sketched out for secondary qualities above). But there are crucial differences here which may well be metaphysically significant. Ascriptions of value do not obviously serve any explanatory purpose with respect to the allegedly valuable things, and this, combined with their obvious relativity to the ascribers' rather narrow interests and purposes, can be taken to show that treating these ascriptions as responsive even to perspective-dependent features is a genuine error. Whatever the merits of this contention it is clear that merely alluding to the possibility of perspective-dependent qualities does not answer it. Each case has to be considered on its own particular merits, even given this subtle possibility. But folk psychology, at least, is safe enough if anything is (and something has to be if the reconciling approach is available). First, there is the existence of Intentional explanation, which presumably works in particular cases just because its ascriptions are grounded in the features that the superpsychologist would disclose. But beyond this, the utter centrality of folk psychology as a source of appreciation of what goes on around and among us cannot be exaggerated. The suggestion, mentioned in section 10 above, that we might succeed in 'getting by' without this cannot be given credibility, whether or not it is intelligible. If things seem otherwise, then I suspect this is because the idea has been confused with another one, namely the idea that we can 'get by' without folk psychology *for explanatory purposes*. If these are construed in a narrowly scientific manner, then (waiving the 'pragmatic' defence) perhaps there is truth in this thought. But once it is recognized that folk psychology is not predominantly explanatory, and also acknowledged, as we are at present supposing it will be, that there are legitimate if non-scientific perspective–relative ways of conceiving things, then the idea that we might 'get by' without folk psychology is simply ludicrous. What could be more important, in non-scientific contexts, than contemplating the ways in which we appear to ourselves and each other? What point could there be in destroying the appearance (if that is possible)?

17. What we have are two solid defences of folk psychology against the Brucish attack, both of which, I have claimed, are enough to keep classical meaning respectable. There is the pragmatic defence described in section 8, which trades on the *de facto* indispensability of the Intentional stance. And there is the 'weak' metaphysical defence just outlined. There is enough here to turn aside all but the hardest of scientistic noses. I shall end up by suggesting that even these should at least stop in their tracks. To resist my last vindication one has to condemn out of hand anything that does not show up in the scientific image, and not make the concessions that are necessary to my 'weak' defence. True, one has to accept the pragmatic point that the Intentional stance is practically indispensable: but this would be done with bad grace. For our opponent would see the point as a mere reflection of our epistemic weaknesses, and consider for example the activities of the classical theorist of meaning as self-indulgent pandering to these, rather than as attempts to articulate the components of a perfectly respectable, if perspective–relative, conception of parts of reality. Perhaps there are not very many scientistic monsters of this sort, once the necessary distinctions have been made. But that would not rob what follows of its main thrust, since we shall see that it works equally well against the Brucish idea that by adopting the design stance one at last gets to see agents as they are in themselves: an idea that is compatible with my 'weak' defence. What results is an even stronger defence of folk psychology.

18. Sellars's 'image' metaphor, in terms of which Bruce's project is best seen, incorporates, roughly, the following picture. We (or 'mind') find ourselves confronted with a (mind-) independent reality

which we see, as it were, through two different lenses (those of science and of common sense). Given the metaphysical priority of the scientific view, then, and given that there are apparent clashes between the two views, certain elements visible through the common-sense lens are taken out of the reality beyond it (which is more accurately represented by the scientific view) and attributed to the nature of the lens itself. We just happen to have, it is said, minds which are fitted with this sort of distorting lens. Whether or not it is concluded that this distortion is the source of error, or just (at least sometimes) perspective–relative bona fide sources of understanding, depends on the moves sketched above. Briefly, what this attempt at a synopsis does is to place the unwanted features into the mind. But then you would expect Bruce to find them there when he starts looking; for *his* project is that of turning the scientific lens around, so to speak, so the mind can get a proper scientific look at itself. But he does not seem able to find some important things. Notoriously, raw phenomena—put into the mind to keep colours and so on out of the world—do not show up on his analysis. Arguably, such properties can vary independently of the causal (etc.) features which are supposed to constitute the essential reality of the mind. Arguably, we cannot (at least yet) so much as conceive how a physical mechanism can have raw phenomenological aspects. And certainly the causal/explanatory vocabulary does not reveal to us the full nature of the states and so on so described.[23] Here are some properties of the mind, then, that Bruce cannot easily accommodate—those that relate to what it is like to be or have one. Yet *its being like something* is surely a fundamental feature of mind-as-it-is-in-itself if anything is. Moreover, this problem concerns more than just raw phenomena. As I tried to emphasize above, it is *like something* to participate with others in such standard folk-psychological activities as communication: communicators cooperate, think of themselves as *we*, and so on. The distinctive feel of this—if you like, its phenomenology—is lost to the outsider who contents himself with a design account of what is going on, and refuses to join in. Yet, once again, the enjoyment of an interactive phenomenology is fundamental to the folk-psychological mind-as-it-is-in-itself if anything is, given that interaction is at the heart of folk psychology. This suggests that Bruce may simply be changing the subject, and not talking of the *mind* at

[23] Cf. Thomas Nagel, 'What is it Like to be a Bat?', in his *Mortal Questions* (CUP, Cambridge, 1979).

all, when he attempts superpsychological breakdowns. And equally, if this is right, hard-nosed scientism is surely wrong. The existence of mental phenomena can hardly be denied; and it is incoherent to try to write them off as illusions brought about by the unfortunate constitution of the mind. So why should we suppose that the Brucish project is going in even roughly the right direction? Genuine metaphysicians should be much more circumspect.

In sum, we can say that there is just no good reason for the dismissive attitudes towards classical meaning that it has been my aim to discredit, at least in so far as they rest upon the superpsychological aspirations that I have described. Much distortion in this area has resulted from an excessively narrow conception of folk psychology which puts Intentional explanation at its heart. The rather brief discussion of sections 7–12 is intended to dispel this illusion. Once it is dispelled, the motivations for an anti-folk-psychological stance become rather hard to find. Moreover, in so far as they rest upon the scientism discussed in the final sections of this paper, they are hardly worth considering. Even more, the scientism itself is in rather a bad way as a basis for theorizing about the central aspects of our most notable possession. Naturally I do not mean to discredit in advance future essays on its behalf, but I hope at least to have put them in their place, and to have indicated what an uncomfortable place that is. What I have said can hardly be seen as a prolegomenon to any future metaphysic of mind. But I shall be satisfied if I help to spread the thought that we still need one.

CHAPTER 3

PHYSICALIST THINKING AND CONCEPTIONS OF BEHAVIOUR*

JENNIFER HORNSBY

1. I start from two pictures. One presents a view of what is involved when we ascribe propositional attitudes to one another. The other presents a view of what is involved when the scientist treats a human being as a physical thing—of what a neurophysiologist sees as going on when he concerns himself with the stimulations of sense organs, with the motor responses in a person's body, and with events and states that intervene between such stimulations and responses.

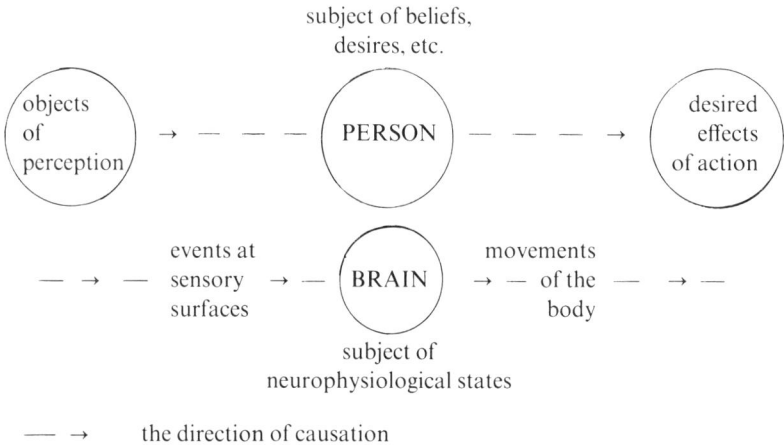

subject of beliefs, desires, etc.

objects of perception → — — — PERSON — — — → desired effects of action

— → — events at sensory surfaces → — BRAIN → — of the — → — movements of the body

subject of neurophysiological states

— → the direction of causation

One has only to look at these two pictures to be tempted to make a superimposition. Two considerations may combine to make the

---

* © Jennifer Hornsby 1986. I have been helped by comments on previous versions from David Lewis, Christopher Peacocke, Philip Pettit, Michael Smith, David Wiggins, and, especially, John McDowell.

temptation irresistible. First, the brain and central nervous system is a part of a person whose proper functioning is a necessary condition of that person's having the effects on the world she desires to have. Second, the causal chains that lead up to and away from a person's psychological states apparently pass through the events depicted in the area that circumscribes the neurophysiologist's study. If you extend the causal chains of the representation of the brain backwards and forwards, what you reach is the elements standing at the left and right of the representation of the person. The dependence of the person's functioning on the functioning of her brain may make one think of the brain as a mechanism inside the person which is responsible for producing the effects in virtue of which she has her distinctive effects on the world. But then the common properties of the brain's states and of the person's mental states—states of each sort being seen as causal intermediaries—may make one think that in placing the brain inside the person one locates the propositional-attitude states there. Many will therefore feel compelled to say that particular beliefs and desires *are* the neurophysiological states of a person.

This line of thought gives a very quick argument for a version of physicalism. Perhaps no one wishes to acknowledge that he takes such a direct or simple route. But I think that there is a widespread presumption that if beliefs and desires have any place in the physical world, then they are internal states of persons, or of their brains; and I think that this presumption can be created by the sort of high-level comparison of pictures I have just imagined. My project in this paper is to question certain versions of physicalism the quick argument may seem to recommend, by challenging the envisaged superimposition of the two pictures. More particularly, I shall challenge the use to which a certain conception of *behaviour* is put. According to this conception, *behaviour* subsumes both a brain's outputs and a person's outputs, and thus provides an area common to both pictures.

2. Naively we think that we can become informed about people's mental states by receiving right answers to such questions as 'Why did she keep to the edge of the pond?' or 'Why did she turn on the burner?'. And we suppose that such answers give psychological explanations of behaviour. But it is often said nowadays that any

account of psychological explanatory states is bound to use a purely bodily notion of behaviour.

Consider, for example, Kim's claims:[1]

[An] action of turning on the burner, insofar as this is thought to involve the burner going on, is not an action that it is the proper business of psychological theory to explain or predict. . . . It is not part of the object of *psychological* explanation to explain why the burner went on. . . . The job of psychological explanation is done once [psychological theory] has explained the bodily action of turning a knob; whether or not this action results in my also turning on the stove, my starting cooking the dinner . . . is dependent on facts quite outside the province of psychology, [which] are not the proper concern of psychological theory.

Kim and others believe, then, that we ought to recognize psychology's proper business to be much narrower than we naively take it to be.

Kim's claim that psychological states cannot serve to explain (for example) why Kim turned on the burner is rested on the premiss that such states do not serve to explain why the burner went on. Both the premiss and the argument here may be questioned. In order to question the premiss, one must take a relaxed view about psychological explanation. Then it will seem that it can be psychologically explained (for example) why a burner went on: 'Why did the burner go on? Is the switch faulty?' 'No: Jane turned it on, she wanted to make some tea'.

To question the argument, one may take a less relaxed view and start with the assumption that any psychological explanation has as its explanandum why some person did what she did. The principle underlying the argument would then seem to be something like this:

Even if the explanation why *p* appears to be the fact that *z*, still if *q* and *r* are necessary for *p* and the fact that *z* does not explain why *q*, then the fact that *z* can only really explain why *r*.

[1] Jaegwon Kim, 'Psychophysical Supervenience', *Philosophical Studies*, xli (1982), 64. (I have changed the order of Kim's sentences.) For a similar argument, given in the course of a defence of functionalism, see Brian Loar, *Mind and Meaning* (CUP, Cambridge, 1981), 88.

But such a principle is surely unacceptable. Suppose that we thought that we could explain why the window broke by saying that a heavy stone hit it at speed. We then notice that the window's breaking required that the window be situated at p and that p be on the stone's trajectory, and that the stone's hitting the window at speed does not explain why the window is situated at p. We do not conclude that after all the stone's hitting the window at high speed cannot really explain why the window broke.[2]

It is a question how narrow the province of what is psychologically explained would become if one endorsed Kim's argument wholeheartedly. Kim himself speaks as if *turning a knob*, unlike *turning on the burner*, were an admissible object of psychological explanation. Yet *turning a knob* is surely proscribed for him: it seems no more to be 'part of the object of psychological explanation' to explain why a knob turned than it is to explain why the burner went on. And we may wonder whether in fact Kim's principle does not rule out psychological explanations even of 'bodily actions'—of why someone moved her finger, say; for it is by no means obvious that someone's moving her finger is not 'dependent on facts which are not the proper concern of psychological theory'. (I return to this at the end of section 3.)

Of course Kim's conclusion about the objects of psychological explanation may not be meant to rely on the principle alone. It may rely on a prior view of psychological states—as internal states of people which are the immediate causal ancestors of movements of their bodies. This view is certainly held by functionalists. And the functionalists' conception of behaviour may be supposed to recommend itself on the merits of functionalism. So it will be worth discovering whether the attractions of functionalism can survive scrutiny of the particular notion of behaviour that that doctrine employs.

---

[2] It may be said that this counterexample is importantly different from the examples that were Kim's concern, because in the counterexample it is only in the presence of the explanans that we come to be able to separate necessary conditions for the obtaining of the explanandum. But this feature may also be present in psychological cases. We can know that someone turned on the burner (and that there is a psychological explanation of that) without knowing what sort of bodily movement on her part resulted in the burner's being on.

3. Functionalists think that the defining feature of any type of mental state is given by describing the causal relations that its instances bear (a) to the environment's effects on a person, (b) to mental states of other types, and (c) to a person's effects on the environment. And they think that mental terms can be simultaneously implicitly defined in a total psychological theory of all the types of mental states. Such a theory contains terms of two sorts, which David Lewis has called the T-terms and the O-terms. The T-terms are, intuitively, mental terms, to be thought of as receiving implicit definition; in a functional theory, their denotations are accorded functional roles that are specified using only the non-mental O-terms. The functionalist thinks of the functional theory (abstracted, as it were, from the psychological theory) as true of, or realized by, the physical states of individuals: physical states occupy the functional roles of mental states.[3]

Functionalism is to be understood here as a thesis in the philosophy of mind, which treats of those states and events that in the ordinary way we attribute to one another, for example in explaining action. We can ask then 'What does the functionalist have to say about the role of the propositional–attitude states in producing action?'. Put in the functionalist's own terms, this is a question about output generalizations ((c) above), which are meant to give an account of the systematic ways in which such states as beliefs lead, as it is said, to behaviour.

We are told that behaviourism is the ancestor of functionalism, and that functionalism inherits the virtues of behaviourism. But the functionalist's notion of behaviour is very much more restrictive than that which some of the behaviourists employed. When functionalists speak of behaviour, they speak, like Kim, of bodily movements, or else they speak of motor responses.[4] When Ryle spoke about behaviour, he meant such characterizations of people's actions as these: 'telling oneself and others that the ice is thin, skating

---

[3] David Lewis, 'Psychophysical and Theoretical Identifications', *Australasian Journal of Philosophy*, 1 (1972), 249 ᵥ58. (Where Lewis uses 'state' I use 'type of state', because, unlike Lewis, I reserve the word 'state' for particulars; and I make no assumption that functionalists are committed to any type identities of Lewis's sort.)

[4] 'Bodily movements' is used by Loar and others; 'motor responses' by Lewis in Psychophysical and Theoretical Identifications'.

warily, shuddering, dwelling in imagination on possible disasters, warning other skaters, keeping to the edge of the pond'.[5] (It is true that some behaviourists were reductionists, and that they used a narrower conception of behaviour than Ryle. But if one is allowed to think of functionalism as inheriting its attractions from a non-reductionist position, then Ryle's everyday use of 'behaviour' ought not to be legislated into invisibility.)

There are two important differences here between the (Rylean) behaviourist and the functionalist. The behaviourist makes allusion to things beyond the agent's body in his specifications of behaviour, but the functionalist does not. And the behaviourist's behavioural items are actions (that is, events of people doing things such as moving their bodies), whereas the functionalist's behavioural items are apparently not actions, but movements of people's bodies (which are either effects of actions, or proper parts of actions, depending upon your views).[6] We need to understand why the functionalists should depart from the behaviourists in these two ways and employ the particular conception that they do.

The functionalist's stated objection to behaviourism is familiar enough: the behaviourist said that to believe something (for instance) is to be disposed to certain behaviour, whereas the functionalist insists that belief cannot be defined in terms of behaviour alone, because allowance has to be made for the simultaneous determination of behaviour by many different mental states. In this point alone, however, there is nothing that evidently constrains one to used a bodily conception of behaviour. And we need to notice something else, which is seldom stated very explicitly by functionalists; the behaviourists' neglect of the interdependencies between mental things was not in fact the only defect of behaviourism that the functionalist needed to correct for. Certainly, if your belief that it is going to rain is to lead you to take your umbrella, then you need (for example) to want not to get wet and to believe that umbrellas keep the rain off, and to have no other countervailing desires or interfer-

---

[5] *The Concept of Mind* (Hutchinson, London, 1949), 129.

[6] There is little here that is uncontroversial. (For an account of the controversy, see my 'Bodily Movements, Actions and Mental Epistemology', in *Midwest Studies in Philosophy*, vol. IX (1985).) What I assume now is that we can distinguish the denotations of descriptions such as '*a*'s raising her arm', which are actions, from the denotations of such descriptions as '*a*'s arm's rising', which are not actions.

ing beliefs. But equally certainly, if your belief that it is going to rain is to lead you to take your umbrella, then you need to believe of something that is your umbrella *that* it is your umbrella. Not only can it not be left out of account what desires a person has (as the behaviourist seemed to suppose), it also cannot be taken for granted that what people believe is true. Avoiding taking this for granted, one might say that someone who believes that *p* is (very roughly) someone who would, *given that p*, realize such desires as prevailed given her other desires and beliefs. But there is a problem about incorporating this into a functionalist psychological theory as it stands. For this does not tell us, in behavioural terms however broadly construed, what someone with a certain belief would ever unconditionally *do*.

There are two ways in which the functionalist might try to make allowance for the fact that it is only where other relevant beliefs of the agent are true that behaviour as we naturally and widely conceive it is predictably matched with particular desires and beliefs. First, he might settle for using what one could call a world-conditioned notion of behaviour, saying, at the behavioural end of an output generalization, that a person would do things of this sort: such-and-such-if-the-world-is-as-it-would-be-if-relevant-beliefs-of-the-agent-were-true. (I return to this idea in section 5.) Second, he might restrict the notion of behaviour, so that something counts as a description of behaviour only if an agent can be expected to satisfy it irrespective of whether her beliefs are true. In talking about behaviour, he then confines himself to those things that an agent would do no matter whether the world were as she believed it to be—things, one might say, that she is *simply able* to do.

This provides the real explanation of why the functionalist should go back to the body in describing behaviour. And perhaps we can now also understand the functionalist's other deviation from the behaviourist—his not treating actions themselves as behavioural items. Even if a person's beliefs about what it is to ϕ are false, she will at least *try* to ϕ if she has overwhelming reason to ϕ (or so a functionalist may say). It seems then that the notion of *trying* or *attempting* can be introduced if one wants a means of saying in 'purely psychological' terms what someone's beliefs and desires in conjunction do produce. One then arrives at a two-stage account of action production, such as can be found in some functionalist writings.[7] At the first stage, one says how beliefs and desires modify one another and mediate the production of attempts; so much is 'pure psychology', in the language of the T-terms. At the second stage, one says what attempts to do things would actually bring about, whatever the truth values of the beliefs that led to those attempts; the idea is that a sufficiently motivated agent who is *simply able* to do something will do that thing. This second stage takes one from the T-terms to the O-terms; and it is here that one is constrained to use the bodily movement vocabulary for describing behaviour, and to speak (not of actions themselves, but) only of things that are the most immediate, bodily effects of a person's attempts.

Something like this functionalist view of action production is presumably shared by Kim (section 2). But what one now gets at the second stage of the account of action production will be instances of:

a tries to ϕ & a is *simply able* to ϕ → there occurs a ϕ-type movement

(where to be a 'ϕ-type movement' is, intuitively, to be a movement of the type associated with actions of ϕ-ing). And this means that, unless we are prepared to say that an agent's being *simply able* to do something is a 'proper concern of psychological theory', the argument that Kim gave in order to encourage us to suppose that only 'bodily action' is genuinely psychologically explicable could be used again now to show that even movements of bodies are not things 'that it is the proper business of psychological theory to explain or predict'. But an agent's being *simply able* to move a part of her body is constituted by the integrity and functioning of the relevant bits of her motor system and the absence of constraints on her body itself, and such things are in no obvious or intuitive sense psychological and would seem to be quite on a par with (for instance) the burner's being such as to light when the knob is turned. Following through on Kim's argument, then, the province of psychological explanation would become even more circumscribed than Kim allowed: the

---

[7] See *Mind and Meaning*, 86–91. Loar uses a technical, theoretical psychological notion of *willing*, where my exposition uses *trying*. Loar's view of theoretical psychology is discussed in section 5. For arguments (in effect) that 'try' has many of the properties needed for the two-stage account of action production, see Chapters 3 and 4 of my *Actions* (Routledge and Kegan Paul, London, 1980).

proper objects of psychological explanation could only be events described as agents' *trying* to do things.[8]

4. Functionalists for their part will probably be happy to allow that conditions relating to agents' *simple abilities* have to be specified using T-terms and be caught up with psychological theory. Their aim is to show how some of the brain's complexity can be seen to mirror the complexity of the propositional–attitude scheme. And it might seem that the use of purely bodily O-terms for describing people's outputs is in no way inimical to that aim. Although a bodily motion of behaviour is more restricted than an everyday one, there is much that can be said about people's bodies' movements, and it may seem that functionalists can avail themselves of anything that can be said about them and proceed to an interesting psychological theory.

But it must not be forgotten that functionalist output generalizations are still meant to be got from what we all know about action-explanation in knowing common-sense psychology. One thing that we know is that ϕ-ing is a proper explanandum of the common-sense

---

[8] Loar's argument for narrowing down psychological explanation (see n. 1) introduces *basic actions*, which Loar calls 'primary explananda'. He says that non-basic things are explained by 'independent facts', that is facts that are not themselves psychologically explained. The question for Loar is quite parallel to that for Kim: is the reason offered for extricating 'independent facts' from non-basic things not also a reason for extricating non-psychological facts even from basic things?

There are two points about Loar's terminology. (a) I have spoken of *basic things* (*done*), rather than *basic actions*, because actions themselves, assuming these are particulars, do not stand to one another in relations of relative basicness. (See *Actions*, Chapter 5, where the relation *more basic than* is taken to hold between descriptions of actions, or, better, my 'Action and Ability', in R. Haller (ed.), *Language, Logic and Philosophy* (Reidel, Dordrecht, 1981), where the relation is taken to hold between the things a person does.) (b) It may be that Loar himself does not distinguish actions from bodies' movements, as my exposition of functionalism has suggested functionalists do.

I state the second stage of a functionalist's account of output as I do because I think that (on occasion) an agent's ϕ-ing is the same as her trying to ϕ and not the same as a movement of the ϕ-type. Still the consequent of the conditional might read '*a* ϕs'— only then the conditional cannot be supposed to take one from cause to effect (unless one denies that, on occasion, events of trying simply are actions). At any rate, the argument addressed to Kim and Loar requires only that some condition relating to the agent's body's functioning, as well as some condition relating to the agent's mind, is necessary for the occurrence of an action. To accept this much, no stand needs to be taken on the controversy mentioned in n. 6, or on the details of a correct formulation of the two-stage account of action production.

psychological scheme only if agents have some beliefs in the ascription of which ϕ-ing could be mentioned. So functionalists are not in fact entitled to use whatever bodily movement terms they like; their resources can include only such terms as could be used in giving the contents of agents' mental states. It seems, then, that they must refrain from using any very detailed bodily movement terms.

In fact it will be controversial exactly how much detail can enter into the bodily movement descriptions of common-sense psychology. If someone turns on a light (say), how detailed can a bodily description be of what she intentionally does, or tries to do? What beliefs about the movements of their bodies do people in practice employ? My own view is that hardly any detail can enter. When we engage in the practice of skills that require the manipulation of objects, for instance, it is unclear that we employ any beliefs which concern purely and simply the movements of our hands. It seems that a person can act as a result of having beliefs and desires, while having next to nothing in the way of beliefs about how her body moves when she acts.[9] And if this is right, then the functionalist, in confining himself to bodily movements, confines himself to an extremely impoverished notion of behaviour indeed.

What is certain is that functionalists don't in fact envisage using a notion of behaviour that would strike us as at all impoverished. Even if common-sense bodily movement descriptions can be richer than I have just suggested, we may still doubt that they can be as rich as those that functionalists actually want to employ. In functionalist writings, one often finds what appear to be gestures towards great complication in accounts of behaviour. Armstrong spoke of 'making certain motions with the hand and so on'; he remarked that this was vague, and said that 'the matter might be investigated in a time-and-motion study for instance'.[10] Lewis speaks of 'Karl's fingers moving

[9] See my discussion of what I there called *teleologically* basic descriptions of actions in Chapter 6 of *Actions*. And notice that I make no assumption to the effect that all beliefs are linguistically expressible by their possessors.

If bodily movement descriptions of actions are not basic, then there will be some *non-bodily* basic descriptions for functionalists to use in describing outputs. But if the functionalist does use output O-terms which touch on regions beyond the agent's body, then (a) it will become more implausible that his 'simple ability' conditions are 'purely psychological', and (b) this will do nothing to supply the richness that functionalists seem to want to find in their notion of behaviour (see below).

[10] D. M. Armstrong, *A Materialist Theory of The Mind* (Routledge and Kegan Paul, London, 1968), 147.

on certain trajectories and exerting certain forces'.[11] It can seem as if the functionalists, feeling that the complexity of the propositional–attitude scheme must indeed demand some richness in the specification of behaviour, simply ignore the common-sense character of the truths about propositional attitudes that they represent themselves as beginning from.

It will be no good saying that, since every bodily movement does have some detailed description of which a student of time-and-motion or a psysiologist could become apprised, any detail that the functionalist's aims require can always be introduced into functionalist theories. For one thing, the student of time-and-motion may discover that the sorts of bodily movements that agents think of themselves as going in for are not connected in systematic ways with the sorts of motions his studies concern.[12] And although it is surely right that there are, occasion by occasion, identities between the (coarse) bodily movement effects of actions and the (refined) bodily movement effects of finely discriminated states of the nervous system, it is unclear that this can help the functionalist who is trying to avoid a notion of behaviour that strikes him as too crude for the use to which he wants to put it. Someone who hoped to use physiological knowledge occasion by occasion to pin down the neurophysiological states that caused some effect of some action would have lost sight of one of the functionalists' aspirations—to use our knowledge of interpersonal psychology to define types of mental state.

5. I suggest that some of the allure of functionalism has resulted from failure to keep track of the use of the simple term 'behaviour'. The elements of common sense that give rise to the idea of a psychological theory seem correct when 'behaviour' is understood in Ryle's way, as including all the many things an agent does. The idea of a functional theory realized in neurophysiological states seems correct when 'behaviour' is understood in (say) the physiologist's way, as an

---

[11] David Lewis, 'Radical Interpretation', at p. 114 in the reprinting in his *Philosophical Papers*, vol. I (Clarendon Press, Oxford, 1983), quoted more fully at n. 26. Many functionalists speak of behaviour in a purely schematic way.

[12] I am relying here on such claims as are made for example by P. F. Strawson and G. J. Warnock in D. F. Pears (ed), *Freedom and the Will* (Macmillan, London, 1963): our system of classifying actions is grounded in quite different interests from any system of bodily movement classification. I do not conclude, as they did, that actions are not bodily movements; but I do take their claim to show the irreducibility of movements-classified-by-someone-interested-in-action to movements-classified-by-the-scientist-interested-in-movements-*per-se*.

agent's moving her body in all kinds of complex fashions. These two notions of behaviour overlap, and when 'bodily movements' is used to catch them both, they are made to appear to coincide. But the two notions do not coincide. And if one wants to preserve both common sense and the idea about functional theories, then one can only conclude that there is a complexity in propositional–attitude psychology that does not derive from any complexity in people's bodily movements conceived in ways available to common-sense psychology.[13]

No doubt many functionalists will say that theoretical psychology has to be enlisted in the service of common-sense psychology. They would make proposals about how theoretical psychological findings could be brought to bear on common-sense psychological states, and they would claim that the proposals will enable us to discover states that must be counted as beliefs and desires even though common-sense psychology unaided would never have recognized them as such.[14] It is as if common-sense psychology had a hidden complexity that the theoretical psychologist could uncover experimentally; as if the superimposition of the picture of the person on the picture of the brain could reveal a sort of complexity in the picture of the person which ordinarily goes unheeded. But why should we think that common-sense psychology, in order to achieve what we can all achieve using it, must really be capable of achieving a great deal more that non-theoreticians will never know about? If common-sense psychology has no concern with how exactly we move our fingers when we turn on lights (say), then this is because we do not have to try to move our fingers in the exact way in which we actually move them in order to turn on a light when we want to. But

---

[13] It may be pointed out that complexity could be derived from complexity in descriptions of *inputs*. (Functionalists insist that stimulus terms as well as behavioural ones are needed to characterize the mental ones: this is a respect in which functionalists are thought to differ from behaviourists which I have not singled out for attention.) But I think that there are things to be said about *perception* which lead in the same direction as the things I have said about *action* and which would show that the functionalist cannot make anything of this point. And the argument I actually give is meant to rely on the fact that my opponents themselves believe that more detail is needed in *output* specifications than (so I say) they are entitled to.

[14] This explains the technicalities in Loar's account (see. n. 7). Loar's suggestion is that if a theory well confirmed by experiments in theoretical psychology and neurophysiology were true of a person, and certain of the functional states of the theory satisfied the full complement of the constraints imposed by common sense as necessary conditions of having beliefs and desires, then it would be correct to count those functional states as beliefs and desires.

where the details of bodily movements are not within common-sense psychology's province, how can that which bears on the details have a bearing on common-sense psychological states? How can theoretical psychology dictate to common sense answers to questions that it is in the nature of common sense not to ask?

Instead of resorting to theoretical psychology, we could suppose that the picture of the brain cannot be superimposed on the picture of the person because the picture of the person has its own fine points which are not such as to be exposed in the structure of the brain. What we should then have to exploit in understanding the felt complexity of propositional–attitude psychology is not the brain's complexity, but our knowledge that common-sense psychology enables us to explain so much more than why there are the movements of people's bodies that there are. The step from a Rylean sort of behaviourism to functionalism will then seem to have been, in a way, a retrograde step. If mental states are to be thought of as dispositions of any sort (or, if you prefer, as states that are parts of systems that exhibit an overall structure), then, to the extent that they are dispositions to behave (or states connected systematically with ways of behaving), the relevant notion of behaviour is the broad one that the philosopher behaviourists used and the functionalists left behind.

If we do employ the ordinary and richer conception of behaviour in specifying the upshots of mental states, we cannot hope to circumscribe mental states in anything like the way that the functionalist envisages. Recall what was wrong with the old behaviourist's conception from the functionalist's point of view. Using that conception, one cannot leave the truth or falsity of agents' beliefs out of account. We imagined that this point might be accommodated by using a 'world-conditioned' notion of behaviour, but left this suggestion rather vague (section 3). Now the ramified character of the interdependencies between mental states, which the functionalist is so anxious to take account of, ensures that any worldly conditions incorporated in a notion of behaviour would ramify in any theory that attempted to accommodate that notion. A person can be expected to do what she tries to do on occasion only if certain beliefs that explain her then trying to do that are true. But the interdependencies between mental things ensure that for any desire or belief whose causal role we might think to define, it is possible that almost any belief might interact with it in the production of some possible event of trying.[15] Thus if the world-conditioned notion of behaviour is introduced by the functionalist, and from case to case he makes it explicit which beliefs are such that their truth or falsity on occasion is relevant to what behaviour is produced, his task turns into the project of giving an account of the structure of rational thought and practice, any exemplification of which is conditioned by a simultaneous view of the world as a subject confronts it. This is not the project of providing descriptions, however abstract, of the brain.

6. It is not a novel claim that explanation in the rational mode cannot be converted into science. As Davidson has said:

Any effort at increasing the accuracy and power of a theory of behaviour forces us to bring more and more of the whole system of the agent's beliefs and motives directly into account. But in inferring this system from the evidence, we necessarily impose conditions of coherence, rationality, and consistency. These conditions have no echo in physical theory.[16]

I take the mismatch Davidson sees between the mental and the scientific physical to show up in the fact that an attempt to incorporate conditions of rationality in a physicalist theory, using a concep-

---

[15] The 'certain' beliefs are (intuitively, and leaving out modifications that would be required to accommodate fortuituously false beliefs) those whose truth is required for the agent's trying to ϕ to result in the agent's ϕ-ing.

It is easy to miss the point about the ramification of worldly conditions if one thinks about explanation as we know it and forgets about the predictive aspirations of functionalists' output generalizations. When we know the explanation of an agent's doing something, we are in a position to specify a small number of beliefs which enter the explanation of her doing that, and only some of these are beliefs whose truth values bear on whether she has actually done the thing. But this is not the position of someone who hopes for a general, predictive theory of what agents would do. Consider a functionalist who hoped to derive actual mental/physical identities for the case of a particular person at a particular time. He might start with a list of types of state which were instantiated in the person at that time. For any type of state on that list, he will say (counterfactually) that its instance would interact thus and so *if* . . . ; for any type of state not on that list, he will say (doubly counterfactually, as it were) that *if* there were an instance of it, then it would interact thus and so *if* . . . . Thus *possible* events of trying must be seen (at *t*) as such as to be produced in a person (at a time later than *t*) by way of beliefs that that person may lack (at *t*). (Some people seem to forget that a functionalist's psychological theory must make mention of all the types of mental state there are. I have put the matter as I have here only because it may help to remind one of this.)

[16] This is from 'Psychology as Philosophy'; see Donald Davidson, *Essays on Actions and Events* (Clarendon Press, Oxford, 1980), 231.

tion of behaviour that is bodily but constrained by common-sense psychology, seems to leave something out. Even to its proponents it seems to leave something out, and they proceed by injecting some extra detail into bodily behavioural descriptions (cf. Armstrong and Lewis). But there is no warrant for the extra detail.[17]

Davidson himself thinks that the mismatch between the mental and the scientific physical shows up in two particular ways at the level of what can be said about people's 'outputs'. First, 'Practical reasoning ... may simply fail to occur'. Second, 'Wanting to do something ... may cause someone to do [the] thing, and yet the causal chain may operate in such a manner that the act is not intentional'.[18] These two claims surely reveal an immediate and insuperable obstacle to constructing functionalists' output generalizations. But I have allowed the argument to progress, believing that the superficial plausibility of the functionalists' contrary claims derives in large part from their free use of a quite schematic notion of *behaviour*.

The idea upon which the arguments here have traded is present in Davidson too, of course—in the claim that the mental is not a closed system. The felt complexity of propositional–attitude psychology will be accommodated only when 'the constitutive role of rationality' is properly acknowledged, and the attempt to see the patterns in a person's mental states embodied in the states of physical science is duly abandoned.[19]

7. The fundamental assumption that has been in dispute is that, in stating the causal powers of mental states, one can prescind from all but the most immediate effects of the actions they produce, and ignore almost everything under the head of 'desired effects of actions'

[17] I say that there is no warrant for the detail. But I should acknowledge that I have an argument only in so far as I am in a position to ask (rhetorically) 'What reason could there be for supposing that the detail is warranted?' ('What reason could there be for supposing that theoretical psychology can dictate to common sense?'). Of course the committed proponent of scientific materialism thinks that there are reasons where I see none: he supposes that metaphysical principles provide the warrant. I try to engage with his position in sections 8–10.

[18] The quotations are from 'Freedom to Act', at pp. 77 and 78 in *Essays on Actions and Events*.

[19] John McDowell also argues that if expositions such as Loar's seem to undermine Davidson's claims about the mental's anomalousness, then that could only be an illusion. He focuses attention on 'internal constraints', where I have focused on 'output generalizations'. See 'Functionalism and Anomalous Monism', in Ernest Le Pore and Brian McLaughlin (eds.), *The Philosophy of Donald Davidson: Perspectives on Actions and Events* (Blackwell, Oxford, 1986).

in the picture of the person (section 1). This assumption underlay the physicalist line of thought sketched at the outset. And we shall see now that it is the same assumption which leads people to accept the supervenience of the mental on the neurophysiological, and which gives rise to another physicalist view of intentional states of mind.

To many it seems (a) that a difference of mental state between two people requires some difference in their behavioural dispositions, and (b) that a difference in the behavioural dispositions of two animal bodies requires some difference in their internal physical machinery. They think, then, that if one were to allow that there could be a mental difference without a difference in brain state, one would be denying that the brain was responsible for the production of behaviour.[20]

Their argument is guilty of the same equivocation on 'behaviour' as the functionalists rely on. Premiss (a) requires for its truth a broad and everyday conception of a behavioural disposition; (b) requires a narrow one. (a) is true if we take it to mean that a change in mental state affects the proper explananda of psychological explanations; (b) is true if we take it to mean that only a change in brain state could affect how a creature moves itself. Nothing in the argument holds these two conceptions of a behavioural disposition together.[21]

Of course it is well known that there are counterexamples to a thesis of the supervenience of the psychological on the neurophysiological. Putnam's Twin Earth examples show that there can be variations in the objects of *de re* states of mind that are not reflected in any dispositions to move the body one way rather than another.[22] Some proponents of the supervenience thesis try to show that these examples do their thesis only negligible damage, as if the existence of *de re* states posed some special, local problem. But we saw that the

---

[20] The argument is in Colin McGinn, *The Character of Mind* (Oxford University Press, Oxford, 1982), 29; though McGinn himself would not endorse the argument just as it stands (see n. 23).

[21] Of course anyone can, if he wants, put common-sense descriptions of behaviour together with scientific descriptions of behaviour, and call what he arrives at descriptions of behaviour. What cannot be guaranteed, however, is that, having assembled a notion of behaviour by reference to two explanatory schemes, one has then accorded some stable sense to 'explanation of behaviour' or 'behavioural disposition'. (I have not said that no one is entitled to the functionalists' conception of behaviour; I have only questioned whether one is entitled to suppose that it can be put to the use to which functionalists put it.)

[22] See Hilary Putnam, 'The Meaning of "Meaning"', in his *Mind, Language and Reality* (CUP, Cambridge, 1975).

so-called holism of the mental is apt to embrace all of those worldly facts which a person's attitudes concern and which her bodily movements confront: the problem for supervenience is not a problem specifically about *de re* states of mind.

In some physicalist writings, this last point is acknowledged, and it is agreed that propositional–attitude states cannot be characterized as the functionalist envisages; but it is then said that these states must nevertheless have causal–explanatory *components*, which components may be seen to coincide with brain states. According to this new view, the picture of a person from which we begin is not itself something upon which any picture of the brain can be superimposed; but the picture of the person can, as it were, be split into two, and one of the resultant parts—the 'internal side' of a person, which is supposed to incorporate explanatory states—is suited to having some picture of the brain fitted on to it.[23]

Yet it is hard to see how anyone is in a position to claim that there are states whose ascription to people is explanatory of their behaviour unless he can demonstrate that the ascription of such states does, or would, cast light upon behaviour. We know of course that such states as we ascribe—beliefs having contents, for instance—do cast light. But it is no help then to be told that there must be states which lurk behind the states we ascribe and which carry their explanatory force. It is a strange idea that the satisfaction yielded by common-sense explanations has its source in something of which the parties to the explanation are quite ignorant—as if light had been cast through a medium that we cannot yet see through. But it would be a quite baffling idea that the explanatory force of an explanation resides in something that is not capable of illuminating anything for us—as if we could be sure that light will one day pass through a medium that is always opaque.

Not only can the picture of the brain not be superimposed upon the person, then: we have no reason to believe in any picture of a person's non-worldly aspect for it to be superimposed upon instead.

8. These conclusions ought not to surprise anyone who accepts that

---

[23] See for example Colin McGinn, 'The Structure of Content' in Andrew Woodfield (ed.), *Thought and Object* (Clarendon Press, Oxford, 1982). McGinn himself argues that the notion of *content* is decomposable into explanatory and truth-conditional aspects. The explanatory states he envisages do not have semantic content by virtue of their explanatory role, and the arguments below apply to his position inasmuch as this is so.

our reason for believing that mental states are occupants of causal roles is given by pointing to the place of mental states in causal explanation. For nothing in the argument here is hostile to the thought that causal roles are constitutive of at least some mental concepts. It can be true that the explanatory task that propositional–attitude ascription serves is a causal one; and it can be true that we cast all the light we can on propositional–attitude concepts by saying (not in functionalist theories, but in the available ways) what explanatory task their ascriptions serve.

It will be said that there is a puzzle here, however. How can the propositional–attitude states be thought of as mediating causally between inputs to and outputs from persons, although nothing with the appropriate causal powers of mental states can be found by scrutiny of a person's interior? Does not our conception of causality compel us to see the states which are cited in causal explanations of (*inter alia*) movements of a body as states which are located on causal chains that can be traced through space and time and that run through space–time volumes incorporating movements of that body? But then are we not obliged to see bodily movements as somehow primary among the explananda of action explanations? (Some line of thought such as this must be what lends plausibility to arguments like Kim's in section 2.)

One will feel tremendous pressure to accept this if one adopts a paradigm of causal explanations, got (say) from the picture of the brain, and takes it that the causal explanations obtained in viewing a person as a person must also conform to that paradigm. But if the causal–explanatory powers of mental states cannot be specified in such a way that a scientist could be led to recognize states that are the subjects of his studies as having those powers, then the belief that common-sense psychological states conform to the paradigm is undermined. The impossibility of specifying the causal–explanatory powers of mental states in ways that would suit a scientist is revealed in the difficulty of finding a notion of behaviour which is both available to common-sense psychology and rich enough to define states that are explanatory according to the paradigm even while they share in the complexities of common-sense psychological states.

9. Why is the idea that propositional–attitude states can be fitted to the scientific paradigm so compelling? I suspect that an unacknow-

ledged allegiance to principles of positivist epistemology must take a share of the blame.

If one begins with a distinction between psychological terms and non-psychological terms, and dresses this up in a distinction between T-terms and O-terms such as Lewis's (section 3), then one comes to think of the O-terms as conveying all the data from which psychological theories could be constructed. Application of the O-terms seems then to be independent of anything one knows about people (*per se*), and common-sense psychology begins to seem to be a theory of such observables as the O-terms describe, a theory distinctive only in its particular concepts.

But reflection on the practice of psychological explanation shows what an extraordinary myth this is.[24] Someone required to explain why some agent has done something has to show how the psychological facts about the agent are consistent with what she ostensibly did. This may require him to become clearer about what went on in the world even as he speculates about her mental states. (Equally of course he may learn about the world by learning of her states of mind.[25]) It is not, as the model of theory and observation might suggest, that he has to arrive at a view about what went on in the agent's head which coheres with some prior account of what happened at the place where her body meets the world.

We ought not then to expect to find any notion of behaviour ('the observable') that is suited to reductionist claims. Certainly Rylean talk of skaters' dispositions to warn other skaters seems laughable if it is read as offering any reduction of believing that the ice is thin. And there is reason to suppose that the features of Ryle's behavioural terms which contaminate them psychologically must in fact be present equally in any terms that figure in any account of mental things. There are two (related) ways in which the application

---

[24] The story that mental terms were actually introduced as theoretical terms is called a myth by David Lewis (op. cit. n. 3). In support of the idea that it is a good myth (sc. that our terms for mental states mean just what they would if the myth were true), Lewis says that if it were a good myth, it would explain the appeal of Rylean behaviourism. But the appeal of Rylean behaviourism cannot be separated from its use of a broad and everyday notion of behaviour; and this is a notion which ought not to be available to one who tells the mythical story. (See below, and n. 26 on Lewis on behaviour.)

[25] That this is a point about psychological explanation, rather than about 'head/world correlations', will be apparent only if one takes a relaxed view of psychological explanation; see section 2.

of everyday behavioural terms is caught up with the application of psychological terms. First, bits, or items, of behaviour, as described by behavioural concepts, are the effects of mental states; but it is impossible to divide behaviour up into bits in such a way that the bits correspond to things that have a psychological history unless we know something about the mental states that actually produce the behaviour. Second, Ryle's descriptions tell us of things that the agent intentionally did; and one is not in a position to take a view of which things are intentionally done by people unless one has some view of their mental states. These two features are bound to be inherited by any behavioural descriptions that are fit for inclusion in an account of mental states: their application must presuppose (a) a psychologically informed method for articulating the events that flow from a person, and (b) a sense of what is psychologically relevant among the events thus articulated.[26]

If one rests content with a naive conception of psychology's province, one cannot then construe 'observable' in positivist spirit and think of behaviour, the objects of psychological explanation, as 'observable'. Helping oneself to 'observable' behaviour, on the other hand, is only a way of ensuring that one ignores the truth about psychological explanation.

10. Section 9 is no doubt inadequate as a diagnosis of the attractions of present-day physicalist accounts of intentional phenomena. Here I suspect that the whole history of the subject is to the point. Philosophers of mind have come to see Cartesian dualism as the

---

[26] Lewis is sensitive to the fact that intentional notions must be precluded from accounts of behaviour if they are to be put to a theoretical use. He wrote (loc. cit. n. 11):

> There is an ambiguity in the term 'behaviour'. . . . I am using it to refer to raw behaviour—body movements and the like— . . . ; not to behaviour specified partly in terms of the agent's intentions. . . . That Karl's fingers move on certain trajectories and exert certain forces is what I call 'behaviour'; that he signs a cheque is not.

What Lewis seems to want to rule out from 'raw' behavioural descriptions is only instances of 'ϕ' such that any event of someone's ϕ-ing is an event of her intentionally ϕ-ing. There is no need to deny that this ruling can give us a notion of behaviour. What I do deny is that such a ruling provides us with a notion that might have been used by someone ignorant of all common-sense psychological truths. I deny, then, that Lewis has found a notion fit for his 'good myth'. (Of course there *is* a notion of behaviour (or anyway of *output*) that we can imagine applied in utter independence of any interest in persons; but with this (very raw) notion, we return to one on which we get no real purchase when we state common-sense psychological accounts.)

great enemy, but have underestimated what they have to contend with. Taking the putatively immaterial character of minds to create the only problem that there is for Descartes' account, they marry up the picture of the person with the picture of her brain, and settle for a view of mind which, though material in its (cranial) substance, is Cartesian in its essence.[27]

Of course the acceptance of immaterial substance *was* one of Descartes' errors. But it does not take a scientific materialism to remedy that error. After all, it has not been said that there are elements of the person picture that science fails to deal with because they are ethereal and unnatural, but only that we have to look for the source of common-sense psychology's complexity elsewhere than at the junction between the central nervous system and the world.

---

[27] What Descartes's commentators are typically most anxious to remind us of is that Descartes should not have held both that mind and body are substances whose essences are distinct, and that mind and body causally interact. Bernard Williams is an exception: he describes a difficulty which is independent of Descartes's treating the mind as soul-like, and depends only upon Descartes's thinking that all the transactions between the mental and the physical happen, as it were, at an interface. See the discussion of *terminal* interactionism (as Williams says we might call it) in *Descartes: The Project of Pure Enquiry* (Penguin, Harmondsworth, 1978), 288–92.

CHAPTER 4

CARTESIAN ERROR AND THE OBJECTIVITY OF PERCEPTION*

TYLER BURGE

Individualism as a theory of mind derives from Descartes. It dominates the post-Cartesian tradition—Locke, Berkeley, Leibniz, Hume—up until Kant. And it has re-emerged in the writings of Husserl and of many English-speaking behaviourists and functionalists. Although a generic similarity of standpoint is discernible in this motley, it is difficult to state clearly and succinctly what these philosophers hold in common. Roughly, they all think that the nature and individuation of an individual's mental kinds are 'in principle' independent of the nature and individuation of all aspects of the individual's environment.

A more precise characterization of individualism that captures the position of many modern functionalists is

Individualism is the view that if one fixes those non-intentional physical and functional states and processes of a person's body whose nature is specifiable without reference to conditions beyond the person's bodily surfaces, one has thereby fixed the person's intentional mental states and processes— in the sense that they could not be different intentional states and processes from the ones that they are.

This characterization is useful. But it is not directly relevant to the non-materialist tradition. Perhaps for some in this tradition (most plausibly, Berkeley and Hume), one could alter the characterization by referring to the person's phenomenological mental phenomena instead of to the person's physical states and processes. So for them individualism would be the thesis that a person's phenomenological, qualitative mental phenomena fix all the person's mental states, including those (like thoughts, desires, intentions) with intentionality or representational characteristics.

* © Tyler Burge 1986. I am indebted to John McDowell, Robert Matthews, and group discussion during the Colloquium at Oberlin College in 1985.

But now the characterization seems strained. It depends on distinguishing two aspects of the mental: phenomenological and intentional. I think it hard to maintain that traditional philosophers were drawing such a distinction cleanly enough to use it as the foundation for a major assumption. In retrospect we can see philosophers in this tradition as tending to assimilate concepts or even thoughts to (sometimes rarefied) percepts, and as regarding percepts as having their referential or intentional features intrinsically, as a result of their non-relational, qualitative, phenomenological natures. But it is doubtful that these philosophers can be seen as having made the distinctions necessary to be attributed a supervenience thesis of the sort just proposed. Moreover, the rationalists purported to lay little weight at all on the phenomenological character of our intentional states.

One could say that

Individualism is the view that a person's mental states and processes have intrinsic natures, in the strong sense that the nature and correct individuation of those states and processes (including individuation of their intentional content) is independent of any conditions that obtain outside that person's mind.

Although this characterization does better for Descartes, it has its own difficulties. These centre on the term 'outside'. It is not just that the term is vague as applied to the mind. The primary problem is that the characterization trades on a crucially unclear point in most idealist, especially most pre-Kantian idealist, theories. With Leibniz and Berkeley (and, on some interpretations, Hume), it is a subtle matter to say what is 'outside' an individual's mind. Of course, in solipsistic theories nothing is outside the individual's mind in any sense. One may argue over whether the theories of Leibniz, Berkeley, or Hume are in some sense 'ultimately' solipsistic. But regardless of what one thinks on this matter, the present characterization is crude at just the wrong point.

Still, the idea that the mind is somehow self-contained seems common to individualists. The idea can be refined, at least somewhat. Although it is difficult to generalize smoothly across Descartes, idealists, and various materialist reductionists, we shall characterize individualism, for our purposes, in roughly the way we began:

Individualism is the view that an individual person or animal's mental state and event kinds—including the individual's intentional or representational kinds—can in principle be individuated in complete independence of the natures of empirical objects, properties, or relations (excepting those in the individual's own body, on materialist and functionalist views)—and similarly do not depend essentially on the natures of the minds or activities of other (non-divine) individuals. The mental natures of all an individual's mental states and events are such that there is no necessary or other deep individuative relation between the individual's being in states, or undergoing events, with those natures, and the nature of the individual's physical and social environments.

Individualism has been motivated in a variety of ways. Explanatory or reductionistic strategies, ontological preconceptions, and various epistemic intuitions have provided undeveloped but nonetheless deep conviction in the truth of the doctrine. The epistemic intuitions, however, were the original ones, deriving as they do from Descartes. They retain considerable power, I think, even among philosophers who instinctively avoid resting weight on Cartesian thought experiments. In the first section of this paper, I shall discuss these intuitions in a sketchy and preliminary way. In the second, I shall propose an argument against individualism that bears fairly directly on those intuitions. The argument centres on perception. The issues at stake here are of some moment; and the present brief discussion should be construed as a sketch, not an appropriately scaled treatment.[1]

1. Descartes imagined himself thoroughly mistaken about the nature and even existence of the empirical world. The thought

---

[1] I have discussed individualism in several other papers: 'Individualism and the Mental', *Midwest Studies*, vol. IV (1979), 73–121; 'Other Bodies', in Andrew Woodfield (ed.), *Thought and Object* (Clarendon Press, Oxford, 1982); 'Two Thought Experiments Reviewed', *Notre Dame Journal of Formal Logic*, xxiii (1982), 284–93; 'Intellectual Norms and Foundations of Mind', to appear in *The Journal of Philosophy*, and 'Individualism and Psychology', to appear in *The Philosophical Review*. There are significant differences among the various arguments against individualism in these papers. Some centre on the role of the linguistic environment, some on the objectivity of theoretical discussion, some on the role of the physical environment. 'Individualism and Psychology' contains the argument that I shall present here in section II. But the argument in this other paper is given in a substantially different context. I think that ultimately the greatest interest of the various arguments lies not in defeating individualism, but in opening routes for exploring the concepts of objectivity and the mental, and more especially those aspects of the mental that are distinctive of persons.

experiments that he proposed are exceptionally vivid and powerful, at least on first encounter. And they have suggested to many—as they suggested to Descartes—that one's mental phenomena are in certain fundamental ways independent of the nature of the empirical and social worlds.

When one considers the thought experiments in any depth, one comes to realize that their details bear heavily on precisely what philosophical theses can be supported by reference to them. This generalization applies with undiminished force to attempts to use Cartesian thought experiments to support individualism. For example, the case for individualism based on the dreaming hypothesis is immediately affected (undermined, I believe) by the fact that an interpretation of dreams presupposes thoughts in a wakeful state. And the fact that it is part of the demon hypothesis that one is being deceived or fooled is of critical importance to any discussion of the relevance of the hypothesis to individualism. But I want to cut through such subtleties as much as possible. The 'Cartesian' cases that I will be imagining make no use of dreams and make no assumptions about demonic deception. I think that laying these aspects of the thought experiments aside strengthens their prima facie usefulness for individualist purposes. I will construe Descartes as capitalizing on the causal gap that we tend to assume there is between the world and its effects on us: different causes could have produced 'the same' effects, certainly the same physical effects on our sense organs. I will interpret him as conceiving a person as radically mistaken about the nature of the empirical world. I shall see him as imagining that there is something causing the given person's mental goings on, but as imagining that the entities that lie at the ends of relevant causal chains (and perhaps the causal laws) are very different from what the person thinks.

The Cartesian hypotheses gain considerable power if one places oneself in the position of the person under the delusion. From the 'inside', from a 'first-person' point of view, one develops an impression of the independence of the nature of one's mental life from outside determining factors. One has a vivid sense of how the world seems; but one remains conscious of the contingency of the relation between the way the objective world is and its effects on us. That is, the same sensory effects could seemingly have been systematically produced by a variety of different sets of causes-cum-laws. Then our vividly grasped thoughts would be mistaken. These sorts of considerations have led many to conclude that individualism must be true.

But let us consider more closely. As we have stated the Cartesian hypothesis, it contains two elements: some epistemic remarks and some remarks about causation.

The causal elements by themselves do not support the individualist position. The possibility that very different causal antecedents could issue in the same physical effects on the individual's body, and perhaps even issue in the same phenomenological mental phenomena, is used as a component in my previous arguments against individualism. (See n. 1.) The strategy of the arguments is to conceive of a person's having certain thoughts (for example, a belief that aluminium is a light metal used in making airplanes). Then, holding the history of the person's body—and perhaps non-intentionally specified, qualitative experiences—constant, one conceives of a relevantly different environment's having substantially the same physical effects on the person's surfaces. (For example, one may conceive of an environment that lacks aluminium altogether, and contains some superficially similar metal instead, but in such a fashion that the person's body is not differently affected in any relevant way.) In such a case, the person plausibly lacks some of the originally specified thoughts. (The person lacks beliefs involving a concept of aluminium.) Differences in the nature of the environment with which the person interacts seem to affect the individuation of a person's thoughts, even though there is no difference in the way the person's surfaces, individualistically and non-intentionally described, are affected.

Thus both the Cartesian thought experiments and my anti-individualistic arguments make use of the possibility that different causal antecedents could have the same effects on the person's surfaces. The Cartesian might want to describe the causal elements in his thought experiments more richly: relevantly different causal antecendents have the same effects on the person's mind. But such a description would blatantly beg the question at issue. Whatever force the Cartesian thought experiments lend to individualism must lie elsewhere.

The epistemic observations centre on the point that one could be drastically wrong about the nature of the empirical world around one. Until this point is made into a claim about the difficulty of justifying one's beliefs, it has no sceptical force. But even in its present form, the point is hardly uncontroversial. It tends to be the target of transcendental arguments. I shall accept it here for heuristic purposes, however, since my immediate aims are not epistemic. I want to grant a fairly strong epistemic conclusion from the thought experiments (one that I would not accept outright), and show, in a setting where scepticism is not at issue, that the conclusion by itself does not support individualism in the slightest.

So let us assume that we know or have reasonable beliefs about what the empirical world is like. And let us grant that the Cartesian thought experiments show that we could be radically wrong in these beliefs. That is, it is epistemically possible that the world be, or have been, very different from the way we reasonably think it is, or even know it is. This may be seen as a concession that we are deeply fallible. We can imagine being, and perhaps even being shown to be, pretty spectacularly wrong. But it is not a concession that there is reason to think that the beliefs that we are conceding might 'in principle' be wrong, really are wrong, or even are unjustified.

So what follows from this concession of the Cartesian epistemic possibility? Nothing immediate that favours individualism. We took our thoughts about the world as a *given* and conceded that they might be radically mistaken. But we conceded nothing about how our thoughts about the world are determined to be what they are. That is the issue before us. To assume that the epistemological intuitions occasioned by the Cartesian thought experiments support individualism is to make a step that needs justification. It is to beg precisely the question at issue.

It is a well-known point that in considering counterfactual situations we hold constant the interpretation of the language whose sentences we are evaluating in the counterfactual situations. It is quite possible to consider the truth or falsity of interpreted sentences even in counterfactual situations where those sentences could not be used or understood. Similarly for our thoughts when we are considering the Cartesian situations. We hold our thoughts constant. We consider situations in which the thoughts that we have would be false. And we concede that we could in principle be mistaken in thinking that the world is not arranged in one of the ways that would make our thoughts radically false. We do not ask how our thoughts' being false in certain ways would affect our thinking them. To ask what language or what thoughts would be possible if the world were in a given counterfactual state is to raise a question different from those raised in the Cartesian thought experiments. Thus there is some tendency for a Cartesian to move without argument from the counterfactual features of the thought experiments to the conclusion that the individuation of thoughts is unaffected by any possible differences in the environment. The move, or conflation, begins with: 'Things might have been radically otherwise without our surfaces being differently affected; and relative to these imagined circumstances, our (actual) thoughts would be subject to numerous and radical errors'. It concludes with: 'Things might have been radically otherwise and our thoughts and minds would remain just as they are'. Taken by itself, the transition is completely without justification.

There is, of course, another factor in the transition. Descartes's individualism rests primarily on his view of the special authoritative character of our knowledge of (some of) our own thoughts. A reconstructed Cartesian argument for individualism might follow these lines: (a) Suppose that one imagines that one's thoughts are subject to error in one of the Cartesian ways. (b) One knows what one's thoughts are, and they would be mistaken. But (c) an anti-individualist position holds that in some of the Cartesian cases we would think thoughts different from those we actually think—we would be in different mental states. (d) This conflicts with our authoritative knowledge about what (some of) our thoughts are and would be: we know authoritatively that our present thoughts would be the same.

This argument equivocates between considering what our thoughts are and what they would be. We can imagine that our thoughts are radically mistaken. So we accept (a) for present purposes. (b) is correct: we know what our thoughts are and we can see that in the counterfactual circumstances, those thoughts would be mistaken. (c) is also correct. I think it true, and compatible with (a), that in some of the Cartesian situations in which our actual thoughts about the empirical world would be mistaken, we would not be thinking the thoughts that we actually are thinking. But contrary to (d) there is no conflict with reasonable characterizations of first-person authority. We are authoritative about some of our actual thoughts about the empirical world; and we can imagine those very thoughts being quite mistaken. Moreover, whatever our thoughts would be if the counterfactual situation were to obtain, we would be authoritative about some of them. But we are *not* authoritative about what our thoughts about the empirical world would be if the counterfactual cases were actual. That is a philosophical issue, not a matter of what one's present mental events actually are. Although it may be settled by special, 'a priori' means, it is not an issue over which anyone has first-person (singular) authority. First-person authority presupposes our thoughts as given; we are then authoritative about those thoughts. But our thoughts are determined to be what they are partly by the nature of our environment. And we are authoritative about neither our environment nor the nature of that determination.

The problem of explicating the nature and source of the authoritative knowledge that we have of some of our present mental phenomena is close to the heart of the larger problem of explicating what is distinctive about persons. Here is not the place to elaborate a position on these matters. In opposing individualism, however, I am opposing the traditional rationalist assumption that in order to be authoritative about one's thoughts, one must be authoritative about (or at least be able to know a priori) all conditions for determining or individuating the nature of those particular thoughts. I believe that there is no simple, cogent defence of this assumption, certainly none that is immediately sustained by the Cartesian thought experiments.

Although all of these points demand development, what I have said so far seems to me to undermine the sense that the Cartesian thought experiments provide simple, direct support for individualism. It is easy to see how we might be involved in either or both of the two conflations that I have just warned against: conflating questions of counterfactually evaluating one's thoughts with questions of what thoughts one would think if one were in the counterfactual situation; and conflating the fact that we are authoritative about our actual thoughts, and would be authoritative about what our thoughts would be in any (relevant) counterfactual situation, with the claim that we are actually authoritative about certain thoughts that we would be thinking regardless of what actual or counterfactual situation we would be in. I think that the belief that the Cartesian cases support individualism usually rests on one or both of these conflations. The individualist needs arguments beyond what the intuitive thought experiments yield.

I want to close this section by mentioning a very common argument for individualism that involves a crude version of the sort of thinking that infers the doctrine directly from the Cartesian thought experiments. It begins by noting that we could have the same perceptual experiences, same perceptual representations, whether these were veridical perceptions, misperceptions, or hallucinations. Similar points can be made for other intentional mental phenomena. The argument concludes from these observations that perceptual experiences are independent, for their intentional natures, of the perceiver or thinker's environment. This inference has no force. Questions of veridicality are judged with respect to given mental states. It is a further question how those states are determined to be what they are. The natures of such states are determined partly by normal relations between the person or organism and the environment. Error is determined against a background of normal interaction. I will develop this idea in the next section.

2. It seems to me that a deeper consideration of perceptual error and veridicality provides powerful grounds for rejecting individualism. I begin with the premiss that our perceptual experience represents or is about objects, properties, and relations that are *objective*. That is to say, their nature (or essential character) is independent of any one person's actions, dispositions, or mental phenomena. An obvious consequence is that individuals are capable of having perceptual representations that are misperceptions or hallucinations: a person may have a perceptual representation even though he or she is perceiving nothing of the kind that is perceptually represented. A stronger consequence of the premiss is that, in any given case, all of a person's perceptual capacities, and indeed cognitive capacities, could in principle be mistaken about the empirically perceivable property (object, relation) being perceptually presented. To put this consequence with some gesture at precision: for any given person at any given time, there is no necessary function from all of that person's abilities, actions, and representations up to that time to the natures of those entities that that person perceptually interacts with at that time (and is capable of perceiving at that time and earlier).

Our second premiss is that we have perceptual representations (or perceptual states with contents) that *specify* particular objective types of objects, properties, or relations *as such*. Representations specify such objective entities as blobs, bars, boundaries, convexity, cones, rough texturedness, being farther from x than from y; and they specify them *as* blobs, bars, boundaries, and so on. The 'logical form' of such perceptual representations is not particularly important to our argument. I am inclined to think that some have the form of 'that boundary'. But as far as our argument is concerned, all could have the form 'that is a boundary', or 'there is a boundary there', or even (what I consider quite implausible) 'there is a boundary there causing this perceptual experience'.[2] The important thing is that the representations specify some particular objective entities (e.g. a boundary) as such (e.g. as a boundary). They do not simply describe those entities in terms of their role in causing perceptual states of a certain kind. For example, I assume that perceptual representations do not all have contents like those of 'whatever normally causes this sort of perceptual representation'—or 'whatever normally has this sort of perceptual appearance', where the description denotes some objective property.

There are a variety of reasons why this latter sort of perceptual representation is not fundamental or canonical. The idea that our perceptual representations make primary reference to themselves is an old philosopher's tale with little or no genuine plausibility. I take it that attribution of such complicated perceptual representations is implausible on its face. And to get the description to apply to appropriate entities (as opposed to antecedent or intermediate occur-

---

[2] The second premiss is in conflict with Descartes's view that one cannot make perceptual errors because one perceives only one's own mental phenomena. According to this view one infers (wills to infer) the existence of objective properties causing those phenomena. Cf. *The Principles of Philosophy*, Pt. II, Principle III; *Meditations* VI. A similar view embraced Russell. Cf. *The Problems of Philosophy* (Oxford University Press, London, 1912), Chapter 3; *The Analysis of Matter* (Dover, New York, 1954). I have discussed these sorts of views briefly in 'Individualism and Psychology', op. cit. John Searle, in *Intentionality* (CUP, Cambridge, 1983), Chapter 2, argues that the content of perceptual states is always self-referential, in the last of the ways listed in the text. I find the argument unpersuasive in that it depends on an undefended conception of 'conditions of satisfaction'. I do not think that there is strong reason to think that perceptual experiences have as complicated contents as he claims, and do not think that those contents are self-referential. (Searle's examples all concern recognition—a very late stage of perception. Cf. David Marr, *Vision* (W. H. Freeman and Company, San Francisco, 1982).) Still, these disagreements are not crucial to my argument. Searle's purportedly individualistic contents contain specifications of objective entities as such—for example 'a yellow station wagon'. So such contents satisfy the requirements of my argument.

Perhaps this is a good place to emphasize that neither this premiss nor any other part of the argument relies essentially on any particular notion of content or representation. I use these notions without apology, but I am aware that there are those who think they see something wrong with this sort of talk. For purposes of the argument this language may be regarded as a variant on talk about the type of intentional state. Clearly perceptual experiences are properly specified and individuated in such intentional terms. The argument concerns the nature and pre-conditions for the states and events thus individuated.

rences, such as arrays of light striking the retina), the descriptions would have to be complicated in ways that have never been fully articulated. Such complications make a bad case worse. There is no reason to think that notions like normality, or causation as a relation between objects and perceivers, or appearance, enter into primary perceptual experience. These notions are developed from meta-reflection on that experience.

Moreover, to be appropriately informative the perceptual representation would have to specify the *sort* of phenomenological type that it itself instantiated: 'this sort' is simply too unspecific to account for the reticulated array of perceptual types that we recognize and discriminate. But the idea that we classify our perceptual phenomenology without specifying the objective properties that occasion it is wildly out of touch with actual empirical theories of perception as well as with common sense. The sorts of complicated representations that we have been discussing seem to me to have little place in perception at all (as opposed to sophisticated, self-conscious, discursive reflection on perception—where they presuppose classifications of perceptual types in terms of public entities). But our argument requires only that they not be the only sorts of perceptual representations that we have.

In a sense, this second premiss is a rejection of what used to be called the representational theory of perception. According to that theory, we primarily perceive, or at least primarily make reference to, *representations* of objective entities; we make reference to objective entities *only* indirectly—by assuming or inferring that there are objective counterparts or causes of the representations that we make direct perceptual reference to. I take it that this theory is discredited and rarely defended nowadays. It is implausible for the reasons I have mentioned. Among our perceptual representations are surely specifications, not merely role descriptions, of objective entities.

Although this second premiss is worth articulating, I think that at a deeper level of argument, it can be dispensed with. I believe that the second premiss is ultimately a necessary consequence of the first: we can make veridical perceptual reference to objective entities of a given type only if we can make perceptual reference to them as such. But I shall not take on the burden of arguing that here.

Our final premiss is that some perceptual types that specify objective types of objects, properties, and relations as such do so partly because of relations that hold between the perceiver (or at least members of the perceiver's species) and instances of those objective types. These relations include causal interaction.[3] If there were no such relations, a perceiver would lack at least some perceptual intentional types that he or she has.

The premiss derives from the fact that perceptual experience, and the formation of perceptual representation, is *empirical*. The intentional nature of some of our perceptual representations—what information they carry, what they mean—depends partly on the way epistemically contingent aspects of the world that occasion them actually are. Our perceptual information and our informational and representational states are worked up out of empirical interaction with an objective world.

The force of this point was obscured in the Locke-to-Hume tradition by a peculiar distortion. The empirical character of perception was depicted as if it were (at most) a purely causal affair. The perceptual types were considered to carry information about the world intrinsically—because of their shape in the image, for example. The role of the objective world was simply to cause appropriate ones among these information-bearing percepts to pop into the mind at appropriate moments.

Behind this distortion was the intuitively powerful but primitive idea (deriving from pre-Cartesian Aristotelians and prominent among post-Cartesian empiricists) that perceptual representations represented by virtue of similarity with their objects. This idea seems now to have little explanatory value. How could similarity alone (even assuming that the relevantly similar respects were articulated) explain perceptual representation? Among post-Cartesian empiricists the answer sometimes relied on the representational theory of perception, which we have just discussed: we represent objective empirical entities by representing subjective counterparts that are similar and by representing or inferring a relation between subjective and objective correlates.

Descartes and his rationalist successors either rejected or laid little weight on explanations in terms of similarity. But they tended to

---

[3] I think that these relations always include intentional application—a notion that I have discussed elsewhere in some detail. Cf. 'Belief *De Re*', *The Journal of Philosophy*, lxxiv (1977), 338–62; and 'Russell's Problem and Intentional Identity', in J. Tomberlin (ed.), *Agent, Language, and the Structure of the World* (Hackett Publishing Company, Indianapolis, 1983). The relation of application to the present set of issues is in fact complex and worth pursuing. But pursuit is inappropriate here.

retain the view that perceptual representational types carry information or have their representational characters in complete independence of the way the empirical world is. Theological and idealist considerations were imported to shore up the objectivity and cognitive value of perceptual representation. And the whole tradition fell prey to Humean scepticism.

In retrospect, this set of ideas seems strange. Not only do our perceptual presentations or experiences have the qualitative features that they have because of the law-governed ways that our sense organs and neural system interact with the physical environment. But their giving empirical information to conscious beings about the environment—their representing it—depends on their qualitative features being regularly and systematically related to objective features of the environment. No matter what their phenomenological character, perceptual presentations can represent objective empirical features beyond themselves as such only through having instances stand in regular causal relations to instances of those objective features.

Granted, certain of our visual representations may be ascribed attributes that are the same as or at least analogous to attributes of the objective entities that they represent. Our perceptual representation-in-the-image of a straight line may perhaps itself be said to be 'straight'. The image may be thought of as like a picture with some elements that have properties (for example geometrical ones) that correspond to some of those that it depicts. (Of course, this line has been vociferously doubted by many philosophers; but I shall grant it for present purposes. Doubters have one less obstacle to agreement with our primary position.) Even where such analogies hold, they do so at least partly because of the laws of optics, the natures of our bodies, and the geometrical characteristics of physical objects. And similarities in the perceptual image are of representational significance only because and only in so far as they are formed through regular interactions with objective entities.

It must also be noted that any such similarities are limited in scope. Whatever similarities perceptual representations of three-dimensional orientations, or of three-dimensional shapes, or of occluding edges, bear to their objects are certainly not sufficient even to suggest a unique match. In such cases, which surely include the bulk of our perceptual representations, there is no other natural way to specify the intentional content of the perceptual experiences than by reference to the types of objective entities that they are normally applied to.

The third premiss states that some of a perceiver's perceptual types take on their representational characters partly because their instances interact in certain ways with the objective entities that are represented. It does not claim that all do. It is plausible that many perceptions are composites of others. In some few cases, the whole may be representational, though it is *never* formed by interaction with actual objects. One thinks of hallucinations of pink elephants or unicorns. Moreover, some representations at the level of recognitional capacity (beyond the level of early vision) may be heavily informed by background theory, in such a way as to acquire representational character independently of any interaction. Again, these cases seem very much the exception. Still, it would be a mistake not to allow for them.

There are other ways that perceptual states may acquire their representational characteristics. Sometimes the evolutionary history of a species may form a perceptual tendency in members of the species that has representational characteristics that depend in some way on interaction between an individual's ancestors and objects of a relevant sort. The intentional content of a perceptual state may be independent of the individual's learning history. Instances of the state could, in an individual, be occasioned in an abnormal way, yielding misperceptions not preceded in that individual by veridical perceptions. Our premiss could be complicated to accommodate such possibilities explicitly. But the basic anti-individualistic thrust of the argument that follows would be unaffected.

The empirical character of perceptual representation formation is evinced in our common methods of interpreting a creature's perceptual experience. When we seek to determine the intentional content or representational types in a creature's perceptual experience, we determine what objective properties are discriminated by its perceptual apparatus. That is, we build up intentional type attributions by determining the types of objective entities whose instances regularly causally affect the creature's sense organs and are normally discriminated perceptually by the creature—or at least by creatures of the same species.

This fact about perception constitutes, I think, a qualified basis for the oft-repeated slogan that error presupposes a background of veridicality.[4] I think that this slogan is sometimes misused. I think that we are not immune from fairly dramatic and wholesale error in characterizing the nature of the empirical world. But I do think that we are nearly immune from error in asserting the existence of instances of our perceptual kinds, and of other kinds that are taught by more or less immediate association with perceptually based applications. I think that (induced) massive perceptual hallucination or a total lack of regularity between an individual's experience and his or her environment are the only possible explanations for an individual's perceptual experiences *always* systematically failing to apply to the world.

Most perceptual representations are formed and obtain their content through regular interaction with the environment. They represent what, in some complex sense of 'normally', they normally stem from and are applied to. It makes no sense to attribute systematic perceptual error to a being whose perceptual representations can be explained as the results of regular interaction with a physical environment and whose discriminative activity is reasonably well adapted to that environment.

So there are our three premises: our perceptual experience represents objective entities; perceptual experience specifies objective entities as such; and the formation of perceptual representation (of perceptual intentional types) is empirical. We are now in a position to argue that individualism is not true for perceptual representation.

We begin with an individual with perceptual experience of objective entities. The person normally perceives instances of a particular type of objective entity (call it '*O*') correctly (as *O*s). But imagine that one or more of his or her perceptual experiences involves misperception. At time *t*, the person misperceives an instance of another

---

[4] The slogan has roots, I think, in Kant's point that the concept of seeming makes sense only in contrast to the concept of being. Cf. *The Critique of Pure Reason*, 'The Refutation of Idealism'. The point regained prominence in Quine's 'Principle of Charity', *Word and Object* (MIT Press, Cambridge, Massachusetts, 1960), Chapter II; and it has been employed in different ways by Donald Davidson, for example in 'On the Very Idea of a Conceptual Scheme', in his *Inquiries into Truth and Interpretation* (Clarendon Press, Oxford, 1984). I am inclined to believe that Quine and Davidson sometimes use this important idea with insufficient discrimination. But the issues here are again complex, and require more development than I can undertake. I should note, however, that in the remarks that follow my terms 'characterization' and 'application' are terms of art. Cf. 'Intellectual Norms and Foundations of Mind', op. cit., and the works cited in n. 3.

type of objective entity (call it 'C') as an O. That is, an instance of C is present and is causing the perceptual experience. Since C and its instance are objective, it is in principle possible that all the given person's sensory modalities together might be fooled. In fact, we may imagine that given what the person knows and can do at the time of the misperception, he or she cannot discriminate the actual situation, at that time, from the one he or she represents. We may even imagine that nothing the person does or is disposed to do up until time t would (on this particular occasion) have discriminated between this instance of C and an instance of O.[5] Our first premiss gives us this much. The objectivity of the objects of perception entails that there is always a possible gap between the proximal effects of those objects on an individual's mind or body (and the sum of what the person represents, thinks, and can do), on one hand, and the nature of the objects themselves, on the other. The same proximal effects, representations, thought, and activity could in certain instances derive from different objective entities.

The first premiss also yields the following counterfactual. We fix those of our person's physical states and discriminative abilities that can be specified non-intentionally and independently of the nature of his or her environment. But we conceive of a counterfactual environment in which the sort of entity O that the person actually represents never occurs. Instead, the sort of proximal stimulations that are actually normally caused by instances of O are counterfactually normally caused by instances of C (or at any rate by something other than instances of O). We may further imagine that members of our person's species have evolved so as to adapt to this situation. They regularly obtain information about instances of C; and we may imagine that their physical movements and discriminative abilities are quite different from the ones they have in the actual circumstances. Only the protagonist's body, non-intentionally and individualistically specified, need remain the same.

---

[5] There is no need to assume that the instance of C is in principle unverifiable or indiscernible as an instance of C. Another person with relevant background information might be able to infer that the instance of C would produce a perceptual illusion. Another person with different dispositions might even be able to perceive the difference between the instance of C and an instance of O. It need not be that all instances of C always look like instances of O to other members of the species. It is enough for the argument that instances of C that our protagonist is exposed to not be discriminable by him or her from the instances of O that he or she has been exposed to.

We assume, using the second premiss, that in both actual and counterfactual situations, our person has perceptual experiences that are or include specific specifications of the relevant objective entities. For example, if in the actual situation, *P* correctly perceives an instance of *O*, the person perceives it as an *O*. By the third premiss, since the objective entities that the person normally interacts with—and perceives as such—differ between actual and counterfactual situations, and since the laws explaining these interactions differ, the perceptual intentional types of the person also differ. Counterfactually, he or she perceives a *C* as a *C*, not as an *O*. Our protagonist's perceptual experience at *t* in the counterfactual situation is not a misperception, but is in fact veridical. (What is important is only that the perceptual state does not specify anything as an *O*.) But the person's physical states, discriminative abilities, and perhaps purely phenomenological (non-intentional) states remain the same between the two situations. So the person's intentional perceptual types are not individualistically individuated.

It is easiest to imagine an example concretely if the case is taken from the more primitive (but still conscious) stages of vision. For then elaborate conceptual or verbal dispositions associated with the visual state need not be brought into consideration. More dispositions complicate the attempt to imagine a case in detail. But they do not affect the logic or soundness of the argument already given. As long as the first assumption about objectivity is in place, there is the guarantee that there is no unique fit between non-intentional dispositions and the represented environment.

To fix an example, we may imagine that the sort of entities being perceived are very small and are not such as to bear on the individual's success in adapting to the environment. An *O* may be a shadow of a certain small size on a gently contoured surface. A *C* may be a similarly sized crack. The individual *P* encounters several *O*s, and they are commonly seen in the environment. In the only case(s) in which *P* encounters a *C*, *P* may have no dispositions that would discriminate the instance of *C* from an instance of *O*—although *P* might in principle have been taught such procedures, and although other individuals may have them. For example, *P* may have no dispositions involving touch that could be used to discriminate them, perhaps because the relevant entities are too small, or because *P* is not disposed to rely on non-visual modalities in such cases, or because touch itself is fooled. Still, if only *O*s normally cause visual representations of the sort P has, if P's having those representations is explained in terms of their relation to Os (characterized as Os), if P can discriminate Os from relevantly different things in the environment, and if P's visual or cognitive systems have some means of distinguishing objective entities from subjective ephemera (most of the time), then P's visual representation may specify Os as such. The misperception of a relevant sort of crack as a relevant sort of shadow may be a result of a one-time causal aberration.

We may assume, if we wish, that in the actual situation—given P's abilities, and the actual laws of optics—P would be capable of visually discriminating some instances of C (cracks of the relevant sort) from some instances of O in ideal circumstances. But we are supposing that P is confronted by only one or a few instances of C; and in those cases, circumstances are sufficiently non-ideal so that all P's abilities would not succeed, in those circumstances, in discriminating those instances of C from instances of O. P misperceives the relevant cracks as shadows.

Now imagine a counterfactual case. Owing to peculiar optical laws or effects, there are no visible Os—no shadows (visible to P's species) of relevantly similar shape and size on gently contoured surfaces. The optical laws are also such that all the visual impressions caused by and explained in terms of Os in the actual situation are counterfactually caused by and explained in terms of Cs—relevantly sized cracks. The cracks are where the shadows were in the actual case. Suppose also that at the (few) time(s) when in the actual situation P is confronted with a C, P is also counterfactually confronted with a C. None of the differences relevantly affects the physical history of P's visual system or any of P's other physical stimulations, physical dispositions, or physical activity.[6] In such a counterfactual situation, P would normally be visually representing Cs—relevantly small cracks—as Cs. P would never be visually representing, or misrepresenting, anything as an O. One can imagine that in the counterfactual case, even if there *were* appropriately sized shadows on relevant surfaces, the different laws of optics in that counterfactual

[6] One may imagine that the dispositions that would, in the actual case under ideal circumstances, have visually discriminated Cs from Os would, in the counterfactual case, be activated in circumstances that provide discrimination of some other type of thing from Cs. Given the very different physical environment and laws, one can imagine these dispositions to have almost any visual meaning that one likes.

case would not enable *P* ever to see them. If this were so, one could hardly take *P*'s visual impressions (physically and perhaps phenomenologically the same as in the actual case—but explained as *normally* caused by cracks) to be misrepresentations of things as the relevant sort of shadows. For we imagine *P*'s visual impressions to be caused in a regular way by the objects *P* is looking at. The visual impressions provide as sound a basis for learning about the environment in the counterfactual case as they do for learning about the (different) environment in the actual case. Counterfactually, *P*'s intentional perceptual states are different: *P* sees *C*s as *C*s.

The general strategy of the argument is simple. The first premiss notes a possible gap between a person's physical states and intentional states, on one hand, and the state of the world that is seen, on the other. Holding the relevant physical effects constant, we imagine different visible objects in the world, and different optical laws normally and regularly relating those objects to the person's physical states. In such a case, it is clear that some of the person's intentional visual states, at least some of those that specify objective entities as such, would be different. The second and third premisses of our argument already jointly indicate that a person's intentional perceptual states are in fact not individuated individualistically. These premisses presuppose the first. The first premiss makes explicit the possibility of error, and thereby indicates that the non-individualist methods of individuation, indicated by the second and third premisses, do not 'in principle' have counterpart methods that are individualistic.

If one relinquishes the claim that a person's perceptions represent objective entities, then the argument collapses. All three premisses are undermined. So as applied to a solipsistic thinker, the argument is powerless.[7] On the other hand, the objective and empirical

---

[7] Perhaps one should see in this light the fanciful examples of beings that are bodily identical to us over a period of time, but that are extended quantum accidents with no regular relations to their physical environment. There is perhaps enough in the mental events of such beings to count them thinkers. (Actually, this seems to me problematic: there are problems about dispositions; but let them pass.) Whatever thoughts they entertain have no determinate *objective* reference. Their mental goings on and their physical movements are compatible with successful adaptation to and regular causation by any one of an infinity of possible environments. Such intentionality as their phenomenological states have should perhaps be seen as making reference to qualitative phenomenological types, not to objects that are in principle

character of perceptual representation seems to guarantee non-individualistic intentional perceptual states, and non-individualistic methods of individuating them.

independent of the individual's thought and perception. For such a being, individualism is perhaps true. But its truth would be bought at the price of interpreting the thinker as a solipsist unawares. I leave the ultimate coherence of such a description an open question.

CHAPTER 5

SINGULAR THOUGHT AND THE EXTENT OF INNER SPACE*

JOHN McDOWELL

1. In defending the Theory of Descriptions, Russell presupposes an interlocking conception of genuinely referring expressions ('logically proper names') and singular propositions: logically proper names combine with predicates to express propositions which would not be available to be expressed at all if the objects referred to did not exist. Thus Russell objects to the idea that a sentence in which a definite description is combined with a predicate should be counted as sharing a form with a sentence in which a logically proper name is combined with a predicate, on the ground that if the description fits nothing, as it may, this assignment of logical form implies that the description-containing sentence is 'nonsense';[1] and it is plain that he might have said 'expresses no proposition'. The point of the alternative logical form proposed by the Theory of Descriptions is to ensure that the proposition which such a sentence is held to express is one available to be expressed in any case, whether or not there is something answering to the description.

It seems clear that Russell's conception of singular (object-dependent) propositions is intended in part as a contribution to psychology: propositional attitudes whose contents are singular propositions are meant to be recognized as a distinctive kind of configuration in psychological reality. But Russell takes this psychological application of the idea to be possible only under a severe restriction on its scope. And more recent philosophers have tended to follow him in this: those who have taken the Russellian idea of a singular proposition seriously at all have acquiesced in something

---

* © John McDowell 1986.

[1] 'On Denoting', *Mind*, xiv (1905), 479–93; reprinted in Bertrand Russell, *Logic and Knowledge*, ed. R. C. Marsh (George Allen and Unwin, London, 1956), 41–56; see p. 46 in the latter.

like Russell's restriction,[2] or else, if they wanted to recognize object-dependent propositions outside Russell's limits, they have located them within the purview of a discipline of 'semantics' further removed than Russell's semantics was meant to be from aiming to delineate the contours of thought.[3] I believe a version of Russell's idea can help with some venerable philosophical difficulties about the relation between thought and reality; but first we must see how its directly psychological application can be detached from Russell's restriction.

2. Russell's restriction results, in effect, from refusing to accept that there can be an illusion of understanding an apparently singular sentence (or utterance), involving the illusion of entertaining a singular proposition expressed by it when, since there is no suitably related object, there is no such proposition available to be entertained. Whenever a strictly singular parsing of a range of sentences (or utterances) would involve postulating such illusions, the apparatus of the Theory of Descriptions is brought to bear, in order to equip sentences (or utterances) of the range with non-singular propositions which they can be understood to express whether or not there is a suitably related object. This generalizes the original argument against counting definite descriptions as genuinely referring expressions. The generalized argument applies also to ordinary proper names, and indeed to nearly all expressions one might intuitively regard as devices of singular reference. The upshot, in Russell's hands, is that we can entertain and express singular propositions only where there cannot be illusions as to the existence of an object of the appropriate kind: only about features of sense-data or items present to us with similar immediacy in memory, and (when Russell recognized them as objects) our selves.

Why should we find it intolerable to postulate the sort of illusion which Russell disallows? Why not say that some sentences (or utterances) of a given range express singular propositions, whereas others present the illusory appearance of doing so (to those not in the know)—rather than, with Russell, devising a kind of non-singular proposition to be associated with all alike? If we suggest that the idea of this sort of illusion is harmless, we risk undermining the Theory of

---

[2] See, for instance, Stephen Schiffer, 'The Basis of Reference', *Erkenntnis*, xiii (1978), 177–206.

[3] This is true of David Kaplan's unpublished 'Demonstratives', and of a great deal of work inspired by it.

Descriptions itself, not just its extension beyond the case of definite descriptions. But we can recover a special plausibility for the original Theory of Descriptions by introducing another piece of Russellian apparatus, the notion of acquaintance.[4]

When the Russellian conception of singular propositions is given its directly psychological application, it implies that which configurations a mind can get itself into is partly determined by which objects exist in the world. One might have expected the topology of psychological space, so to speak, to be independent of the contingencies of wordly existence: Russell's thought is that we can intelligibly set that expectation aside, but only when the mind and the objects are related by what he calls 'acquaintance'. The real point about definite descriptions can then be this: although someone who understands a sentence (or utterance) in which a definite description occurs *may* be acquainted with the appropriate object, the way in which the description is constructed out of independently intelligible vocabulary makes it absurd to require acquaintance with an object, on top of familiarity with the words and construction, as a condition for entertaining a proposition as what the sentence (or utterance) expresses. (This is less plausible for some uses of definite descriptions than others; but I am not concerned with evaluating the argument.)

This opens the possibility that we might equip Russell with a defence of some form of the Theory of Descriptions, strictly so called, on the ground that an appeal to acquaintance would be out of place in an account of how at least some definite descriptions (or utterances of them) are understood; while at the same time we might consistently resist Russell's own extension of the Theory of Descriptions to other cases, with the idea that acquaintance makes it possible to entertain singular propositions and illusions of acquaintance generate illusions of entertaining singular propositions, so that there is no need to look for non-singular propositions to suit both sorts of case. But we cannot make anything of this abstract possibility until we give more substance to the notion of acquaintance.

When Russell defends the claim that one can entertain a singular proposition about an object only if one is acquainted with the object, he equates that claim with the claim that one can entertain such a proposition only if one knows which object it is that the proposition

---

[4] See 'Knowledge by Acquaintance and Knowledge by Description', in Bertrand Russell, *Mysticism and Logic* (George Allen and Unwin, London, 1917), 152–67.

concerns.[5] The equation betrays insensitivity to the grammatical difference between the use of 'know' implicit in 'is acquainted with' and the use in 'knows which ...';[6] but the grammatical conflation is theoretically suggestive. The underlying idea is that to entertain a proposition one must know how one's thinking represents things as being. If the proposition is singular, one can satisfy that requirement only by knowing which object is represented, and how it is represented as being; and half of this condition is Russell's requirement in the 'know which ...' version. The notion of acquaintance with an object, now, is the notion of an immediate presence of object to mind such as would make it intelligible that the mind in question can entertain singular propositions, targeted on the object in the special way in which singular propostions are, in conformity with that requirement. I shall illustrate this idea in a not strictly Russellian application, and then comment on the divergence from Russell.

A Russellian paradigm of acquaintance is perception. As I mentioned, Russell allows as objects of perceptual acquaintance only features of sense-data. But we can extract the notion of acquaintance from that epistemological framework and apply it to at least some perceptual relations between minds and ordinary objects. A typical visual experience of, say, a cat situates its object for the perceiver: in the first instance egocentrically, but, granting the perceiver a general capacity to locate himself, and the objects he can locate egocentrically, in a non-egocentrically conceived world, we can see how the experience's placing of the cat equips the perceiver with knowledge of where in the world it is (even if the only answer he can give to the question where it is is 'There'). In view of the kind of object a cat is, there is nothing epistemologically problematic in suggesting that this locating perceptual knowledge of it suffices for knowledge of which object it is (again, even if the only answer the perceiver can give to the question is 'That one'). So those visual experiences of objects that situate their objects can be made out to fit the account I suggested of the notion of acquaintance: abandoning Russell's sense-datum epistemology, we can say that such objects are immediately present to the mind in a way that, given the connection between location and identity for objects of the appropriate kind, makes possible the targeting of singular thoughts on the objects in conformity

[5] See *The Problems of Philosophy* (Oxford University Press, London, 1912), 58.
[6] See my 'Identity Mistakes: Plato and the Logical Atomists', *Proceedings of the Aristotelian Society*, n.s. lxx (1969–70), 181–95.

with the Russellian requirement in its 'know which . . .' version. Anyone who knows Gareth Evans's seminal work will recognize that what I have done here is to read Russell's notion of acquaintance into a simplified form of Evans's account of perceptual demonstrative modes of presentation.[7]

The most striking divergence from Russell is this: the position I have just sketched leaves it an evident possibility that one can be under the illusion of standing in a relation to an object that would count as acquaintance, the impression being illusory because there is no such object. There would be an independent justification for Russell's disallowing this possibility if some such principle as this were acceptable: a capacity or procedure can issue, on a specific occasion, in a position that deserves some epistemically honorific title (for instance 'acquaintance with an object') only if it *never* issues in impostors. But it is not acceptable—indeed, it is epistemologically disastrous—to suppose that fallibility in a capacity or procedure impugns the epistemic status of any of its deliverances. There is no independent justification, from general epistemology, for refusing to allow that there can be illusions of entertaining singular propositions.[8]

3. Russell envisages singular propositions having as constituents, besides what is predicated of their objects, simply the objects

---

[7] See *The Varieties of Reference* (Clarendon Press, Oxford, 1982), Chapter 6. I have tried to formulate the position in such a way as to suggest the lines of an answer to Christopher Peacocke's complaint of 'a curiously unmotivated asymmetry' in Evans's proposal: *Sense and Content* (Clarendon Press, Oxford, 1983), 171. But this is not the place to elaborate.

[8] In a fuller treatment, it would be necessary at this point to consider in detail the possibility of liberalizing the notion of acquaintance outside the case of perceptually presented objects. Topics for discussion here would include the non-compulsoriness of Russell's assumption that acquaintance with a self could only be acquaintance with a Cartesian ego (see Evans, *The Varieties of Reference*, Chapter 7, for material for an argument against that assumption); a liberalization of the notion's application to memory, parallel to the liberalization I have suggested for its application to perception (hinted at perhaps in the Appendix to Chapter 8 of *The Varieties of Reference*, but not achieved in the body of that work because of what is arguably an excessive concern with recognition); and the idea of an autonomous variety of acquaintance constituted, even in the absence of other cognitive relations to an object, by mastery of a communal name-using practice (rejected by Evans at pp. 403–4 of *The Varieties of Reference*, but perhaps on the basis of an excessive individualism). But in this paper I am concerned with the general structure of a possible position rather than the details of its elaboration, and the perceptual case should suffice as an illustration.

themselves.[9] This has the effect that there cannot be two different singular propositions in which the same thing is predicated of the same object. The upshot is that we cannot make singular propositions beyond Russell's restriction figure in the direct delineation of the contours of thought without flouting a principle we can associate with Frege: that if some notion like that of representational content is to serve in an illuminatingly organized account of our psychological economy, it must be such as not to allow one without irrationality to hold rationally conflicting attitudes to one and the same content. As long as Russell's restriction is in force, it seems unlikely that Russellian singular propositions will generate violations of this principle: a feature of a sense-datum, say, will not be liable to figure in one's thinking twice without one's knowing that it is the same one—which would protect one, assuming rationality, from the risk of conflicting attitudes about it. But singular propositions about, say, ordinary material objects, on Russell's account of their constituents, would be too coarsely individuated to conform to the Fregean principle. Is this a justification of Russell's restriction?[10]

No. Russell's idea of the constituents of propositions reflects a failure to understand Frege's distinction between sense and reference; it is not essential to the real insight which his notion of singular propositions embodies. The insight is that there are propositions, or (as we can now put it) thoughts in Frege's sense, which are object-dependent. Frege's doctrine that thoughts contain senses as constituents is a way of insisting on the theoretical role of thoughts (or contents) in characterizing a rationally organized psychological structure; and Russell's insight can perfectly well be formulated within this framework, by claiming that there are Fregean thought-constituents (singular senses) which are object-dependent, generating an object-dependence in the thoughts in which they figure. Two or more singular senses can present the same object; so Fregean singular thoughts can be both object-dependent and just as finely individuated as perspicuous psychological description requires. So the Fregean principle does not justify Russell's restriction on object-dependent propositions.

---

[9] See, for instance, 'The Philosophy of Logical Atomism', in *Logic and Knowledge*, 177–281, at p. 245.

[10] An affirmative answer is implicit in Simon Blackburn's remark, at p. 328 of *Spreading the Word* (Clarendon Press, Oxford, 1984), that the considerations to which Frege is sensitive are 'the primary source of argument' against regarding thoughts as intrinsically object-dependent.

The possibility of Fregean singular senses which are object-dependent typically goes unconsidered. As if mesmerized by the Theory of Descriptions, philosophers typically assume that Frege's application of the distinction between sense and reference to singular terms is an anticipation of the Theory of Descriptions in its extended form, without even Russell's exception in favour of logically proper names—so that there is no such thing as an object-dependent Fregean thought.[11] But as far as one can tell from the mysterious passage in 'On Denoting' where Russell discusses the distinction between sense and reference,[12] this does not seem to have been Russell's own view of Frege's intention.[13] And it is notoriously difficult to make this reading of Frege cohere with at least one seemingly central strand in Frege's thinking, namely the idea that reference-failure generates truth-value gaps: this seems most smoothly understood on the view that thoughts of the appropriate kind are, precisely, object-dependent, so that where there is reference-failure there cannot be a thought of the appropriate kind to bear a truth value.[14]

Admittedly, Frege occasionally offers, as specifying the sense of, say, an ordinary proper name, an expression to which Russell would

[11] Even Blackburn, who has not the excuse of being ignorant of Evans's work, strangely proceeds as if the object-independence of Fregean senses were uncontentious. See n. 10; and note how on p. 317 he represents 'the singular thought theorist' as holding that the identity of a singular thought 'is given by the object referred to', which suggests a Russellian rather than Fregean conception of the constituents of singular thoughts. Whatever explains this, it may in turn partly explain why Blackburn does not see that he would need to demolish (among other things) the neo-Fregean account of object-dependent perceptually demonstrative thoughts given in Chapter 6 of *The Varieties of Reference* before being entitled to conclude, as he does at p. 322 on the basis of a discussion of the arguments about communication in Chapter 9 of that work, that the question whether we should count someone who uses an empty singular term as expressing a thought can only turn on 'some semantic thesis concerning *expression*' and is 'a boring issue'. (I find Blackburn's discussion of the arguments about communication unsatisfactory also, but I cannot go into this here.)

[12] *Logic and Knowledge*, 48–51.

[13] At pp. 330–1 of *Spreading the Word*, Blackburn represents Russell as complaining that a Fregean thought could not be closely enough related to the right object. But the complaint in Russell's text seems to be the reverse: a Fregean singular thought is so closely related to its object that Russell cannot see how it maintains its distinctness from a Russellian singular proposition, with the object rather than a sense as a constituent.

[14] See my 'Truth–Value Gaps', in *Logic, Methodology and Philosophy of Science* VI (North-Holland, Amsterdam, 1982), 299–313; and, for a convincing account of Frege's general semantical framework, Evans, *The Varieties of Reference*, Chapter 1.

certainly want to apply the Theory of Descriptions. But we can see
this as manifesting, not an anticipation of the extended Theory of
Descriptions as applied to, say, ordinary proper names, but a converse assimilation: a willingness to attribute object-dependent senses
to all members of Frege's wide category of singular terms (*Eigen-
namen*), including even definite descriptions. It is characteristic of
Frege's lofty attitude to psychological detail that he should think in
terms of singular (that is, object-dependent) thoughts without devot-
ing attention to the nature of any necessary epistemological background, and hence without arriving at the thought, formulated
above in terms of acquaintance, which makes this assimilation unattractive.

Admittedly again, Frege often writes of singular terms having
sense but lacking reference. This may seem to show that the attribution of sense to singular terms reflects something parallel to the
motivation of the extended Theory of Descriptions: a desire to ensure that 'singular' utterances are assigned thoughts that they can be
credited with expressing whether or not appropriately related objects exist. But this appearance can be at least partly undermined by
noting, first, that Frege is prepared to count the serious utterance of
a sentence containing an empty singular term as a lapse into fiction;
and, second, that in at least one passage he treats fictional utterances
as expressing 'mock thoughts'. Mock thoughts should have only
mock senses as constituents. If the purpose of Frege's saying that
empty singular terms have senses would be better served by saying
that they have mock senses, then what is in question here is not
going along with the motivation for the extended Theory of Descriptions, but rather disarming it—registering that it will *seem* to a
deluded user of an empty singular term that he is entertaining and
expressing thoughts, and (so to speak) supplying merely apparent
singular thoughts for these to be, rather than real non-singular
thoughts.[15]

Of course this does not straightforwardly fit what Frege says; at
best this may be what he is driving at, in an anyway unhappy region
of his thinking. But in any case the question should not be whether
Frege himself clearly embraced the idea of object-dependent

---

[15] For an elaboration of this reading, with citations, see Evans, *The Varieties of
Reference*, 28–30.

singular senses, but whether the idea is available, so that we can recognize object-dependent thoughts outside Russell's restriction without flouting the Fregean principle about the topology of psychological space. And the dazzling effect of the Theory of Descriptions should not be allowed to obscure the fact that there is nothing in the notion of sense itself to preclude this. But something deeper, whose nature will emerge in due course, tends to sustain the usual reading of Frege.

4. It is not plausible that Russell sees his restriction as dictated extraneously, by the result of applying some independently compulsory general epistemological principle, such as the one canvassed in section 2 above, to the notion of acquaintance. Rather, Russell finds it evident in its own right that the illusions which the restriction disallows must be disallowed, and the epistemology of acquaintance shapes itself accordingly into a rejection of fallibility. (General epistemological preconceptions would make this come more naturally to Russell than it does to us.)[16] If we lift Russell's restriction, we open the possibility that a subject may be in error about the contents of his own mind: he may think there is a singular thought at, so to speak, a certain position in his internal organization although there is really nothing precisely there.[17] It seems that Russell would reject this possibility out of hand; that will be why he finds it clearly absurd to say that sentences which people think they understand are 'nonsense'. This makes it plausible that the ultimate basis for Russell's

---

[16] In a post-Russellian epistemological climate, there is something bizarre about Daniel C. Dennett's suggestion that 'Russell's Principle' (the 'know which . . .' requirement) leads inevitably to Russell's restriction: see pp. 87–8 of 'Beyond Belief', in Andrew Woodfield (ed.), *Thought and Object* (Clarendon Press, Oxford, 1982), 1–95. Dennett's conception of the epistemology of acquaintance is shaped to suit an independently accepted restriction on the scope for object-dependent thought, not something that could serve as a ground for the restriction.

[17] Nothing precisely there; of course there may be all sorts of things in the vicinity. See Evans, *The Varieties of Reference*, 45–6; which gives the lie to Blackburn's implication, at pp. 318–22, that Evans (and I) would 'deny that there is thinking going on in the empty world'. Anyone who believes in singular thoughts in the sense of this paper will (by definition) hold that they are 'not available' in the absence of an object; at p. 318 Blackburn implies misleadingly that this position is characteristic only of 'strong singular thought theorists', who represent the mind as simply void when a seeming singular thought lacks an object. It is not clear to me that there are any strong singular thought theorists in Blackburn's sense.

restriction is a conception of the inner life, and the subject's knowledge of it, which it seems fair to label 'Cartesian'.[18]

One reason, then, to pursue a less restricted conception of object-
dependent propositions is the interest of its radically anti-Cartesian
implications. In a fully Cartesian picture, the inner life takes place in
an autonomous realm, transparent to the introspective awareness of
its subject; the access of subjectivity to the rest of the world becomes
correspondingly problematic, in a way that has familiar manifes-
tations in the mainstream of post-Cartesian epistemology. If we let
there be quasi-Russellian singular propositions about, say, ordinary
perceptible objects among the contents of inner space, we can no
longer be regarding inner space as a locus of configurations which
are self-standing, not beholden to external conditions; and there is
now no question of a gulf, which it might be the task of philosophy
to try to bridge, or declare unbridgeable, between the realm of subjectivity and the world of ordinary objects. We can make this vivid
by saying, in a Russellian vein, that objects themselves can *figure in*
thoughts which are among the contents of the mind; in Russell himself, formulations like this attach themselves to the idea that singular
propositions are individuated according to the identity of their objects rather than modes of presentation of them, but a Fregean
approach to singular thoughts can accommodate such locutions—
firmly distinguishing 'figure in' from 'be a constituent of'—as a
natural way of insisting on object-dependence.

Russell credits Descartes with 'showing that subjective things are
the most certain';[19] presumably he would not think it impugned the
acceptability of his restriction to suggest that it has a Cartesian
basis. But the climate has changed; contemporary sympathizers
with Russell will usually disclaim a Cartesian motivation.[20] I want
to maintain nevertheless that, independently of Russell's own un-
ashamedly Cartesian stance, the point of recognizing object-dependent thoughts outside Russell's restriction, with the Fregean fineness
of grain needed for them to serve in perspicuous accounts of how
minds are laid out, lies in the way it liberates us from Cartesian
problems. To make this plausible, I need to digress into a general
discussion of the nature of Cartesian philosophy.

[18] See Evans, *The Varieties of Reference*, 44–6.
[19] *The Problems of Philosophy*, 18.
[20] See, for instance, Schiffer, 'The Basis of Reference' (see n. 2); and Blackburn,
Spreading the Word, 324–5—on which see section 7.

5. The feature of the classically Cartesian picture to focus on is the effect I have already mentioned, of putting subjectivity's very possession of an objective environment in question. It is hard for us now to find Descartes's purported regaining of the world, in the later stages of his reflections, as gripping as we can easily find his apparent loss of it in the opening stages.

What generates this threat of loss? We cannot answer this question simply by appealing to a generally sceptical tendency in Descartes's epistemological preoccupations. Not that they have no such tendency, of course. But ancient scepticism did not call our possession of a world into question; its upshot was, less dramatically, to drive a wedge between living in the world and (what is meant to seem dispensable) knowing about it.[21] What, then, was distinctive about the scepticism that Descartes ushered on to the philosophical scene, to make this comfortable distinction no longer available?

I doubt that we can construct an adequate answer out of the detail of Cartesian epistemology. Barry Stroud, for instance, plausibly traces the Cartesian threat of losing the world to this principle: one can acquire worldly knowledge by using one's senses only if one can know, at the time of the supposed acquisition of knowledge, that one is not dreaming.[22] This sets a requirement which Stroud argues cannot be met: no proposed test or procedure for establishing that one is not dreaming would do the trick, since by a parallel principle one would need to know that one was not dreaming that one was applying the test or procedure and obtaining a satisfactory result. So Stroud suggests that if we accept the requirement we cannot escape losing the world.

Now one drawback about this for my purposes is that it does not address the question raised above: why does the threatened conclusion that the senses yield no knowledge of the world seem, in Descartes, to threaten loss of the world, given the ancient sceptics' alternative that it is not by way of knowing about the world that we are in possession of it? But it is more to my immediate purpose that if losing the world is to seem inescapable on these lines, we need to be persuaded not to claim conformity to the requirement on the

---

[21] On the contrast between ancient scepticism and Cartesian scepticism, see M. F. Burnyeat's very illuminating paper, 'Idealism and Greek Philosophy: What Descartes Saw and Berkeley Missed', in Godfrey Vesey (ed.), *Idealism Past and Present* (CUP, Cambridge, 1982), 19–50.

[22] See Chapter 1 of *The Significance of Philosophical Scepticism* (Clarendon Press, Oxford, 1984).

following ground: one's knowledge that one is not dreaming, in the relevant sort of situation, owes its credentials as knowledge to the fact that one's senses are yielding one knowledge of the environment—something that does not happen when one is dreaming. Of course this does not meet the requirement as Descartes understands it; the Cartesian requirement is that the epistemic status of the thought that one is not dreaming must be established independently of the epistemic status of whatever putative perceptual knowledge of the environment is in question, serving as a test case for the possibility of acquiring such knowledge at all. But why must the direction of epistemic support be like that? We are not allowed to depend on our possession of the world for knowledge that we are not dreaming at the relevant times; so our grip on the world must have been loosened already for the Cartesian epistemological reflections to take the course they do.

I have followed M. F. Burnyeat on the newly radical character of Cartesian scepticism. In a perceptive discussion, Burnyeat identifies one Cartesian innovation which certainly helps account for this: in ancient scepticism, the notion of truth is restricted to how things are (unknowably, it is claimed) in the world about us, so that how things seem to us is not envisaged as something there might be truth about, and the question whether we know it simply does not arise (although appearances are said not to be open to question); whereas Descartes extends the range of truth and knowability to the appearances on the basis of which we naively think we know about the ordinary world. In effect Descartes recognizes how things seem to a subject as a case of how things are; and the ancient sceptics' concession that appearances are not open to question is transmuted into the idea of a range of facts infallibly knowable by the subject involved in them. This permits a novel response to arguments which conclude that we know nothing from the fact that we are fallible about the external world. Whatever such arguments show about knowledge of external reality, we can retreat to the newly recognized inner reality, and refute the claim that we know nothing on the ground that at least we know these newly recognized facts about subjective appearances. Notice that the epistemological context in which, on this account, the inner realm is first recognized makes it natural that the first of its inhabitants to attract our attention should be perceptual experiences, with other inner items at first relegated to the background. I shall stay with this focus for some time.

To the extent that this response to scepticism leaves the old arguments unchallenged, it may seem to suffice already for the characteristically Cartesian willingness to face up to losing the external world,
with the inner for consolation.[23] But, although the introduction of
subjectivity as a realm of fact is an essential part of the story, we still
do not have a complete account of what is special to Descartes. We
are still faced with a version of the question which ancient scepticism
makes pressing: even if the inward step to a region of reality where
we can call a halt to scepticism involves conceding that we have no
knowledge of outer reality, why should that threaten us with the
conclusion that we have no access to outer reality at all? Why should
the availability of infallible knowledge about the newly recognized
inner region of reality encourage us to such defeatism—as opposed
to either the ancient option of deeming knowledge inessential to our
hold on the world, or an even less concessive approach whose suppression needs explaining: namely trying to construct a conception
of fallibly acquired outer knowledge which could peacefully coexist
with a conception of infallibly acquired inner knowledge?[24]

Simply accommodating subjectivity within the scope of truth and
knowability seems, in any case, too innocent to account for the view
of philosophy's problems that Descartes initiates. We need something more contentious: a picture of subjectivity as a region of reality
whose layout is transparent—accessible through and through—to
the capacity for knowledge that is newly recognized when appearances are brought within the range of truth and knowability.[25]

Short of that picture, the newly countenanced facts can be simply
the facts about what it is like to enjoy our access, or apparent access,

[23] Descartes himself thinks he can do better than this, but, as I remarked, it is difficult to find this part of his thinking convincing.

[24] Besides the extending of truth and knowability to what thereby comes to be conceivable as the realm of subjectivity, Burnyeat mentions as a Cartesian innovation the
preparedness to count one's own body as part of the external world. So long as scepticism does not seem to threaten loss of the world, one's own body will not naturally
come within the purview of one's sceptical doubts (after all, one needs a body to engage with the world). This suggests that the externalizing of the body is not something
independently intelligible, which could help to explain why Cartesian scepticism induces the threat of losing the world. The direction of explanation should be the reverse: if we can understand how the threat of loss of the world comes about, we
should be equipped to see why Descartes's conception of the external world is so rev-
olutionary.

[25] Burnyeat's phrase 'a new realm for substantial knowledge' (p. 49, n. 53) does
not distinguish the specifically Cartesian conception of the new realm from the innocent alternative.

to external reality. Access or apparent access: infallible knowledge of how things seem to one falls short of infallible knowledge as to which disjunct is in question. One is as fallible about that as one is about the associated question how things are in the external world. So, supposing we picture subjectivity as a region of reality, we need not yet be thinking of the newly recognized infallibly knowable facts as constituting the whole truth about that region. Of facts to the effect that things seem thus and so to one, we might say, some are cases of things being thus and so within the reach of one's subjective access to the external world, whereas others are mere appearances.[26] In a given case the answer to the question 'Which?' would state a further fact about the disposition of things in the inner realm (a disposition less specifically mapped by saying merely that things seem to one to be thus and so); since this further fact is not independent of the outer realm, we are compelled to picture the inner and outer realms as interpenetrating, not separated from one another by the characteristically Cartesian divide. Arguments designed to force the admission that one cannot know that it is the first disjunct that is in question would be powerless, in face of this position, to induce the threat of losing the world. Even if we make the admission, it does not go beyond the ancient sceptics' renunciation of knowledge of external reality. There is nothing here to exclude the ancient option of living comfortably in the world without aspiring to know it. And it should seem a good project, in this position, to try to resist the admission by breaking the link between knowledge and infallibility.

We arrive at the fully Cartesian picture with the idea that there are no facts about the inner realm besides what is infallibly accessible to the newly recognized capacity to acquire knowledge. What figures in the innocent position I have just outlined as the difference between the two disjuncts cannot now be a difference between two ways things might be in the inner realm, with knowledge of which is the case available, if at all, only with the fallibility that attends our ability to achieve knowledge of the associated outer circumstance. Such differences must now be wholly located in the outer realm; they must reside in facts external to a state of affairs which is common to the two disjuncts and which exhausts the relevant region of the inner realm. We cannot now see the inner and outer realms as interpene-

---

[26] See my 'Criteria, Defeasibility, and Knowledge', *Proceedings of the British Academy*, lxviii (1982), 455–79; and J. M. Hinton, *Experiences* (Clarendon Press, Oxford, 1973).

trating: the correlate of this picture of our access to the inner is that subjectivity is confined to a tract of reality whose layout would be exactly as it is however things stood outside it, and the common-sense notion of a vantage point on the external world is now fundamentally problematic. The ancient option of giving up the claim that knowledge is among the ties that relate us to the world no longer seems to the point, since the very idea of subjectivity as a mode of being in the world is as much in question as the idea of knowing the world. And it no longer seems hopeful to construct an epistemology which would countenance not only infallible knowledge of how things seem to one but also knowledge acquired by fallible means. Once we are gripped by the idea of a self-contained subjective realm, in which things are as they are independently of external reality (if any), it is too late for such a move (worthy as it is in itself) to help—our problem is not now that our contact with the external world seems too *shaky* to count as knowledgeable, but that our picture seems to represent us as out of touch with the world altogether.[27]

I approached this fully Cartesian picture of subjectivity by way of the thought, innocent in itself, that how things seem to one can be a fact, and is knowable in a way that is immune to familiar sceptical challenges. Short of the fully Cartesian picture, the infallibly knowable fact—its seeming to one that things are thus and so—can be taken disjunctively, as constituted either by the fact that things are manifestly thus and so or by the fact that that merely seems to be the case. On this account, the idea of things being thus and so figures straightforwardly in our understanding of the infallibly knowable appearance; there is no problem about how experience can be understood to have a representational directedness towards external reality.

Now the fully Cartesian picture should not be allowed to trade on these innocuous thoughts. According to the fully Cartesian picture, it cannot be ultimately obligatory to understand the infallibly knowable fact disjunctively. That fact is a self-standing configuration in the inner realm, whose intrinsic nature should be knowable through and through without adverting to what is registered, in the innocuous position, by the difference between the disjuncts—let alone

---

[27] It is superficial to chide Descartes for not contemplating the possibility of a fallibilist epistemology, as if Cartesian scepticism was merely the result of judging all putative knowledge by the standards of introspection. The course of Cartesian epistemology gives a dramatic but ultimately inessential expression to Descartes's fundamental contribution to philosophy, namely his picture of the subjective realm.

giving the veridical case the primacy which the innocuous position confers on it. This makes it quite unclear that the fully Cartesian picture is entitled to characterize its inner facts in content-involving terms—in terms of its seeming to one that things are thus and so—at all. Ironically, when reverence for the authority of phenomenology is carried to the length of making the fact that internal configurations are indistinguishable from the subject's point of view suffice to establish that those configurations are through and through the same, the upshot is to put at risk the most conspicuous phenomenological fact there is. The threat which the Cartesian picture poses to our hold on the world comes out dramatically in this: that within the Cartesian picture there is a serious question about how it can be that experience, conceived from its own point of view, is not blank or blind, but purports to be revelatory of the world we live in.

6. I have stressed that there is a less than Cartesian way of recognizing subjectivity as a realm of knowable truth. This makes it necessary to ask why the distinctively Cartesian way is as gripping as it is. The realm of subjectivity comes to our notice initially by way of our noting a range of infallibly knowable facts. But however seriously we take the picture of a region or tract of reality, that seems insufficient to explain why it should be tempting to suppose that the whole truth about the tract in question should be knowable in the same way.

We can approach an explanation by bracketing the directly epistemological character of the Cartesian picture, and focusing initially on the idea of the inner realm as self-standing, with everything within it arranged as it is independently of external circumstances. Why might Descartes have found this idea tempting? And why should the temptation have first become pressing around Descartes's time? Both these questions can be answered in terms of a plausible aspiration to accommodate psychology within a pattern of explanation characteristic of the natural sciences. (Of course the aspiration need not have struck Descartes in just those terms.) It seems scarcely more than common sense that a science of the way organisms relate to their environment should look for states of the organisms whose intrinsic nature can be described independently of the environment: this would allow explanations of the presence of such states in terms of the environment's impact, and explanations of interventions in the environment in terms of the causal influence of such states, to fit into a kind of explanation whose enormous power to make the world intelligible was becoming clear with the rise of modern science, and is even clearer to us than it would have been to Descartes. It is plausible that Descartes's self-standing inner realm is meant to be the locus of just such explanatory states.

Now this intellectual impulse is gratified also in a modern way of purportedly bringing the mind within the scope of theory, in which the interiority of the inner realm is literally spatial: the autonomous explanatory states are in ultimate fact states of the nervous system, although, in order to protect the claim that the explanations they figure in are psychological, they are envisaged as conceptualized by theories of mind in something like functionalist terms.[28] This conception of mind shares what I have suggested we should regard as the fundamental motivation of the classically Cartesian conception; and I think this is much more significant than the difference between them.

The most striking divergence is that the modern position avoids Cartesian immaterialism. But how important a difference is this? In one way, it is obviously very important: the modern position simply escapes a metaphysical and scientific embarrassment which the classically Cartesian picture generates. But in another way it need not be very important, because we can understand Cartesian immaterialism as derivative rather than fundamental: the natural upshot of trying to satisfy the common impulse at a certain juncture in the history of science.

One submerged source of immaterialism may be a sense of the problem canvassed at the end of section 5: that once we picture subjectivity as self-contained, it is hard to see how its states and episodes can be anything but blind. Magic might seem to help, and magical powers require an occult medium.[29]

Another explanation of immaterialism reintroduces the bracketed

[28] See, for instance, Brian Loar, *Mind and Meaning* (CUP, Cambridge, 1981).
[29] I intend this to echo some thoughts of Hilary Putnam's: see his *Reason, Truth and History* (CUP, Cambridge, 1982), 3–5. However, I believe that Putnam misses the full force of his insight: rather than rethinking the conception of what is in the mind that leads to the temptation to appeal to magic, as I urge in this paper, he retains that conception (see, for instance, p. 18), avoiding the need to appeal to magic by making what is in the mind only a partial determinant of content. I argue below (sections 8 and 9) that positions with this sort of structure cannot avoid the problem about inner darkness that makes the appeal to magic seductive. (In a fuller discussion, I should wish to connect the temptation to appeal to magic with elements in Wittgenstein's approach to meaning; but I cannot elaborate this now.)

epistemological concerns. It is helpful to revert to the contrast between the fully Cartesian picture and the less than Cartesian picture which I described. By itself, there is nothing dangerous about the idea that how things seem to one is a fact, knowable in a way that is immune to the sources of error attending one's capacity to find out about the world around one. We can think of this 'introspective' knowledge as a by-product of our perceptual capacities, available on the basis of a minimal self-consciousness in their exercise. There is no particular incentive to think of the facts which the newly countenanced knowledge-acquiring capacity finds out as configurations in an immaterial medium. (Not that it is natural to conceive them specifically as material. There is simply no reason to find the question 'Material or not?' pressing.) It is a related point that, short of the fully Cartesian picture, there is nothing ontologically or epistemologically dramatic about the authority which it is natural to accord to a person about how things seem to him. This authority is consistent with the interpenetration of the inner and the outer, which makes it possible for you to know the layout of my subjectivity better than I do in a certain respect, if you know which of those two disjuncts obtains and I do not. In this framework, the authority which my capacity for 'introspective' knowledge secures for me cannot seem to threaten the very possibility of access on your part to the facts within its scope.

In the fully Cartesian picture, by contrast, with the inner realm autonomous, the idea of the subject's authority becomes problematic. When we deny interpenetration between inner and outer, that puts in question the possibility of access to the external world from within subjectivity; correspondingly, it puts in question the possibility of access to the inner realm from outside. 'Introspective' knowledge can no longer be a by-product of outwardly directed cognitive acitivities, with nothing to prevent its objects being accessible to others too. The idea of introspection becomes the idea of an inner vision, scanning a region of reality which is wholly available to its gaze—since there is no longer any room for facts about the subjective realm which the subject may not know because of ignorance of outer circumstances—and which is at best problematically open to being known about in other ways at all. It is difficult now not to be struck by the question how such a tract of reality could possibly be a region of the familiar material world; immaterialism seems unavoidable.[30]

---

[30] Note that these considerations simply bypass the standard objection to Descartes's argument for the Real Distinction.

We can understand Cartesian immaterialism, then, as the result of trying to accommodate features which seem essential to subjectivity—representational bearing on the world and availability to introspection—within a conception of the inner realm as autonomous; if we think of the temptation to appeal to magic as sufficiently submerged, we can say 'within a conception of the inner realm as a suitable subject for science'. It seems clear that Descartes intended his conception of the inner to figure in a scientific account of the world: this emerges from his willingness to worry about the physics, as it were, of the interaction between mind and matter. At the time it would not have been contrary to reason to hope for an integrated psycho-physics which would incorporate immaterial substances into a fully scientific view of the world. Now, with the physical conservation laws well entrenched, that looks simply out of the question. But of course that need not cast suspicion on those intuitive marks of subjectivity: Cartesian immaterialism, and the closely associated picture of the inner realm as knowable through and through by introspection, reflect a distortion which those marks undergo when forced to combine with the scientifically motivated conception of the inner realm as autonomous.

This makes it worth wondering whether it is the insistence on autonomy which is the real disease of thought, with the superficially striking peculiarities of Descartes's own picture of mind no more than a symptom that something is amiss. In the modern version of the insistence on autonomy, something on the lines of functionalism in effect takes over the purpose served by what, in conjunction with the insistence on autonomy, generates Cartesian immaterialism: namely to make it plausible that the envisaged conception of an autonomous inner realm is at least a partial conception of the mind.[31] As I have granted, this frees the insistence on autonomy from the immediately uncomfortable postures of a fully Cartesian metaphysic. But it is a serious question whether the improvement—which is undeniable—is more than the suppression of a symptom.

---

[31] The qualification in 'at least a partial conception' is meant to accommodate positions like that of Colin McGinn, 'The Structure of Content', in Woodfield (ed.), *Thought and Object*, 207–58. I do not mean to suggest that the Cartesian marks of subjectivity (introspectability and the presence of representational content) are simply missing from the modern version of the insistence on autonomy. But there are complications about their status and position, some of which will emerge below (sections 7 and 9): they can no longer do exactly the work they are credited with in my reconstruction of the Cartesian picture.

7. It has been easiest to expound the classically Cartesian picture by concentrating initially on perceptual experience. But the picture will not look like a picture of the mind unless it is enriched to include at least propositional attitudes.

Now it is clear that object-dependent propositional content, at least outside Russell's restriction, cannot be an intrinsic feature of states or episodes in a self-standing inner realm. Self-standingness disallows this, independently of the specifically Cartesian conception of inner knowledge that seems to be operative in Russell's own imposition of the restriction. However, it is worth examining a particular way of pressing the insistence on self-standingness against intrinsic object-dependence in thoughts which exploits considerations closely parallel to the fully Cartesian conception of experience.

I distinguished an innocuous disjunctive conception of subjective appearances from the fully Cartesian picture, in which a difference corresponding to the difference between the disjuncts is external to the inner realm, with the only relevant occupant of that realm something wholly present whether things are as they seem or not. There is a parallel contrast between two ways of conceiving singular thought: first, the idea that if one seems to be thinking about an ordinary external object in a way that depends on, say, its appearing to be perceptually present to one, the situation in one's inner world is either that one is entertaining an object-dependent proposition or that it merely appears that that is so; and, second, the idea that a difference corresponding to the difference between those disjuncts is external to the layout of one's inner world, which is for these purposes exhausted by something common to the two cases.[32]

Simon Blackburn has tried to pinpoint the motivation for the view that, at least outside Russell's restriction, thoughts which one might want to ascribe in an object-involving way are not object-dependent in their intrinsic nature. Blackburn's argumentative strategy is what he calls 'spinning the possible worlds'.[33] In the sort of circumstances in which it is plausible to speak of singular thought and singular communication, a situation in which one object figures can be indistinguishable, from the subject's point of view, from a situation in which a different object figures or one in which no object figures in

---

[32] We can continue to think of the inner world as the realm of appearance, but with the introduction of propositional attitudes the notion of appearance loses the connection it has hitherto had with perceptual experience in particular.

[33] *Spreading the Word*, 312.

the right way at all, though there is an illusion of, say, perceptual presence. According to Blackburn, this constitutes an argument for saying that the intrinsic character of the thoughts in question is something which can be constant across such variations; so that object-dependence is not an intrinsic feature of thoughts, but reflects a style of ascription of thoughts which takes account not only of their intrinsic nature but also of their external relations.[34]

Blackburn anticipates the charge that this argument is Cartesian. He rejects the charge on the following grounds:

> The *doppelganger* and empty possibilities are drawn, as I have remarked, so that everything is the same from the subject's point of view. This is a legitimate thought-experiment. Hence there is a legitimate category of things that are the same in these cases; notably experience and awareness. Since this category is legitimate, it is also legitimate to ask whether thoughts all belong to it.[35]

But in the context of my pair of parallel contrasts, these remarks seem to miss the point. The uncontentiously legitimate category of things that are the same across the different cases is the category of how things seem to the subject. In the case of experience, the less than Cartesian position I described, exploiting the idea that the notion of appearance is essentially disjunctive, establishes that although that category is certainly legitimate, that does nothing to show that worldly circumstances are only externally related to experiences; to think otherwise is to fall into a fully Cartesian conception of the category. Analogously with the parallel contrast: the legitimacy of the category of how things seem is consistent with an essentially disjunctive conception of the state of seemingly entertaining a singular thought, and is hence powerless to recommend the conclusion that thoughts are only extrinsically connected with objects. Extracting such a recommendation from the phenomenological facts to which Blackburn appeals betrays a conception of the realm of appearance more philosophically contentious than anything that sheer phenomenology could deliver.

Notice how, instead of 'Everything seems the same to the subject',

---

[34] As Blackburn notes, the argument belongs to the genre of Twin Earth thought experiments introduced into philosophy by Putnam: see 'The Meaning of "Meaning"', in Hilary Putnam, *Mind, Language and Reality* (CUP, Cambridge, 1975), 215–71.

[35] *Spreading the Word*, 324.

Blackburn uses locutions like 'Everything is the same from the sub-ject's point of view'. This insinuates the idea—going far beyond the fact that there is a legitimate category of how things seem to the subject—of a realm of reality in which samenesses and differences are exhaustively determined by how things seem to the subject, and hence which is knowable through and through by exercising one's capacity to know how things seem to one. That idea seems fully Car-tesian. (It should be clear by now that immaterialism is beside the point of this charge.)[36]

8. In disconnecting experience from the external world, the fully Cartesian picture makes it problematic how the items it pictures can be anything but dark (see section 5 above). Independently of any general empiricism about the materials for concept-formation, it seems plausible that if we conceive propositional attitudes on the same principles, as occupants of the same autonomous inner realm, we make it no less problematic how it can be that they have a repre-sentational bearing on the world.

In the physicalistic modern version of the insistence on autonomy, the self-standingness of the inner realm suffices to exclude intrinsic involvement with the world, without any need for an appeal to phenomenology. And in the most clear-sighted form of the position,

---

[36] At pp. 324–5 of *Spreading the Word*, Blackburn offers a different way of res-ponding to the charge of Cartesianism, in terms of the idea that we should 'see the facts about a subject's thoughts as facts about his relation to the environment', but insist that 'the relevant features of an environment are themselves universal'. But with this idea (which Blackburn does not himself endorse) the empty case is no longer sup-posed to be one in which the intrinsic nature of the subject's psychological state is the same. And that makes it hard to see any intelligible motivation for the position's 'universalism'. To put the point in terms of experience: if the actual presence of some cat or other (say) is necessary for an experience as of a cat of a certain character, what can there be against saying that such a 'universalistic' description applies in virtue of the experience's being an experience of that particular cat? In another case the same 'universalistic' description may apply in virtue of a relation to a different cat; but if the 'universalistic' description cannot apply in the empty case, there is no threat here to a position according to which the 'universalistic' description supervenes on non-'universalistic' descriptions of the intrinsic nature of experiences. (Discussing experi-ence at p. 311, Blackburn omits the empty case; the argument for 'universalism' seems seriously incomplete until the empty case is introduced.) Perhaps the gap in this argu-ment can be filled somehow; but it would still be quite mysterious how this could con-stitute a defence of the original phenomenological argument—which trades essentially on the empty case—against the charge of Cartesianism.

the darkness of the interior is institutionalized. The intrinsic nature of inner states and events, on this view, is a matter of their position in an internal network of causal potentialities, in principle within the reach of an explanatory theory that would not need to advert to relations between the individual and the external world. Representational bearing on the external world figures in a mode of description of those states and events which takes into account not only their intrinsic nature but also their relations to the outside world.[37] Light enters into the picture, so to speak, only when we widen our field of view so as to take in more than simply the layout of the interior.[38]

Since there is light in the full composite picture, it may seem absurd to suggest, on the basis of the darkness in the interior, that this position leaves us squarely in the Cartesian predicament without resources to deal with it. The composite picture is offered as, precisely, a picture of the mind in full and intelligible possession of its perspective on the external world. If we want to consider the mind's relation to the world, according to this position, we ought not to worry about the nature of the internal component of the picture taken by itself.

What makes this unsatisfying, however, is the way in which the internal component of the composite picture, and not the compositely conceived whole, irresistibly attracts the attributes that intuitively characterize the domain of subjectivity. Consider, for instance, the idea of what is accessible to introspection. If introspection is to be distinguishable from knowledge at large, it cannot be allowed access to the external circumstances which, according to this position, partly determine the full composite truth about the mind; so its scope must be restricted to the internal component (remarkably enough, in view of the darkness within).[39] Again, consider the topological constraint derived from Frege (see section 3 above). It is in the internal component that we have to locate the difference which Frege's constraint requires us to mark between pairs of (say) beliefs which in the full composite story would be described as involving the attribution of the same property to the same object, but which have

---

[37] The clearest formulation of a position like this that I know is McGinn, 'The Structure of Content' (see n. 31 above).

[38] Here one of those intuitive marks of subjectivity (see section 6, and in particular n. 31, above) shifts its location in our picture of mind.

[39] See McGinn, 'The Structure of Content', 253–4. Here the other of those intuitive marks of subjectivity undergoes a sea change.

to be distinguished because someone may without irrationality have one and not the other. There is nowhere else to locate the difference once the picture of the mind is structured in this way. So Frege's notion of a mode of presentation is supposed to have its use in characterizing the configurations of the interior (remarkably enough, in view of the fact that they are in themselves blind).[40] But a mode of presentation should be the way something is presented to a subject of thought. The same point emerges more generally in the way it is natural, in this two-component picture of mind, to speak of an item's role in the strictly internal aspect of the composite truth about the mind as its *cognitive* role:[41] something's cognitive role should be its role in the cognitive life of (surely) a subject of thought. It is impossible not to be concerned about the boundary around the internal component of the two-component picture, and the darkness within it, if one is concerned at all about the relation between subjectivity and the objective world.

Quite generally, nothing could be recognizable as a characterization of the domain of subjectivity if it did not accord a special status to the perspective of the subject. But we create the appearance of introducing light into the composite picture precisely by allowing that picture to take in all kinds of facts which are *not* conceived in terms of the subject's point of view. So if the composite picture contains anything corresponding to the intuitive notion of the domain of subjectivity, it is the dark interior. The difficulty is palpable: how can we be expected to acknowledge that our subjective way of being in the world is properly captured by this picture, when it portrays the domain of our subjectivity—our cognitive world—in such a way that, considered from its own point of view, that world has to be conceived as letting in no light from outside? The representational content apparently present in the composite story comes too late to meet the point. The difficulty has an obviously Cartesian flavour, and it seems fair to suggest that the answer to the question I raised and left open at the end of section 6 is 'No'. It is possible to embrace the modern position with a clear scientific conscience, something that is no longer true of the full-blown Cartesian picture of mind. But if the result is merely a materialized version of the Cartesian

---

[40] See, for instance, McGinn, 'The Structure of Content', 230 (sense as 'intra-individual role'; cf. 220–1, 223–4).

[41] See McGinn, 'The Structure of Content', 219 (cognitive role as 'an entirely intra-individual property').

picture, complete with characteristically Cartesian problems about our relation with external reality, the philosophical advance is unimpressive.[42]

It may not be to everyone's taste to accept an invitation to reflect philosophically about the position of subjectivity in the objective world, with Cartesian pitfalls as a real danger, calling for vigilance if we are to avoid them.[43] Modern analytic philosophy has to some extent lost the sense of the Cartesian divide as a genuine risk for our conception of ourselves. But I suspect that the reasons for this are at least partly superficial. It is true that we have epistemologies whose drift is not towards scepticism. But these can seem to yield a stable picture of our cognitive grasp on reality only if the Cartesian divide is genuinely overcome; and modern fallibilist epistemologies typically do not embody any clear account of how that is to be done, but rather reflect a (perfectly intelligible) refusal to persist in a task which has become too plainly hopeless to bother with. In any case, it should be clear by now that the Cartesian danger is not specifically a threat to our knowledge of the external world; the problems of traditional epistemology are just one form in which the Cartesian divide can show itself.

9. Modern philosophical thinking about the relations of thoughts to objects was for a long time captivated by the extended Theory of Descriptions. Saul Kripke's 'Naming and Necessity'[44] and Keith

---

[42] McGinn's anti-Cartesian remarks, at pp. 254–5 of 'The Structure of Content', betray an insensitivity (by my lights) to the genuineness of the concerns about subjectivity (contrast McGinn's 'third person viewpoint') which generate the Cartesian danger. McGinn's soundly anti-Cartesian intentions cannot save him from the Cartesian danger because he does not see the point at which it impinges on his position.

[43] McGinn's remarks about the 'third person viewpoint' (see n. 42 above) suggest a refusal to acknowledge a problem characterizable in these terms. See also Jerry A. Fodor, *The Language of Thought* (Harvester, Hassocks, 1976), 52, for a refusal to allow that the distinction between the personal and the sub-personal matters for 'the purposes of cognitive psychology'. Fodor seems to me to be right (and more clearsighted than others here) that cognitive science should not seek to involve itself in issues of this sort; but by the same token quite wrong to suppose that cognitive science can take over from the philosophy of mind. Freud, whom Fodor cites, cannot be appealed to in support of the idea that psychology (in the sense of discourse, with a theoreticity suitable to its subject matter, about the mind) can simply disown an interest in subjectivity (or the personal); Freud's point is rather that there are aspects of one's subjectivity that are not transparent to one.

[44] In Donald Davidson and Gilbert Harman (eds.), *Semantics of Natural Language* (Reidel, Dordrecht, 1972), 253–355, 763–9; issued as a monograph by Basil Blackwell, Oxford, 1980.

Donnellan's 'Proper Names and Identifying Descriptions'[45] inaugurated a revolt, the tenor of which was this: in accommodating almost all cases of singular thought under the descriptive model (according to which the object, if any, on whose doings or characteristics the truth or falsity of a thought depends is determined by conformity to an object-independent specification which figures in the content of the thought), philosophers had given insufficient attention to the possibility of a different kind of case, where what matters is not the object's fitting a specification in the content of the thought but its standing in some suitable contextual relation to the episode of thinking.[46]

Richard Rorty has suggested that when this recoil from the descriptive model is accorded deep philosophical significance, we are confronted with a piece of broadly Cartesian philosophy—that is, philosophy whose problems are set by the Cartesian divide—in what we ought to hope is its terminal phase: fearing that the descriptive model leaves thought out of touch with reality, proponents of the alternative model want reference to constitute an extra-intentional relation between language or thought and objects. Rorty can plausibly stigmatize this as a matter of succumbing to a hopeless 'demand ... for some transcendental standpoint outside our present set of representations from which we can inspect the relations between those representations and their object'.[47] Apart from the imputation of hopelessness, this view of the philosophical significance of the anti-descriptivist revolution is shared by many of its adherents. But it is not compulsory.

What generates the appearance of a hopeless transcendentalism is an assumption to this effect: the intentional nature of a thought could determine, as a factual matter, that it was about a certain object only in the manner codified in the descriptive model.[48] The

---

[45] In Davidson and Harman, op. cit., pp. 356–79.

[46] I exploit 'tenor' to permit myself to adapt what Kripke and Donnellan actually say to my purposes, in particular to formulate their intuitions in terms of thought rather than language. (For an opposed reading of Kripke, see Evans, *The Varieties of Reference*, Chapter 3.)

[47] *Philosophy and the Mirror of Nature* (Basil Blackwell, Oxford, 1980), 293.

[48] At pp. 288–9, Rorty (*in propria persona*) implicitly disallows the possibility of something both intentional and (in the manner of a genuine relation) object-dependent. I transpose Rorty's reading into a concern with thought rather than, in the first instance, language, in parallel with my sketch of Kripke and Donnellan.

revolt against descriptivism is largely fuelled by counterexamples—cases in which we know more than someone else, and a routine application of that assumption yields unilluminating accounts of him: we want to say, for instance, that he has and expresses false thoughts about something that could not be determined as the object of his thoughts in that way, since the materials available for such determination would take us to a quite different object if they took us to anything at all. In Rorty's account, there is nothing wrong with this impulse towards redescription; although 'it does not mark an invocation of our intuitions concerning a matter of fact',[49] so the 'intentionalist' assumption, formulated as above, can be sacrosanct. What is problematic, according to Rorty, is this thought: the superiority of the redescriptions shows that what is wrong with, say, the extended Theory of Descriptions is an implication to the effect that 'the more false beliefs we have the less "in touch with the world" we are'.[50] What happens here is that descriptivism is allowed to induce a quasi-Cartesian fear of loss of contact with objects, which 'the new theory of reference' seeks to assuage by picturing thought and objects as connected by a substantial extra-intentional relation.

This reading is shaped by the initial assumption, which is admittedly prevalent among anti-descriptivist revolutionaries and descriptivist counter-revolutionaries alike. What makes the assumption seem compulsory is the way of thinking which underlies the usual reading of Frege (see section 3 above). That should suggest the general character of a radical alternative to Rorty's reading. According to the alternative, the intuitive disquiet which led to the revolt against descriptivism reflected an insight—not at first available for sharp formulation—to the effect that the assumption should be dismantled; the revolt should culminate in a conception of object-dependent thought extended outside Russell's restriction, and enriched with Fregean fineness of grain, like the one I outlined at the start of this paper.[51] The trouble with descriptivism, on this view, is indeed a quasi-Cartesian loss of connection between thought and objects; but the response is not, in Cartesian vein, to try to bridge an

---

[49] *Philosophy and the Mirror of Nature*, 291.
[50] *Philosophy and the Mirror of Nature*, 288.
[51] A fuller treatment would need to incorporate a critique of the conception of truth implicit in Blackburn's distinction, at p. 341 of *Spreading the Word*, between 'thoughts, identified as the truths and falsehoods about the world' and 'thoughts identified as the objects of propositional attitudes'.

acknowledged gap, but to undermine the way of thinking which opens it.

It is worth noting a couple of detailed divergences from Rorty which this permits. In Rorty's reading, 'the new theory of reference' conceives itself as fulfilling the task which Cartesian epistemology attempted with familiar discouraging results.[52] But in the different reading, there can be no question of trying to bridge an epistemological gulf between mental states whose nature is independently determined and a reality which threatens to be beyond their grasp: the upshot of the revolution is that scepticism about the existence of the objects of seeming singular thoughts is equally scepticism about the layout of the mental realm. Secondly, the counterexamples can now be integrated with the complaint that descriptivism leaves thought out of touch with objects. The counterexamples are a natural, if oblique, way of recommending the intuition that object-dependence, understood in terms of relations of acquaintance, can be a feature of the intentional nature of a thought, on the ground that the materials otherwise available for intentional determination of the object of a thought seem incapable of generally getting the answer right. There is no need to deny that getting the answer right here is establishing a matter of fact, as Rorty does—with a view to insulating the counterexamples from the idea that descriptivism threatens the connection between thought and objects—on the basis of a curiously old-fashioned restriction of the factual to, in effect, the value-free.[53]

Predictably, the anti-descriptivist revolt has led to a descriptivist counter-revolution. A sympathetic consideration of this movement can bring out the character of the way of thinking which underlies the usual reading of Frege, and suggest the liberating potential of the alternative.

Consider a case in which, according to the anti-descriptivist revolution, it is the contextual presence of an object itself which determines it as the object of a thought. As long as it is assumed that this fact cannot enter into the thought's intentional nature, it follows that the thought's intentional nature is insufficient to determine

[52] *Philosophy and the Mirror of Nature*, 293–4.

[53] I believe that Rorty's view of 'the Cartesian problematic' is in general weakened by an over-concentration on epistemology; and that his view of the prospects for epistemology and philosophy of mind is debilitated by his restricted conception of what can be a matter of fact.

which object it is that makes the subject's thinking true or false, and consequently insufficient to determine what it is that the subject thinks. But now this complaint seems natural: if we try to see intentionality as at most partly determining what it is that a subject thinks, we leave ourselves without anything genuinely recognizable as a notion of intentionality at all. The two-component picture of mind discussed in section 8 aims to codify the thesis that in these cases intentionality is only a partial determinant of what the subject thinks; and the complaint can be focused by noting that the internal component is the only place in the two-component picture for the ideas associated with that aspect of intentionality which concerns the directedness of thought to specific objects: the Fregean idea of modes of presentation, and the idea of (as it were) cognitive space which regulates the application of the idea of modes of presentation. Directedness towards external objects enters the picture only when we widen our field of view to take in more than the internal component. So on this conception there is no object-directed intentionality in cognitive space.[54] (Note that there is no object-directed intentionality, conceived as at most partly determining what it is that the subject thinks, anywhere else in the two-component picture either. If we allow ourselves the whole composite story, we have all the determinants of content in view.)

It is a version of the point I made in section 8 to say that this seems

---

[54] This is clear in McGinn, 'The Structure of Content'. Less clear-sighted versions of the two-component picture obscure the point (holding back from a wholesale form of the relocation mentioned in n. 38 above) by purportedly locating 'narrow contents' in the interior considered by itself. These 'contents' could not yield answers to the question what it is that someone thinks; there is really no reason to recognize them as *contents* at all. Importing that notion serves merely to mask the distance we have come from an intuitive conception of mental phenomena. (See Evans, *The Varieties of Reference*, 200–4.) These remarks apply to the supposed results of what Dennett calls 'hetero-phenomenology': 'Beyond Belief' (see n. 16 above), 39. Hetero-phenomenology brackets the involvement of mental states with specific objects, stuffs, and so forth (a version of the insistence on autonomy); it arrives at specifications of 'notional attitudes' by asking questions like 'In what sort of environment would this cognitive system thrive?' (not taking a 'brain's eye view'—see p. 26: this is why it is *hetero*-phenomenology). This generates the appearance that we can find (narrow) content-bearing states in the interior considered by itself. But the idea looks self-deceptive. If we are not concerned with the point of view of the cognitive system itself (if, indeed, we conceive it in such a way that it has no point of view), there is no justification for regarding the enterprise as any. kind of phenomenology; the label serves only to obscure the fact that, according to this picture, all is dark within. To put the point another way: Dennett fails to accommodate his philosophy of mind to his own insight that 'brains are *syntactic engines*', not '*semantic engines*' (p. 26).

unrecognizable as a picture of the mind's directedness towards external objects; and, with the assumption in place, that can seem to
necessitate staying with the descriptivist view of how thought relates
to objects.[55] So we can understand the counter-revolution as motivated by a partial form of an insight: that, because of essentially
Cartesian difficulties, the two-component conception of mind fails
to supply a satisfying account of the mind's directedness towards the
external world.[56]

But any seeming stability in the descriptivist upshot depends on
not taking this insight far enough. The descriptivist counter-revolutionaries do not entertain the possibility that object-dependence
might be a feature of a thought's intentional nature, and this shows
their adherence to a conception of cognitive space which matches that
of the two-component theorists in this respect: it is a conception of a
realm whose layout is independent of external reality. The counter-
revolutionaries take this to be undamaging so long as content is restricted to the purely descriptive; as if the two-component picture
succeeded in allowing light into the mind by way of the *predicative*
element in a singular thought, so that what is called for might be
simply enriching cognitive space with more of the same sort of thing.
But the fact is that the principles of the shared conception keep light
out of cognitive space altogether. Content in general, not just the
focusing of thoughts on objects, requires directedness towards
reality. We achieve a representation of something not wholly unlike
that directedness when we situate this narrowly circumscribed cognitive space in the world around it. But when we consider the inhabitants of cognitive space from their own point of view—a stance
which it is irresistible to contemplate, since the narrowly circumscribed cognitive space is as near as these pictures come to giving us

[55] 'Descriptivist' need not imply that the specification, conformity to which is supposed to determine the object of a thought, must be linguistically expressible. It
should be clear by now that my objection to the view is not—what that concession
pre-empts—that we sometimes lack linguistic resources to express the 'descriptive'
modes of presentation that it envisages; the point of the label 'descriptivist' is to stress
(by way of allusion to the Theory of Descriptions) the crucial point that these modes
of presentation are not object-dependent. (Cf. Blackburn, *Spreading the Word*, 316,
323.) Rather than 'descriptivist', I would use Blackburn's term 'universalist', except
that I am not sure whether his 'universalist thoughts' are meant to be the bearers of
truth values in their own right envisaged by the position that I am describing here or
the bogus 'narrow contents' envisaged in some versions of the two-component picture
(see n. 54); the differences must not be blurred.

[56] A counter-revolutionary who makes essentially this motivation very clear is
John R. Searle: see Chapter 8 of *Intentionality* (CUP, Cambridge, 1983).

the idea of the domain of subjectivity—we cannot find them anything but blank. (We must guard against a temptation to avoid this by an appeal to magic.)[57] Pushed to its logical conclusion, then, the insight which motivates the descriptivist counter-revolution undermines it, revealing the counter-revolution as mired in the same essentially Cartesian problems.[58] We should reject the shared picture of cognitive space, which is what disallows object-dependence as a feature of intentionality and holds the usual reading of Frege in place.[59]

Notice that, although countenancing object-dependence as a feature of intentionality is a direct response to a threatened loss of contact with objects on the part of singular thoughts in particular, it promises a more general exorcism of Cartesian problems. The idea of cognitive space—the space whose topology is regulated by the Fregean principle—is clearly metaphorical. Allowing intrinsic object-dependence, we have to set whatever literally spatial boundaries are in question outside the subject's skin or skull. Cognitive space incorporates the relevant portions of the 'external' world. So its relations to that world should not pose philosophical difficulties in the Cartesian style.

---

[57] Cognitive science manages to find content in the interior as it conceives that; but it does so by situating cognitive space (on its conception) in the world, not by considering things from the point of view of cognitive space. So it is beside the point here to say (quite correctly) that cognitive science is not an appeal to magic. I confess myself baffled to understand McGinn's suggestion ('The Structure of Content', 215) that 'purely "qualitative"' content could be strictly internal; is it perhaps a trace of the seductive power of a magical conception of content?

[58] This is why I am unconvinced by Schiffer's protestations, in 'The Basis of Reference' (see n. 2), that there is nothing Cartesian about the counter-revolution. Schiffer does not consider the conception of object-dependent modes of presentation that I am recommending in this paper, but one can infer how he would argue against it from his argument against causal chains as modes of presentation (not an idea I want to defend); the argument assumes that modes of presentation would have to be a matter of intra-individual 'cognitive role', and so rests on a version of the insistence on the autonomy of the inner, which I have been suggesting we should regard as the essence of a Cartesian picture of mind.

[59] The nemesis of the counter-revolution is almost explicit in Searle's remarkable claim (*Intentionality*, 230) that we are brains in vats. As Dennett says (see n. 54), the brain is only a syntactic engine. If we were brains inside our own skulls we would have no inkling of the outside world, in a particularly strong sense: there would be no content available to us. It is an insight on Searle's part that intentionality is a biological phenomenon (see *Intentionality*, Chapter 10). But intentionality needs to be understood in the context of an organism's life in the world; we cannot understand it, or even keep it in view, if we try to think of it in the context of the brain's life inside the head.

So long as we make the assumption which shapes Rorty's reading of the anti-descriptivist revolution, we are stuck with the conception of what thought is like, considered in intentional terms, which generates the fear of being out of touch with objects; and only the transcendental move that Rorty describes could so much as seem to assuage the fear. If we succumb to the move, we are embarking on a piece of philosophy in a recognizably Cartesian mode. Rorty brings out very clearly how discouraging the prospects are. But with the assumption in place, however well we appreciate the hopelessness of our predicament once we allow ourselves to feel the Cartesian fear, that does not seem enough to confer intellectual respectability on suppressing it. We have to be shown how to make ourselves immune to the fear of losing the world; but with the assumption about intentionality maintained, the best we can do seems to be to avert our gaze from a difficulty which we choose (intelligibly, by all means) not to bother with. The point of the conception of singular thought that I have been recommending is that it treats the Cartesian fear of loss in a different, and fully satisfying way: not by trying to bridge a gulf between intentionality and objects, nor by a cavalier refusal to worry about the problem, while leaving what poses it undisturbed, but by fundamentally undermining the picture of mind that generates the Cartesian divide.

CHAPTER 6

ON SINGLING OUT AN OBJECT
DETERMINATELY*

DAVID WIGGINS

1. When something is singled out, an object impinges on a conscious subject, and, in having the *de re* thought that he has when he is so impinged upon (the thought, say, 'That bald man has been standing in the snow for four hours'), the subject takes the object for something that it is (say, a man). He apprehends it in at least one way correctly, in however many ways he misapprehends it. I label this claim (I). We can also say (II)—more strongly—that, when a subject singles out an object, he has a thought that is answerable for its correctness to the nature and condition of that object, the thought is the thought it is by virtue of being corrigible by reference to that object, and it is only by reference to the content of such a thought that it is determinable what object it is that impinged upon the mind of the subject.[1] It is not just a question of what bumped into his sensory apparatus: all sorts of things may have done this at that time.

One sort of philosopher may be unhappy with a strict and literal construal of 'impinge' as it occurs here, carrying the connotations it may appear to carry in (I) of a material-cum-causal transaction such as denting or die-stamping, even if he is prepared to take pleasure in the important concession that (II) could be seen as representing to his viewpoint, so soon as the word 'impinge' was interpreted there to meet his requirements. For the sake of having a name, let us call this philosopher an idealist. Another more familiar kind of philosopher

* © David Wiggins 1986.

[1] Cf. my *Sameness and Substance* (Blackwell, Oxford, 1979, with errata for 1980 paperback), 101 and Chapter 5. The present paper continues those themes, treading yet closer to the hazards that lie at every point off the straight and narrow route to the unspectacular truths that the theory of individuation has here to strain after, but not overreach. I am indebted to Jennifer Hornsby, Mark Sainsbury, Martin Davies, and the editors for comments on an earlier version, and to John McDowell for a further suggestion about the penultimate draft.

will be fully content with (I) but not happy to allow that it is *only* by reference to a *de re* thought conceived irreducibly thus that it can be fully determined what object impinged on the consciousness of the subject. Let us call this philosopher a programme-materialist. But let us call anyone happy to accept (I) and (II) together, as literally understood, and happy to say that a fuller development of (I) would deliver something simply entailing (II), a conceptualist or a conceptualist-realist. Conceptualism itself may be thought of as comprising three claims: first, that the singling out of an object in experience depends upon the possibility of singling it out as a *this such*; second, that there is no surrogate or reductive level (for instance, the level of description of retinal stimulation or whatever), that is, no level distinct from that at which we have objects of this sort and thoughts of them conceived in genuine reciprocity with one another, such that, at that reductive level, you could determine what object it was that the subject was impinged upon by; and third, that our cognitive access to reality is always through conceptions that are conceptions of what it is to be this or that sort of thing, these conceptions being a posteriori and at every point corrigible by experience, yet present in advance of the recognition of any particular object as a this such.

2. The thought of the object is the thought it is, then, by virtue of being answerable to that object and the condition of that object. That is one dependence. And there is an opposite if unequal dependence. The object is what it is, whether or not it is singled out: *but it does not simply individuate itself or, in and of itself, differentiate itself from other things.*[2] There are no 'lines' in nature (even though, after the imposition of lines, there are edges for us to find there). It is we, sharing the benign illusion that there is just one way to do this, who impose lines on nature, not arbitrarily or in just any way, but in ways that are determined for us by our constitution and ecology, by the scale appropriate to our physical size in relation to the rest of the world, and by our intellectual and practical concerns. (No doubt the concerns themselves are partly determined by what there is for creatures such as we are to find in the world.) And it is only to be expected, if so much is correct, that, for any object we are to differentiate, this object will be differentiated as an *f* or a *g* or . . . ,

---

[2] Here (I am aware) I yield to the temptation to try to convey something by issuing the denial of something that is really nonsense. What *would it even be* for an object to *differentiate itself*? (Cf. *Sameness and Substance*, Chapter 5 passim.) I confess I should urge a cognate criticism against the next sentence in my text.

where f, g ... are the relevant sorts that our practical and cognitive purposes suggest to us for singling things out in experience. Here however I would stress that in so far as it is the conceptualist's claim that what sortal concepts we apply to experience determines what we can find there, the claim is to be understood in the unexciting way in which one understands the statement that the size and mesh of a net determine not what fish are in the sea but which ones we shall catch.

3. So much for conceptualism or conceptualist realism and so much for the difference between conceptualism and idealism. For the conceptualist, x is a genuine object if and only if, in a sense of 'single out' to be gradually refined, x can in principle be singled out as this such and such or this so and so, and singling out is something that is answerable to multiple constraints that are at once empirical and conceptual and logical.

4. In working out this conception in *Sameness and Substance*—the 'two-way flow' conception of singling out—a preoccupation with the problem of giving equal weight to the a posteriori character of thing kinds f, g ... that participate thus in individuation and to the a priori exigency of identity and objecthood moved me to insist that, in any case where it is indeterminate what has been singled out, we should not say that what has been singled out is something indeterminate.[3] Rather, I said, 'no substance at all has been singled out until something makes it determinate which entity has been singled out'; and, for this to be determinate, 'there must be something in the singling out [something from the sides of the object and the thinker] that makes it determinate what principle is the principle of individuation for the entity'.[4] The singling out of a substance s at time t always, I claimed, 'reaches backward and forward to all the times before and after t at which s exists'.[5] Conceiving the activity or achievement as logically constrained in this way, I thought that singling out simply could not give us an entity that was individuatively indeterminate; it could not give an entity that was a creature of

---

[3] Cf. *Sameness and Substance*, 140 n. 14.

[4] And therefore determinate under what family of sortally concordant individuative concepts it is to be subsumed. See *Sameness and Substance*, 140.

[5] *Sameness and Substance*, 6.

time *t* and 'synchronically' perfectly identical with itself but 'dia-chronically' possibly less than perfectly identical with all sorts of more or less 'other' things. (A picture that would be merely laugh-able if one did not constantly teeter on the edge of being charmed and then finally seduced by it.) That would completely subvert and destroy reference to the things there are in the empirical world.

At the time of making these assertions I was not aware of the argu-ment published by Gareth Evans in 1978, for the impossibility of a vague object;[6] and I was unaware how fatally attractive the failure (as I see it) to grasp the central insight of conceptualism was destined to render the idea of objects that are indeterminate with respect to identity. Still less did I imagine that there could be any philosophical motive to welcome rather than redescribe examples that lent comfort to this idea. In the continuing conviction that the idea of an object such that it is indeterminate which object it is simply cannot coexist with reference to continuants and the individuation of continuants, what I offer here is a version of Evans's argument designed to counter at least some of the objections and criticisms that his article has aroused. Having approved Evans's implied standard for individua-tion, I try to show how readily the conceptualist idea of an object of reference as the correlate of a certain logically and empirically con-strained variety of *de re* thinking (the singling out kind) can accom-modate the logical thesis that if *a* is *b* then *a* is definitely *b*. It may be that conceptualism is unique in being able to accommodate this nearly incontrovertible claim. (That is my own undemonstrated conviction.)

5. It will appear that the world presents us with many apparent counter-examples to the incontrovertible claim. Before offering the argument I have promised to give for it, I note three such. (*a*) Ima-gine a monstrous birth with what seem to be two heads but having only one trunk, heart, liver. . . . 'It is indeterminate', it may be sug-gested, 'whether this is one animal or two animals. So, by suitable pointings supported by suitable explanations, it will be possible to have a case where it is indeterminate whether *this* ostended thing is the same as *that* ostended thing.' (Michael Ayers has insisted on the need to consider such examples: I am indebted to him for suggesting this one.) (*b*) 'Circumstances can arise that make it unclear whether or not a club started at some date is the same as a club that exists at some later date . . . The question of identity has no answer; the facts

<hr/>

[6] 'Can there be Vague Objects?', *Analysis*, xxxviii (1978), 208.

do not determine one.'[7] (*c*) Hobbes offers a story in which Theseus' ship is gradually repaired with new spars, while the old spars are simultaneously collected and reassembled in a reconstruction of the original ship.[8] Suppose someone wishes to maintain (as I myself have) that in such cases an entity can persist through some measure of disassemblage, reassemblage, and replacement of parts, but that there are further extremes of simultaneous disassemblage, reassemblage, and replacement of parts that are too extreme (relative to the proper reference point, which is the original condition of the entity)—indeed definitely too extreme—for that entity to count as having persisted through them. Then it may be said that there must be relatively late stages in the story of the single enduring entity at which it is indeterminate whether the original entity has survived.

6. Why, it will be asked, when we are faced with such impressive-seeming examples, should we regard it as a point in favour of a theory of individuation that it can escape the need to acknowledge the existence of objects that are indeterminate in respect of identity (objects such that it is indefinite which things they are)? Why is it a point in favour of a theory that it can pay full respect to the claim that if *a* is *b*, then *a* is definitely *b*? Because we can prove this.

Suppose that *a* is *b*. Then, given Leibniz's Law, whatever is true of *a* is true of *b*. Now *a* is definitely *a*.[9] But if so, then *b* is definitely *a*. So, by conditional proof and the symmetry of identity, if *a* is *b*, *a* is definitely *b*. In which case there is no future in the supposition that one could say that *a* was *b* but refuse to affirm that it was definitely *b*.

Putting the matter more formally, and letting 'Δ' mean 'definitely' and employing a pattern of proof made familiar by R. Barcan, we have

(i) $a = b$ (Hyp)
(ii) $\Delta(a = a)$ (Truism)
(iii) $\Delta(a = b)$ ((i), (ii), Leibniz's Law)
(iv) $(a = b) \to \Delta(a = b)$ (C.P.)

---

[7] Cf. John Broome, 'Indefiniteness in Identity', *Analysis*, xliv (1984), referring to Derek Parfit.

[8] For references to Hobbes, Plutarch, Plato, and others, see *Sameness and Substance*, 92 ff.

[9] Cf. Evans op. cit. But note that I am *not* using his definitions of 'Δ' and '∇'.

7. Evans wanted to establish not only the connection of identity and definiteness but also the definiteness of *non*-identity. His proof is not available within the framework I have preferred. But here for the record is another proof, taking '∇' as the dual of 'Δ',[10] and exploiting an analogy that impressed Evans between the pair Δ and ∇ and the pair □ and ◇.

(v)	$\sim(a=b)$	(Hyp)
(vi)	$\Delta\nabla\sim(a=b)$	((v), compare S5 $\vdash(A \to \Box\Diamond A)$)
(vii)	$\sim\nabla\sim\nabla\sim(a=b)$	((vi), intersubstitution of logical equivalents, using the duality $\sim\nabla\sim A \equiv \Delta A$)
(viii)	$\sim\Delta\sim(a=b)$	(hypothesis to be refuted)
(ix)	$\nabla(a=b)$	((viii) and $\sim\Delta\sim A \equiv \nabla A$)
(x)	$\nabla(\Delta(a=b))$	((ix), intersubstitution of logical equivalents, using (iv) and $\Delta(a=b) \to (a=b)$)
(xi)	$\nabla\sim\nabla\sim(a=b)$	(resting on (x) and the duality of ∇ and Δ, hence resting on (viii))
(xii)	$\nabla\sim\nabla\sim(a=b)$ and $\sim\nabla\sim\nabla\sim(a=b)$	((xi) and (vii) = contradiction)
(xiii)	$\sim\sim\Delta\sim(a=b)$	(RAA on hypothesis (viii))
(xiv)	$\sim(a=b) \to \sim\sim\Delta\sim(a=b)$	(Conditional proof, discharging (v))
(xv)	$\sim(a=b) \to \Delta\sim(a=b)$	(Elimination of double negation (= DN))
(xvi)	$\nabla(a=b) \to (a=b)$	(contraposition, DN, ∇Δ interdf., (xv))
(xvii)	$\sim\Delta(a=b) \to \sim(a=b)$	((iv) contraposed)
(xviii)	$\sim\Delta(a=b) \to \Delta\sim(a=b)$	((xvii) and (xv), transitivity of '→')

8. As will appear, it is well worth distinguishing (iv) from (xviii), which is much easier to disbelieve. Disregarding (xviii), therefore, let us clarify the meaning of (iv) and rebut an objection or two before returning to (*a*), (*b*), and (*c*).

It is important to see that (iv) does not entail that every true identity sentence will remain true when prefixed with 'definitely'. For identity sentences may contain descriptions, and vagueness may result from a vagueness of these descriptions. Consider the not implausible claim 'The greatest ruler was the wisest ruler'. Very likely there is indeterminacy in this claim. Once, however, we prevail sufficiently over this indeterminacy to identify *candidates* x and y for the two descriptions (but not before that), what (iv) predicts is that if x is y at all then x is definitely y. The matter is open or shut. (We may

---

[10] Thus '∇' and 'Δ' are *consistent*.

say, if we wish, that the 'definitely' in 'If *a* is *b* then *a* is definitely *b*' has a smaller scope than any description that stands in the places marked by '*a*' or '*b*'.)[11]

9. One sort of sceptic may argue that, if *a* is a vague object, then we cannot claim that *a* is definitely *a*. It is here he will say (that is, at (ii)) that all derivations of principles like (iv) are bound to fail. But to this I should reply that, even if identity were a matter of degree, and *a* were a vague object, we still ought to be able to obtain a (so to speak) perfect case of identity, provided we were careful to mate *a* with exactly the right object. And surely *a* is exactly the right object to mate with *a*. There is a complete correspondence. All their vagueness matches exactly. (I aim here of course to speak in terms that my opponent will find it more difficult to reject as unintelligible than I need to find it.)

A related idea that may exert some adverse influence in this dispute and may make (ii) seem more dubious than it is is the thought that 'definitely' cannot be prefixed at all, without destroying full truth, to a sentence in which vague expressions occur. But this is a thought one will dismiss immediately as soon as one considers familiar cases innocent of all suggestion of vague objects and well outside the disputed area, where vaguenesses manifestly trade off:

Definitely, it is raining if and only if it is raining.
Definitely, the evening star is as famous as the morning star is.

And a similar response[12] may be directed against the complaint that Leibniz's Law $(a = b) \rightarrow (\phi a \equiv \phi b)$ is suspect within this controversy, because (as someone has said to me) it was never formulated to manage vague predicates. Any vagueness in the open sentence for which 'ϕ' holds a place in the equivalence '$(\phi a \equiv \phi b)$' will surely trade off against a similar vagueness in the same open sentence on the other side. Just if *a* is *b*, we may surely expect it to be true, and definitely true, that $(\phi a \equiv \phi b)$.

There is no clear limit to what remains to be said about the logic

---

[11] Thus the central question about the definiteness of the *relation of identity* will evade the approach of, for example, Richmond Thomason, 'Identity and Vagueness', *Philosophical Studies*, xxxvii (1981), 329 ff. Note here Evans's use of abstraction, and cf. *Sameness and Substance*, 109 ff.

[12] Contrast Broome op. cit., esp. 7–8, and compare John Alexander Burgess 'Vagueness and the Theory of Meaning', Oxford D.Phil. thesis 1980.

of 'definitely'. But for all present purposes I think it is enough to point out that the argument for (iv) does not presuppose anything very substantial about the logic of 'definitely'. Rather, it constrains the attempt to find or formulate such a logic. (The principles we are now using to get (iv) are strictly minimal. There would be no intuitionist objection to them.) In any case, the question that really concerns me is not so much how to defend (iv) against every conceivable objection, by fuzzy logicians and others, but how the commitment to it will work out within the conceptualist framework, and how it is to be defended against (*a*), (*b*), and (*c*). We must ask how we can avoid the appearance that here at least our experience forces vague objects upon us, and then inquire what consequences this avoidance will have for the theory of individuation.

10. Example (*a*). In a case like this, further inquiry may suggest that the right thing to say is that we have here one non-viable animal and it has two heads. Or it may suggest that there are two animals each as capable as Siamese twins are of separate life or conation. In that case what was born—hereafter 'the birth'—comprises two animals.[13] So far there is no relevant sense in which we have a vague object. All we have is a birth such that either it is identical with one animal or it comprises two animals. We do not have a thing singled out that is such that it is indefinite which thing it is. But what if there is simply no point in insisting that one of these options is the better one? And what if someone exploits their equal acceptability to say that it is indefinite whether this object (this birth) is or is not the same as that object (that two-headed non-viable animal)? Well, then the time has come to protest that even if (*ex hypothesi*) you can take each option, that does not entail you can take both at once. If *there is* a two-headed animal in the offing, then what was born *is* a two-headed animal. Relative to that decision the identity is definite. Or if that seems wrong because the identity is *not* definite (for example, because a mere decision is not enough to make it definite), then there is no identity. (Contrapose (iv).) But that entails that, so far from the

---

[13] Perhaps then we have an *animal* that comprises two animals. This is simply a case of homeomery, not of vague objecthood. For a small but in this connection indispensable supplement to the Fregean view of number concepts, see *Sameness and Substance*, 43–4.

options being equally good, the other option is actually better. The birth comprised two animals. More generally, it is just an illusion that each 'this' can make as good a reference as you like, as well backed as you like, and that they can do so simultaneously even though the identity question *still* remains indeterminate.

11. Example (*b*). Suppose it is alleged that the association of persons meeting in 1985 is indeed the same as a club that appeared to its members to be lapsing (or to have lapsed) in 1963. The first question is whether there is any good reason to allege this identity. It cannot be made to hold by a simple decision on the part of those meeting in 1985 (even if decisions on the part of the founders are relevant to the question). On what terms did the club dissolve? What were the articles of association? What needs to be made out is the point of the claim of identity and the case *for* the identity. If the case is not good enough, then what (iv) reminds us is simply that the clubs are not the same. Why object to that?

12. Example (*c*) is a more complex matter and confused by the thought that, in cases like this, the search for objects can be informed by radically different interests and preoccupations. These seem to generate conceptions of Theseus' ship that are radically different; and the trouble is that there is apparently no way to arbitrate empirically between them.

What does the question of identity turn on here? Without using the idea of identity I cannot say. But using it freely, perhaps I can contrive to say something that is better than useless. First, we have a reference to Theseus' ship; and then (let us suppose) we have a reference to the ship whose late arrival in 399 BC delayed Socrates' drinking of the hemlock. Behind each reference stands the singling out of the object of that reference. What exactly did each of these singlings out catch hold of? We have to find some common way of further amplifying, developing, and specifying each singling out,[14] reaching backwards and forwards along the life span of each object, working towards a more and more complete answer to this question. In the end, we shall either find that we have rendered it completely manifest

---

[14] This stipulation, which ensures the comparability and commensurability of the singlings out as further amplified, corresponds to the 'there exists a sortal concept *f* such that . . .' clause in the statement of principle **D** given at p. 48 of *Sameness and Substance*.

that, as fully spelt out, these are the singlings out of one and the same ship, or we shall find that we have collected an *x* and *y* such that, for some ϕ, ϕx and not ϕy.

On what principle, then, must we determine the temporal extent of Theseus' ship's life span? Well, it depends in the first instance on what ships are and what that ship was. We can allow for the occasional disassembly of the ship; we can allow for a measure of replacement of parts; we can even allow for modifications of the ritual or religious functions of the ship, with or without structural alteration. But what we cannot allow, if *Theseus' ship* is to be that which is being singled out, is arbitrarily much of all three kinds of change. (If we do allow arbitrarily much of all three, we may find we have Hobbes's competitorship.) Perhaps each such change is *pro tanto* insignificant: but what matters at each point is the *overall distance* of the new condition at that point from the original condition of the ship. (If we are careful about this, then no rival ship will develop during the time of Theseus' ship.) And in the end we must say *no* (or refuse to say *yes*) when too many such changes are too variously combined with one another. (This point about the *Sorites* respects the vagueness of predicates that *are* vague.)

13. The question that remains is how well such a view of examples like (*a*), (*b*), and (*c*) will consist with the determinacy of identity. What I claim is that the view is compatible with it, and that the thesis (iv) regulates our thought entirely helpfully here. What the determinacy of identity enforces is that each and every positive decision of identity must be judged by the same strict standard as we ought to require for definite identity. That ruling is special to identity. But what is so unfair or so unmanageable about it? Suppose that in reaching forward to later times we get to a point *t after which*, using that standard, we cease to be satisfied that the very same thing is being singled out. Then we shall say that what we have *at t* is indeed Theseus' ship. But, for this or that item picked out by reference to times *later than t*, we shall refuse to affirm that Theseus' ship is definitely this. Contraposing (iv), we shall say that Theseus' ship is not the item singled out. Before we thought about what identity involved, we might have been in doubt. But having once thought about what it involves, why should we not permit the logic of identity and individuation to regulate our thinking in this way?

14. Well, what might seem unreasonable, given cases like that of

Theseus' ship, is that there should be a cut-off point up to which we definitely have Theseus' ship and after which we have something definitely distinct from it. If up to *t* we definitely had Theseus' ship and as soon as you like after *t* we *definitely did not*, it might seem intolerable that there should be any vagueness at all about where the strict standard ceased to be satisfied. (Intolerable even that there should be vagueness about where to make a Dedekind section.) But here let us revert to the distinction between (iv) and (xviii). Unless we have good independent reasons not only to explore the analogy between $\nabla\Delta$ and $\Box \diamond$ but also to commit ourselves to an S5 framework for 'definitely' logic, we may well doubt the prior commitment to assert the principles $(\nabla A) \to (\Delta\nabla A)$ and $(\text{not } \Delta A) \to (\Delta \text{ not } (\Delta A))$. If so, neither the judgement that not definitely $a=b$ nor any of the judgements that the judgement commits one to, for example (not $a=b$) and (∇ not $(a=b)$), commits us to (Δ not $(a=b)$).

15. The commitment to (iv) falls well short then of a commitment to the definiteness of non-identity—but intelligibly so. Individuation is the mind's work; and wherever there is work for the mind, it will be good to find tasks that we can take to be manageable by minds with our sorts of powers and capacities. But, if we accept (iv) and refuse to accept (xviii), then we can see how it is that singling out is such a task: because nothing then remains to prevent individual thinkers and the societies that breathe life into the individuative practices of individual thinkers from delimiting definitely what they single out,[15] and counting as quite clear what they have singled out, *without* making absolutely everything definite about the frontier between that thing and that which is not that thing. For if we accept (iv) without (xviii), then it can be definite what a thing is without its needing to be definite in every way and at every point what it is not. And why not accept (iv) without (xviii)? After all, whatever thing you take, there is one thing it is, even if there are limitlessly many things that it is not.

16. Individuation is the mind's work,[16] we have claimed. But this is work of construal not construction.[17] No doubt, different practical or cognitive purposes may make different sorts of construal

[15] Provided that it is there to be found. Cf. *Sameness and Substance*, 141–2.

[16] This is what the 'materialist' of section 1 denies.

[17] This is the contrast (and choice) that needs to be brought home to the 'idealist' of section 1.

necessary, and these can be expected to issue in different 'versions' of reality.[18] But that does not mean that everything is a correct version, or a version correct by its own lights (which would lose us the world altogether). Every sentence, by being the sentence it is and having the sense it has, sets itself a goal that it either attains or fails to attain. But, in doing this, it does not set the verdict on whether that goal has been attained. In the same way, every singling out of a thing, being the singling out of this f or that g, construes reality in a certain way. But it does not construct the f or the g from its own a priori materials, as if to validate itself—no more than the focusing of a camera fixed in a certain spot creates that which it records when set at that focus. A *de re* thought that is a singling out thought uses tested a posteriori materials to set a standard for itself that the world can disappoint or gratify, according as there is or is not to be discovered the very object the thought purports to be a thought *of*. But the object is there anyway, even if it took a particular sort of empirically and logically constrained looking to light it up there. The mind *conceptualizes* an object that is there to be conceptualized, even as the object *impinges* upon the mind that has the right thought to single out that object.[19]

---

[18] But not, in my view at least, in *conflicting* versions. Emancipation from the correspondence model of objective truth is one thing. Emancipation from truth or logic is another.

If two versions conflict, not both are right. But *if* they conflict they must of course have the same subject matter. Whereas in different versions with different a posteriori concepts applied for different practical or cognitive purposes, different things will be singled out, and different subject matters will be proposed.

[19] The sentence is adapted from *Sameness and Substance*, 101. Against one possible misunderstanding, see n. 25 there, and compare 141–2.

CHAPTER 7

WHAT DETERMINES TRUTH
CONDITIONS?*

CHRISTOPHER PEACOCKE

There are two dimensions to the propositional content of a given sentence or of a given mental state. On the one hand, there is a dimension which carries information about such matters as the conditions which may lead a thinker to accept such a content, and its consequences in thought once accepted. On the other hand, there is the truth condition of the content. An investigation of the first dimension might have as its goal an adequate description of the conditions under which certain contents are in fact accepted; or it might have as its goal a correct statement of normative conditions relating to those contents. I will be concerned here only with normative conditions: henceforth, by an 'acceptance condition' of a given content, I will mean a correct statement of a normative condition concerning that content. A question then arises about the relation between these two dimensions of content: what, in general, is the relation between a content's acceptance conditions and its truth condition?

The word 'content' which occurs in this question is used here for something conforming to essentially the same principles Frege took to govern Thoughts.[1] Contents are individuated by considerations of cognitive significance; they are the objects of propositional

* © Christopher Peacocke 1986. I have been helped by the comments of Joseph Almog, Martin Davies, Michael Dummett, Richard Grandy, Brian Loar, Graeme Forbes, Stephen Schiffer, Stephen Stich, and the editors. Some of the present paper is programmatic: I intend to publish more on the programme later. Most of this paper was written when I was a Fellow of the Center for Advanced Study in the Behavioral Sciences at Stanford in 1983–4. For financial support in that period I am grateful to the Center, the National Science Foundation (grant BNS 76–22943), and the British Academy. The paper was completed when I was a Visiting Research Associate of the Center for the Study of Language and Information in Stanford: I am also most grateful for its support.

[1] See for instance G, Frege, *Logical Investigations*, translated by P. T. Geach (Blackwell, Oxford, 1977).

attitudes; they have absolute truth values, without relativization to anything else; they are composite, structured entities; and it can be that different thinkers judge, argue about, or have other propositional attitudes to the very same content. That there can be anything conforming to all these Fregean conditions is controversial. But the claim that there can be is not essential to what I shall be arguing. I will use the Fregean framework only for ease of formulation. Even if the Fregean framework is superseded, we can still formulate the question I want to ask about the relations between acceptance conditions and truth conditions. In any plausible theory, there will be something which is the object of propositional attitudes; and in any plausible theory what is believed must somehow determine a truth value. So in the apparatus of any plausible theory, we can ask: what is the relation between the acceptance conditions of what is believed and the conditions for what is believed to determine the truth value *true*?

I will be arguing in support of, though will by no means prove, the conjecture that there is a conception of a content's acceptance conditions on which those acceptance conditions determine its truth condition. More specifically, I will be arguing in support of this Conjecture:

There is a class of contents whose truth conditions are directly determined by certain of their acceptance conditions; the truth conditions of contents outside this class are determined ultimately by their relations to contents inside this initial class.

In the next section I will argue for the Conjecture in the case of certain observational contents; following that I will argue for it in connection with universally quantified contents.

The first part of the Conjecture as displayed would be instantly endorsed by someone who holds that truth itself is to be elucidated as some form of ideal fulfilment of evidential conditions: in fact such a theorist will hold that the first part covers all cases. But that is not the way in which I will be arguing for the Conjecture. I will not, on the one hand, be stating the acceptance conditions of a content solely in terms of the actions of a being with powers greater than, or different from, our own: such an approach is powerless by itself to illuminate the relations between *our* acceptance of a content and its truth conditions. Nor, on the other hand, will I be paring down truth conditions in some way which guarantees in advance of investigation of any particular type of content that the Conjecture must be correct. I will not be presupposing an anti-realistic theory of truth. What I will be supporting is something which has in a full theory to be established by detailed argument about the actual acceptance conditions and the pre-theoretical truth condition of the content, in the absence of independent reasons for thinking these are defective. Such an argument has to be given for each type of content in our conceptual repertoire. We may, though, hope that there are some general forms of argument that can be used for several different types of content in establishing the Conjecture.

We need to avoid trivialization of the Conjecture. It would be trivialized if we allowed as an acceptance condition of 'Men are mortal' the condition that it ought to be accepted only if men really are mortal: and who is to gainsay the correctness of that normative requirement? The relevant acceptance conditions must, then, be further restricted—to those for which we have an immediate account of how a thinker can manifest the fact that he is following their norms, rather than some others. Whenever I give acceptance conditions for a particular content, I will aim to show that this further restriction is met. If the Conjecture is correct, of course, conformity to the norms of an acceptance condition which does use the truth condition outright can after all be manifested: but on the conception I will be outlining, the account of manifestation of such conformity proceeds via acceptance conditions for which we have a direct account of manifestation.

The acceptance conditions I will be discussing commonly concern in part the world external to the head of the thinker; they will not be restricted to psychological states which have no implications for the subject's environment. So these acceptance conditions for a content should not be identified with what many who have used the notion would call the conceptual role of a mental state with that content.[2]

---

[2] Harry Field, 'Logic, Meaning and Conceptual Role', *Journal of Philosophy*, lxxiv (1977) 379–409, at p. 380; Brian Loar, 'Conceptual Role and Truth Conditions', *Notre Dame Journal of Formal Logic*, xxiii (1982), 272–83, at p. 280; see further Colin McGinn, 'The Structure of Content', in Andrew Woodfield (ed.), *Thought and Object* (Clarendon Press, Oxford, 1982), Stephen Schiffer, 'Intention-based Semantics', *Notre Dame Journal*, ibid., 119–56, and also the latter's 'Truth· and the Theory of Content', in H. Parret and J. Bouveresse (eds), *Meaning and Understanding* (De Gruyter, Berlin, 1981). For a conceptual role theory which is not internal in the sense of the text, see Gilbert Harman, 'Conceptual Role Semantics', *Notre Dame Journal of Formal Logic*, xxiii (1982), 242–56.

On such an internal notion of conceptual role, the conceptual role of a state is concerned only with that state's relation to stimulation, to behaviour, and to other internal states: it is immediate that such internal conceptual roles by themselves will in almost all cases fail to determine truth conditions, which will generally concern the external world. The project of elucidating the acceptance conditions which will concern me and the project of elucidating internal conceptual role are distinct from one another.

The two projects may, of course, be surrounded by claims which do make the projects conflict. A theorist of internal conceptual role who says that it is *only* at the level of internal conceptual role that the dimension of content which captures acceptance conditions can be characterized would certainly be saying something competing with the account I will be offering.[3] So equally would a theorist—of either internal or wider conceptual role—who claims that in so far as he can make sense of the possibility at all, the determination of truth conditions by evidential or other acceptance conditions is a trivial matter, not something needing argument for each particular type of content.[4] Before we can assess those further claims, we need to know more about the position they exclude: here I will devote myself to further elaboration of a notion of an acceptance condition and its relation to truth conditions which those further claims would exclude.

1. We take first contents in which an observational concept is predicated in the present tense of an object demonstratively presented in perception: we will be concerned with cases in which the object is of such a size that it can, in our actual circumstances, be determined by perceiving the object whether or not it falls under the observational concept. Such contents or Thoughts would be expressed in English by 'That block is cubic', 'This plate is oval', 'That surface is blue'; but possession of attitudes to these contents is not necessarily restricted to creatures who have a language. Concepts are here taken

---

[3] For a statement of something which would be a consequence of this further claim, see Loar, op. cit.: 'I doubt that on *any* use theory (anything on which meaning is a matter of rules, verification procedures, etc.) whatever constitutes a sentence's meaning would explain or vindicate assigning our preferred truth-conditions to that sentence' (282–3). Loar's more detailed views, on which that formulation would be qualified for observational beliefs, are given in his *Mind and Meaning* (CUP, Cambridge, 1981), esp. Chapter 8.

[4] Harman is a representative of this second attitude: cf. his 'Conceptual Role Semantics', op. cit.

as constituents of contents. So they are conceived as conforming to a Fregean condition on informativeness, a version of the condition which for Frege would correspondingly have governed the senses of predicative words: if the content 'An object is φ if and only if it is ψ' is potentially informative, then φ and ψ are distinct concepts. If we do not cut at least this finely, we will leave out too much that is distinctive of cognitive phenomena.

Contents within the chosen range have the following components. In the first component, the perceived object is presented in a certain way W in perception; some concept F—'block', 'plate', 'surface'—is commonly used in individuating the object presented; and there is the presented object itself, x say. So the first component can be captured in the notation $[W, F(\ )_x]$. Second, there is the observational concept φ. Third is the time, t say, given as the present in these contents: we can write this component of the content $[\text{now}_t]$. The whole content 'That F is φ' is $[W, F(\ )_x]^\wedge[\varphi]^\wedge[\text{now}_t]$: here '$^\wedge$' stands for the component-forming operation on constituents of contents which corresponds, in this simple case, to concatenation on linguistic expressions for those constituents.[5]

If someone judges one of these contents, what commitments does he thereby incur? In asking this, I am asking about one particular sort of acceptance condition. In particular, I am asking about the spectrum of non-defeasible commitments attributable to a thinker in virtue of his judging just that content, as opposed to commitments which may be incurred given auxiliary hypotheses by which the thinker connects that content with others. Because they are associated with the content itself, these commitments may also be labelled *canonical*. As a first approximation for the spectrum of canonical commitments we might try:

(C)   The spectrum of canonical commitments of one who judges a content at t 'That block is cubic' is that: for any position from which the block were to be perceived at t by a minimally functioning perceiver in normal external conditions, the block would be experienced from that

---

[5]   In what follows, nothing essentially turns on having x and t themselves as constituents (albeit under modes of presentation) of the content. Any pairing of a context together with something which, applied to the context, yields x and t can be adapted to the purposes below. The constituent $[\varphi]$ could also be further decomposed. The square brackets around the 'φ' are only for stylistic uniformity in the formal representation.

position as cubic, or as a cubic object would be from that relative position.[6]

In a fuller theory this specification of the canonical commitments, like that for any other type of content, should be derivable from a specification of the contribution to canonical commitments made by the constituents of the given content. The idea behind this first effort is that in perceiving the block as cubic, a subject can confirm that one of the many instances of the displayed universally quantified condition is true. In the context of auxiliary hypotheses about what happens when he moves, the other instances may be inductively confirmed. What the thinker has to do to keep track of the object as he or it moves depends in part on how it is presented to him in perception, in part on its kind. Not only does the thinker actually confirm in his perceptual experience only a fragment of the spectrum of commitments; he does not know infallibly that he has confirmed that fragment, since he does not know infallibly about the state of his perceptual mechanisms or environmental conditions, and moving around the object in any case takes time. But, infallibility aside, instances of this spectrum of canonical commitments can be confirmed. The thinker need not, of course, have these specifications of canonical commitments consciously in mind, or be capable of formulating them. What matters is that they correctly describe his commitments. That they are his commitments will be shown by the circumstances in which he is willing to withdraw a judgement of the content. Suppose a thinker is not questioning the normality of his environment, nor the operation of his perceptual mechanisms: then the pattern of his actual and counterfactual acceptances or rejections of 'That block is cubic' in rational response to his perceptual experiences can make it reasonable to ascribe to him the spectrum of commitments in (C).

Two thinkers may vary greatly in their inductive boldness, but may still judge the very same content. The bolder thinker may re-

---

[6] This applies only to monadic observational predications of perceptually presented objects. A variant account is needed even for some observational relations, particularly when one of their terms is the perceiver himself. It can hardly be required for fulfilment of the canonical commitments of a first-person thought 'I am in front of that (perceptually presented) house' that if I were in any different nearby position, I would still have an experience as of myself being in front of the house. The requirement would have to concern the perceived relation from other positions between the place I was previously located and the house.

quire much less than the more timid thinker in the way of evidence that the canonical commitments of one of our observational contents are fulfilled. But the commitments he incurs, on a narrower evidential base, are the same as those of the timid thinker in judging the same content: I will be arguing that this is what makes it the case that they are judging the same content.

In the case of the concept of being cubic, and other concepts of primary qualities, there is no one sense modality such that possession of these concepts demands a specified sensitivity to perceptions in that particular sense modality. Both a visual and a tactile experience can represent something in one's hand as being cubic, or two nearby edges as parallel, or as pointed. What matters here is the relative order of the modal operator and the quantifier. There is no modality such that, for possession of these concepts, sensitivity to perceptions in that modality is necessary: but it is necessary that there be perceptions in some modality such that there is a certain rational sensitivity of judgements containing the concept to those perceptions, if the concept is to be observational. My discussion will mainly mention visual experience: but it will, in the case of an observational concept of a primary quality, be sufficient for possession of it that the conditions mentioned for visual experience be correspondingly fulfilled for experiences in some other sense modality. Primary qualities can be accessed through different modalities precisely because they are concepts of objective properties whose nature is independent of any particular form of sense experience.

This objectivity is in fact not fully captured in that first approximation to the spectrum of canonical commitments. We can conceive of something which changes shape as a normal perceiver moves around it; and we can conceive of its doing so in such a way that from any position it looks cubic to the perceiver, even though it never is in fact really cubic. The full spectrum of canonical commitments offered in the first approximation could be fulfilled without exhausting the real commitments of one who judges the content. The real commitments exclude the state of affairs just described. It is not right to say that the point is already accommodated by the appeal to normal conditions in the first approximation. Consider a curious sceptic who maintains that things around us do often change shape as we move around them. Can we really answer him by saying 'But these are normal conditions we are in, so your scepticism is unintelligible'? On the contrary, there is no problem in understanding (as opposed to believing) this sceptical hypothesis. What, in the case of the concept of being cubic, has been omitted from the canonical commitments is this: it has to be the object's actual shape in present circumstances which is responsible in the counterfactual circumstances mentioned for the perceptual experiences. What happens in counterfactual circumstances in which the object has a different shape from that it actually possesses is irrelevant to the fulfilment of *these* commitments. The judgement that the presented object is cubic must be withdrawn if it becomes clear that the actual shape is not responsible for the relevant experiences, even if all the counterfactuals in the first approximation are true—as they could be under the curious sceptic's hypothesis. (Equally, if a (surface) colour concept is predicated of a surface, some actual property of the surface of the object must in the counterfactual circumstances cause the experiences mentioned in the canonical commitments.) It also matters that in the improved statement of the canonical commitments, we say that it is the object's actual shape which is responsible for the experiences, rather than saying that it is the fact that the object is cubic which is so responsible. The latter, though true, trivializes the Conjecture: the former does not.

What is a 'minimally functioning perceiver'? Is it a necessary condition of a subject's being a minimally functioning perceiver that if his experience represents his environment as being a certain way, it is so? But this matching requirement is too strong. Someone may wonder as follows: 'I know my perceptual mechanisms are in order, and the lighting is normal, but are those things which I see as square perhaps not really square?' This is a coherent speculation. A philosophical account of a minimally functioning perceiver must accommodate the fact, so familiar to psychologists and artists, that, for example, even with the normal behaviour of light, many different irregular trapezoids can cause a visual experience as of something square in the environment. These different shapes have in common that they cause the same pattern of retinal stimulation. If we imposed the matching requirement on minimally functioning perceivers, our wondering subject would be entertaining something a priori incoherent, which he is not.

Rather than impose the matching requirement, we can proceed thus. A description of things in the environment of a subject is *in the projection class* of a given pattern of retinal stimulation just in case the existence of things in the environment falling under that description could, with the normal behaviour of light, be part of the causal explanation of the occurrence of an instance of that pattern of retinal stimulation. A description of the form 'a door of such and such shape, colour, and texture at such and such orientation and distance relative to the subject' is in the projection class of the pattern of retinal stimulation which you normally receive when you look at such a door. That same class will also have as a member a description of a carefully painted façade at a very different angle which contains no real door or any salient segment which is door-shaped, but which with the normal behaviour of light produces the same pattern of retinal stimulation. With this notion, we can then say that a subject is a minimally functioning perceiver only if two conditions are met when he has a perceptual experience in normal external circumstances: (a) the description under which the experience represents things in the environment as falling is in the projection class of the pattern of retinal stimulation which causes the experience; and (b) suitable relations of causal explanation obtain between the occurrence of that pattern and the experience (the details do not matter here). A minimally functioning perceiver will not necessarily be very efficient—he could be much less efficient than humans—but the following is true of any minimally functioning perceiver. By viewing an object from different positions, he obtains a class of descriptions of what is in his environment which are in the projection classes of *all* the successive patterns of retinal stimulation. This will in general be a much narrower set than the projection class of any one such pattern. In particular, a description of the environment as containing an irregular trapezoid will not be in the projection class of all the successive patterns when a square is viewed from different angles. That is why views from different positions still matter. Similarly, features of objects causally inoperative in producing experiences when the subject is at one location may come into their own when he moves.[7]

In the statement (C) of canonical commitments, the whole universally quantified condition beginning 'For any position . . .' is to be understood as falling within the scope of the thinker's commitment in judging 'That block is cubic'. Suppose the thinker continues to believe the content 'That block is cubic' in the face of one of his experiences of the block which represents it as curved, say. Then he is

---

[7] These examples and points substantially modify the claims about differential explanation and the definition of perception in my *Holistic Explanation* (Clarendon Press, Oxford, 1979), Chapter 2.

committed to believing that either external conditions are not normal or that his perceptual mechanisms are not functioning properly. Again, he does not need to be able to formulate this explicitly: that he has incurred these commitments will be shown in the actual and counterfactual ways he tries to make his judgements coherent.

So much for preliminaries. How does this bear on the relation between acceptance conditions and truth conditions? I claim that for contents of the sort which are our current concern

(S.Obs) For any such content, if all its canonical
        commitments are met, then it is true.

(S.Obs) is so-called because it gives a sufficient condition for the truth of one of our observational contents. I also claim

(N.Obs) For any such content, if it is true, then
        all its canonical commitments are met

—so-called because it gives a necessary condition. If (S.Obs) and (N.Obs) are true, then for this restricted class of contents, certain acceptance conditions—the canonical commitments—determine the truth conditions. (S.Obs) ought to be the more controversial case. For any particular observational concept φ, one would argue for instances of (S.Obs) involving it by contraposition: remember that we are still concerned here only with concepts ϕ such that as things actually are, it can be determined by perception of something whether it is ϕ. The argument for (S.Obs) is then that if external conditions are normal, anything which is not φ actually has a property which would, from some position, cause it not to be experienced by a minimally functioning perceiver as an observably φ thing would.[8] As promised, this argument does not proceed from some general prior identification of truth with ideal fulfilment of evidential conditions, but makes points specific to the kind of content in question. The argument is, for example, inapplicable altogether to concepts which do not possess the connections with perceptual experience distinctive of observational notions. It would also be inapplicable to

[8] A more general argument relevant to instances of (*S*) concerning shape concepts could also be built from a striking theorem of Ullman's: see his paper 'The Interpretation of Structure from Motion', *Proc. Royal Soc. of London* B 203 (1979), 405–26. He shows that three distinct orthographic views of four non-coplanar points on a rigid object suffice to determine its three-dimensional shape (up to a reflection). An efficient perceptual system will exploit this fact: we should not expect a vast number of views to be needed to determine three-dimensional shape.

any ways of thinking of a natural kind which do involve some perceptual component, but which require also a certain internal or theoretical constitution of its instances.[9]

The argument just given draws upon three notions concerning content without elucidating them. It takes for granted the conceptual content of experience. It also employs the idea of one external object rather than another being the one demonstratively presented and thought about. Finally, it simply uses the notion of the commitments being fulfilled, that is, true. These surely all need further elucidation, and they all need it by appeal to the relations between the thinker's states and external things. So the account of the relation between acceptance and truth which (S.Obs) and (N.Obs) give is partial. Nevertheless it matters that we can give this account, for by giving it we fulfil the need to have an account which possesses what we can call *internal determinacy*. For it would be problematic if, even when we are allowed to help ourselves to what I have taken without earning, the truth conditions of these simple contents outstripped their acceptance conditions.

We will sometimes regard as true a content such as 'If I were in the next room, it would still be the case that that (perceptually presented) table is rectangular' ($[W, \text{table}(\ )_x]^\wedge \langle \text{being rectangular} \rangle$ $^\wedge[\text{now}_t]$). This is not equivalent to 'If I were in the next room, a content of the form $[W, \text{table}(\ )_\xi]^\wedge \langle \text{being rectangular} \rangle^\wedge[\text{now}_\eta]$ judged by me there would be true'. So how do we explain the role of our observational contents in such embeddings? In general, for each content of the form $[W, F(\ )_x]^\wedge[\varphi]^\wedge[\text{now}_t]$ there is a corresponding proposition $\langle x,P,t \rangle$ consisting of the perceived object x, the property P presented by the observational concept φ in the content, and the time presented (a Russellian proposition). For the purposes of evaluating these counterfactuals, the truth of the content with respect to non-actual circumstances requires that the object x have property P at t, that is, that its corresponding proposition be true. Unless there is some difficulty about which object and property are so presented,

---

[9] We have not established that the acceptance conditions determine the truth conditions even for all contents of our chosen observational form: for we were operating under the restriction that the object perceptually presented is one the applicability to which of the observational concept can be perceptually determined. The restriction is genuine: consider 'That star is spherical'. To establish the Conjecture for all contents of this type would require arguments of a quite different sort, dealing with theoretical inferences to (for instance) shape in the very small or very large which play no part in the cases of the text.

principles giving the canonical commitments of these contents will
suffice, if we use the notion of the corresponding proposition, for the
determination of what has to be the case for the content to be true in
any arbitrary circumstance.

If the conjunction of (S.Obs) and (N.Obs) allows us to say that
canonical commitments determine truth conditions, we can hardly
deny that in the same sense truth conditions here determine canonical commitments. But this must not be misunderstood. (S.Obs) says
that the *fulfilment* of the commitments ensures the *fulfilment* of the
truth conditions, and (N.Obs) says the converse: neither (S.Obs) nor
(N.Obs) says anything explicitly about uniqueness. In particular,
(N.Obs) does not guarantee that with each truth condition, if (for
the purposes of this paragraph only) that is taken in these examples
as given by the ordered triple of an object, property, and time, there
is associated a *unique* pattern of canonical commitments. (N.Obs)
ensures only this: if the truth condition for a content obtains, the
spectrum of commitments for that content is fulfilled. This is quite
consistent with the non-existence of a route back from reference to
sense: for it can be informative to say of two spectra of commitments
that the one is fulfilled if and only if the other is. So there can still be
a unique content-determining association of a spectrum of canonical
commitments with a given content. Thus suppose we could both feel
heat and see it with infra-red vision. If the terms 'heat$_1$' and 'heat$_2$'
are introduced for the physical properties presented in these two
ways, the thought that something is hot$_1$ if and only if it is hot$_2$ can
be informative. Correspondingly, consider the two thoughts that an
object, presented in a given way, is hot$_1$ and that it is hot$_2$. The canonical commitments of the first thought are all fulfilled if and only if
the canonical commitments of the second thought are: but this an a
posteriori truth. The canonical commitments will indeed be uniquely
determined by an object, property, and time under suitable modes of
presentation. But on the conception underlying this paper, that is
unsurprising: for the conception is that a substantive theory of sense
can be given by appealing to acceptance conditions, of which a specification of canonical commitments is but a special case.[10]

[10] A genuine question for further work is whether there is a corresponding uniqueness in the case of (S.Obs): that is the question of the indeterminacy of the association
of truth conditions with acceptance conditions. For scepticism about determinacy on
a rather different notion of evidential conditions and conceptual role, see Schiffer,
'Truth and The Theory of Content', op. cit.

When the predicative component of one of our observational contents is a primary-quality concept, the content is one that can be barely true, in Michael Dummett's sense adapted to contents: for him, a barely true statement is one for which there is no non-trivial answer to the question 'What makes it true?'.[11] Dummett has also said that our model for knowledge of what it is for a statement capable of being barely true to be true is the ability to use it to give a report of observation.[12] This may need qualification if we allow contents about the entities postulated by the physical sciences to be barely true: but for observational contents, what I have argued so far supports Dummett's claim. The point is not that whenever, for instance, a minimally functioning subject has an experience as of something cubic in normal external circumstances, his experience will be caused by the perceived object's being cubic: we have already seen that to be false. What *is* true is that the only property of the presented object which would explain its appearing cubic (or as a cubic object would) from all relative positions is its being cubic. This feature may be unique to the primary-quality observational contents; and it helps to explain how we can grasp one range of contents which can be barely true.

Two different thinkers may confirm, to their satisfaction, that the canonical commitments of a given observational content are fulfilled. But since each confirms that they are met in the case of his own experiences, the question arises how they can be judging exactly the same content. Why for instance are they not rather judging contents of the same kind? The determination of truth conditions by acceptance conditions helps to answer this question. The truth condition, which concerns the actual, causally operative properties of the presented object, is not person-relative. If the commitments in (C) are fulfilled with respect to any one thinker's experience, they are fulfilled with respect to that of any other thinker. So the ambiguity in (C) of the phrase '*a* minimally functioning perceiver' does not matter. In arguing this, we are arguing for the fulfilment of a condition of adequacy on an acceptance-condition account of content which must always be met, namely: if the content-determining acceptance conditions for a content are in some way thinker-relative, while its truth condition is not, we must be able to establish that if the

---

[11] See his 'What is a Theory of Meaning? (II)', in Gareth Evans and John McDowell (eds.), *Truth and Meaning* (Clarendon Press, Oxford, 1976), 89 ff.

[12] Ibid. p. 95.

acceptance conditions are met for any one thinker, then they are met for every thinker.

There would be several other consequences of the determination of truth conditions by canonical commitments. One would be that a theorist who aims to individuate content by certain acceptance conditions (including canonical commitments) could consistently accept Dummett's arguments that a content (a Thought) is essentially something which, together with the world, determines a truth value.[13] Dummett's arguments suggest that it is an adequacy condition on a theory of sense that it treat contents (Thoughts) as essentially determiners of truth values, given the way the world is. If acceptance conditions do determine truth conditions, then a theory which uses acceptance conditions to individuate content can meet this adequacy condition. Another consequence concerns the claim that the achievement of understanding of a language, or grasp of certain contents, is in part a matter of acquiring a suitable rational sensitivity to acceptance conditions (which may include evidential conditions). This claim need not compete with, but in fact would actually entail, the thesis that these achievements are equally describable as the attainment of grasp, in a particular way, of the truth conditions of the contents.[14] This makes it important to ask whether some form of the present model can be applied to other types of content.

2. The observational contents we have been considering form a very special case. But the relation between truth and acceptance conditions in this case is an instance of a more general form. The more general form is that for each content there is a spectrum of commitments such that the content is true if and only if all those commitments are fulfilled. In the observational case these commitments involved perceptions which represented the world as being a certain way, a way systematically linked to the main concept of the content; but for other contents the correlating operation which determines the commitments from the content may be different. One direction

---

[13] Michael Dummett, *The Interpretation of Frege's Philosophy* (Duckworth, London, 1981), 47.

[14] For a sharply contrasting view, see Brian Loar, 'Conceptual Role and Truth Conditions', 276 ff. and especially n. 4.

in which we could generalize the initial model of the relations between truth and acceptance to a new, non-observational range of contents would be this:

> There is some operation C such that for each content p in the range:
>
> (a) $C(p)$ gives the canonical commitments of p, and
>
> (b) p is true if and only if all the conditions in $C(p)$ obtain.

While one range of contents may be individuated by their canonical commitments, another range may be individuated by their canonically *committing* conditions, by their canonical grounds rather than their canonical consequences. For a range of contents individuated by their canonical grounds, we can say:

> There is some operation G such that for each content p in the range:
>
> (a) $G(p)$ gives the canonical grounds of p, and
>
> (b) p is true if and only if some condition in $G(p)$ obtains.

That a content has certain canonical grounds will be shown in the conditions a thinker takes as sufficient for its holding.

A more refined version of each of these models could accommodate some dependence, in the determination of the truth condition, on the attitudes of the individual thinker. Provided that the nature of this dependence is uniformly given from the content p, this need not in any fundamental way make truth conditions person-relative. On one refined version of the commitment model, for instance, there would be an additional operation B:

> There are operations C and B such that for each content p in the range and for each thinker x:
>
> (a) $C(p)$ gives the canonical commitments of p, and
>
> (b) p is true if and only if all the conditions in $C(p)$ and all the conditions in $B(p, x)$ obtain.

I will give an instance of this model later. One can envisage many less restrictive variations on this theme.

Our question now is: can some form of one of these schematic models be applied to contents which are universal objectual quantifications 'All Fs are G' ($\forall x(Fx, Gx)$)?[15]

---

[15] The reasons for preferring the binary notation given in parenthesis to the standard '$\forall x(Fx \rightarrow Gx)$' are summarized in Martin Davies, *Meaning, Quantification, Necessity* (Routledge and Kegan Paul, London, 1981), 123–36.

In the spirit of Ramsey, we might try to build a theory around the idea that one who believes that all F things are G is disposed, given as a premiss a thought that m is F, to infer that m is G.[16] A theory built in this spirit must solve two problems. The first is that the theory must explain how quantificational contents embed within more complex operators. On this first problem, the theorist can say the following. Suppose the inferential disposition of one who believes that all Fs are G has been satisfactorily characterized. We can ask what condition has to hold in the world for exercise of this disposition never to lead to false belief. This will be the resultant truth condition for the content: and this truth condition can be input, in the extensional cases, to which other operators are applied when a quantification is embedded in more complex contents.[17] This is an adaptation of a tactic already adopted in the observational case. The second problem is that as the theory stands, the disposition it offers would also be possessed by a thinker whose quantification 'All Fs are Gs' has the truth condition that all the objects of which he has, or will have, modes of presentation of any sort in his repertoire are G. The theorist has to offer an account which uniquely determines objectual quantification over *all* objects of the given kind.

Accounts of quantification rarely address the question of what makes a subject's thought one containing unrestricted objectional quantification, rather than some analogue for thought of substitutional quantification. Gareth Evans, for instance, in an illuminating discussion, wrote 'the proposition that some F is G is conceived to be such that it would be rendered true by the truth of some proposition of the form $\ulcorner \delta$ is $G \urcorner$, where δ is a fundamental Idea of an F.'[18] It is no objection to this that the phrase 'some proposition of the form . . .' is within the scope of 'conceived to be such that . . .': Evans was not trying to give an eliminative analysis of grasp of existential quantification, but rather a principle describing it. But there need be no Idea or mode of presentation δ in the thinker's present or future repertoire which verifies a true existential quantification which the

[16] '$(x)\varphi x$ expresses an inference we are at any time prepared to make': F. P. Ramsey, *The Foundations of Mathematics* (Routledge and Kegan Paul, London, 1931), 238.

[17] Here the theorist departs from Ramsey, who seems to have held that quantified sentences do not express propositions in just the same sense in which their purely singular instances do: cf. *The Foundations of Mathematics*, 240.

[18] *The Varieties of Reference* (Clarendon Press, Oxford, 1982), 108.

thinker judges.[19] If we are puzzled about the nature of mastery of unrestricted quantification over objects, the statement that such a quantification is conceived to be true in virtue of a condition which involves unrestricted quantification over fundamental Ideas of those objects should not remove all our puzzlement. We might be tempted to say that we are considering an ideal thinker such that for each F, there is some fundamental Idea or mode of presentation of it in his repertoire. But then we must explain how our actual, non-ideal thought achieves the truth conditions of the thoughts of the ideal thinker; and in doing so we must also explain our grasp of the thought 'For each F, there is some fundamental Idea of it in the ideal thinker's repertoire'.

This problem is of course not special to the universal and existential quantifiers. It arises for any second-level operator whose truth conditions ineliminably involve the full range of objects falling under some concept: it arises equally for the definite description operator, and for such second-level predicates as 'rare', as it occurs in 'Albinos are rare'. What we must give is an elucidation of the phenomenon which Dummett characterizes by saying 'We understand the universally quantified statement because we have, as it were, a *general* grasp of the totality which constitutes the domain of quantification—we, as it were, survey it in thought as a whole . . .'.[20]

We seek an account of grasp of objectual universal quantification in terms of canonical commitments. The account should be one which determines the objectual truth conditions, and thus explains the remarkable fact that humans are capable of grasping a content which requires for its truth something about *all* objects of a given kind. Now there will certainly be differences, accessible to a radical interpreter, between one whose quantifications are objectual and one whose quantifications are substitutional. The empirical conditions which make it reasonable to judge an objectual universal quantification are much more demanding than those making it reasonable to judge a substitutional quantification.[21] On some definitions of validity, there will also be differences in the logic to which

[19] As Evans noted: ibid., 108–9. ·

[20] *Frege: Philosophy of Language* (Duckworth, London, 2nd edn. 1981), 517.

[21] I assume that all the terms in the substitution class denote. If they do not, there will still be other empirical differences between quantifiers read in each of the two ways.

the two quantifiers conform.[22] But these indisputable points do not give us quite what we were seeking: they either come too late, or they raise the same problems. We are asking for a certain form of account which explains how it is that a content can concern all objects. Given that it does, its doing so will have the mentioned consequences which differentiate it from substitutional quantifications. But these particular consequences do not constitute an account of what makes it the case that the content does range over all objects: it has certainly not been shown that they determine the truth condition.

On the other hand, some *ideal* radical interpretation procedure for identifying specifically objectual universal quantification, rather than those particular features differentiating the objectual from the substitutional, might be proposed as supplying what we seek. The ideal procedure would specify what, at the level of facts accessible to the radical interpreter, has to be the case for someone to mean universal objectual quantification by something. If our initial Conjecture is correct, it is indeed reasonable to expect that an ideal radical interpretation procedure for such quantification and an account of its canonical commitments or grounds will be equivalent: they are just accounts from different perspectives, the internal and the external, of what makes it the case that a thinker is judging one content rather than another. But such an ideal radical interpretation procedure we still do not have—in effect it is, from a different perspective, what I am trying to supply.

We initially confine our attention to unrestricted quantification

---

[22] Saul Kripke observes that, if we define validity for substitutional formulae in a way which takes as the range of substitution classes arbitrary sets of expressions of the appropriate category, then substitutional validity and classical objectual validity coincide: a formula is substitutionally valid iff it is classically valid. ('Is There a Problem about Substitutional Quantification?', in Evans and McDowell (eds.), *Truth and Meaning*, at p. 336.) This is not, though, the only definition of validity possible; and there are also ways of elaborating the idea of something being accepted as a law which would be tied to another definition of validity. In particular, as Davies notes, if the substitution classes quantified over in the definition of validity are restricted to those containing expressions already in the language, a wider class of formulae is valid ('A Note on Substitutional Quantification', *Nous*, xiv (1980), 619–22). In a language whose only individual constants are a and b, and whose only term-forming functors are f and g, any instance of the schema $[Fa \,\&\, Fb \,\&\, \forall xF(f(x)) \,\&\, \forall xF(g(x))] \to \forall xFx$ is valid under that altered definition. A reflective thinker who is using substitutional quantification will accept all instances of this schema; a thinker using objectual quantification will not do so. There are also differences in the relation of logical consequence on the altered definition of validity. (J. M. Dunn and N. D. Belnap, 'The Substitution Interpretation of the Quantifiers', *Nous*, ii (1968), 177.)

over physical objects which exist at the present time. Each such object is individuated by its current location and its kind. If we can explain quantification over all places, we can explain quantification over all such objects: for all Fs to be G it has to be that for every place the F (if any) at that place is G.

What is our conception of the range of unrestricted variables over places? I suggest that it is governed, *inter alia*, by two principles. (a) It is closed under such functions as those given by phrases of the form 'the place bearing spatial relation R to place π', when these functions are applied to places already in the domain. Of course in the case of some relations R, there will be no place bearing R to a given place already in the domain—for instance if the universe is finite and bearing R to π entails the relation of being more than a certain distance away from π. But *if* there is such a place, it is in the range of the unrestricted variables over places. (b) Understanding unrestricted quantification over places does not consist in the existence of a finite list of relations of which the understander appreciates that the range of places is closed under just those relations. Rather, the understanding is open-ended: for any new spatial relations with which he is presented, the understander will take the range of places as closed under those relations. This allows for arbitrary fineness of discrimination of smaller regions, and for the discrimination of distinct places at great distances.[23]

According to what we will call the Revised Account, to judge that all (physical, currently existent) Fs are G is to be committed to judging, should the question arise, any instance of the schema (1):

(1) If there is an F at the place (if any) bearing R to π, it is G.[24]

---

[23] This should not necessarily be equated with the range being indefinitely extensible, in Dummett's sense. (A concept is indefinitely extensible if 'for any definite characterization of it, there is a natural extension of this characterization, which yields a more inclusive concept': *Truth and Other Enigmas* (Duckworth, London, 1978), 195 ff.) If we are allowed to use the real numbers in the specification of the spatial relations, there will be characterizations of the range of places which are maximally inclusive. There may be, though, philosophical reasons for holding that the totality of real numbers cannot be explained except by using some indefinitely extensible notion—perhaps 'concept true or false of natural numbers'. So the thesis that the range of unrestricted quantification over places is either indefinitely extensible or has to be elucidated using some indefinitely extensible notion is still in the field.

[24] In the special case of generalizations of the form 'All *places* are G', (1) should be replaced by 'The place (if any) bearing R to π is G'.

Here any term replacing 'π' denotes a place already thought of as being in the domain of places. The judgemental disposition in question may be described as open-ended, in a sense corresponding to that in which the conception of the range of relations under which the domain of places is closed is open-ended. That is, it is enough for a thinker's now judging that all Fs are G that he now judges something which precisely commits him, when presented with what he takes to be a new spatial relation, to accept the corresponding instance of (1). He need not now know of all such relations. The phrase 'what he takes to be' matters here. A thinker may believe there are spatial relations other than those there actually are: without irrationality, he may be disposed to judge any instance of (1) involving a real spatial relation, without judging that all Fs are G. Conversely, if he believes of something which is a genuine spatial relation that it is no such thing, he may correspondingly judge the universal quantification without having that disposition with respect to everything which really is a spatial relation.[25]

The Revised Account preserves an attractive feature of the original Ramseyan theory. It offers an explanation of why there is such a gap between judging that $\forall x(Fx, Gx)$ and judging that Ga & Gb & ... & Gt, where a ... t are in fact all the Fs there are. To accept that last conjunction is by no means to have the general and indefinitely extensible disposition required by the Revised Account if one is to be judging the universal generalization. Indeed there is no particular singular mode of presentation such that a thinker must, in virtue of judging a universal generalization, already have it in his conceptual repertoire: this is as it should be, and is a second virtue of any neo-Ramseyan account.

If all the canonical commitments, according to the Revised Account, for 'All Fs are G' are fulfilled, must it then be true that all Fs are G? Not quite: for the canonical commitments concerned the *recognized* spatial relations, which may diverge from the real spatial relations. All we can say is that if all those canonical commitments

---

[25] A thinker may consistently judge both that all Fs are G, and that *if* there is an F in such and such region, then it is *not G*. But this does not contradict the account built around (1). On the Revised Account, there is no inconsistency either in this thinker or in our description of him. On the Revised Account, he is committed to believing both 'If there is an F in such and such a region, then it is G' and 'If there is an F in such and such a region, it is not G'. Hence on that account he is committed to believing there is no F in such and such a region; and indeed he is so committed.

are fulfilled, all the *F*s the thinker *believes* to exist will be *G*. But let us remember the refined version of the commitment model, which contained a clause about *B(p)*, an operation which may concern the individual thinker's attitudes. It is true that if all the canonical commitments for 'All *F*s are *G*' are fulfilled, *and* the thinker is disposed to recognize a relation as a spatial relation just in case it really is a spatial relation, then all *F*s will be *G*. This is the promised instance of the refined version of the model.

These points presuppose that every place within the range of the thinker's quantifiers is individuated by some extension of the thinker's conceptual resources for specifying spatial relations. These extensions will involve the application of mathematics to the real world. If someone believes that a subject's quantifications sometimes include in their range objects not capturable this way, we can ask him what features of that subject's thought make this fact manifest. If he can cite such features, the strategy of one who proposes the Revised Account will be to adapt his theory to accommodate those features. If no such features can be cited, he will be sceptical that any objects which ought to be captured remain uncaptured by his account.

Have I been cheating? At two points, I have used second-level objectual operators in giving a content grasp of which I presupposed on the part of the thinker when explaining the commitments of universal quantification. First, I exploited the equivalence, for predicates of material objects, of 'All *F*s are *G*' with 'For every place, the *F* (if any) at that place is *G*'. Then there was also the occurrence of 'There is . . .' in (1). But this accusation of cheating presupposes that the enterprise in which I have been engaged has reductive aspirations of a kind which in fact it need not possess. I have been trying to show how the canonical commitments of a universal quantification illuminatingly determine its classical truth condition. This remains a reasonable goal even in the context of an account of universal quantification in which such quantification is used within the scope of the attitudes of the thinker whose grasp of the notion is in question. In such a context, the present account is indeed incomplete. Consider the property of a second-level operator picked out as follows: one takes the conjunction of all the canonical commitments of a universal quantification, and replaces throughout occurrences of the universal quantifier within propositional–attitude contexts by an appropriately typed variable *V*; if the result is __*V*__, the

property we will be concerned with is picked out by the term
$\lambda V[\underline{\quad} V \underline{\quad}]$, which is a property of second-level properties. Now the
account is incomplete because one ought in addition to show one of
two things which I have not shown: either that universal quantifica-
tion is the only operator with the property $\lambda V[\underline{\quad} V \underline{\quad}]$, or that there
are additional constraints on universal quantification, and these
together with the property $\lambda V[\underline{\quad} V \underline{\quad}]$ are jointly possessed only by
universal quantification. However, in either case the account in
terms of commitments can be an essential part of an account of mastery of universal quantification.

The Revised Account may be contrasted with what we can call
relocation theories. Relocation theories try to explain acceptance of
$\forall x(Fx, Gx)$ in terms of conditionals the thinker actually accepts
about the properties of Fs he would encounter at other places. Suppose the relocation theorist says that to believe the present-tense 'All
Fs are G' is to accept such conditionals as (2):

(2) If I travel north for a day, and there learn something of the form
     'The m here is F', that F thing will also be G.

Does the relocation theory give as commitments only those conditionals whose antecedents concern a place a subject could, consistently with the laws of nature, travel to, or is there no such
restriction? If there is no such restriction, we have to suppose that
one who judges that all Fs are Gs is committed to counterfactuals
concerning what would happen if he were at a place he could reach
only by travelling at some earlier time faster than light. It is hard to
believe that the highly obscure question of how such counterfactuals
are to be evaluated has to be settled before one can rationally believe
all Fs to be Gs. So suppose the relocation theorist instead cites as
commitments only those conditionals whose antecedents mention
places the believer could reach. Then the problem is that these commitments fail to determine the truth conditions. Their fulfilment
would require all the Fs at places the thinker could reach to be G;
they would not require all Fs whatsoever to be G. Thus consider
someone who believes that all the planets other than Earth (in some
solar system or other) which he could encounter are uninhabited; he
need not also believe that *all* planets other than Earth are uninhabited, but according to the latest version of the relocation theory

he would be counted as doing so.[26] The Revised Account treats objects which are accessible to the thinker and those which are not as uniform in respect of their relevance to unrestricted quantification: if the inaccessible places are thought of as bearing certain spatial relations to the thinker, they will still be within the range of his quantifiers.[27]

The Revised Account was outlined for currently existing physical objects. But it is an instance of a general form which can be applied to some other ranges of object. In the case of quantification over times, for example, we would equally want to say that we conceive of this domain as closed under such operations as 'the time bearing

[26] As one might anticipate, these difficulties also arise for Jaakko Hintikka's game-theoretic semantics for the quantifiers. These semantics include such clauses as

> (*G.E*) If [a formula] *G* is of the form $(\exists x)A$, I choose a member of [the domain] *D*, give it a name, say '*n*' (if it did not have one before). The game is continued with respect to $A(n/x)$ . . . the result of substituting '*n*' for '*x*' in *A*.

(*Logic, Language–Games and Information* (Clarendon Press, Oxford, 1973), 100: I have changed the notation in unimportant ways.) Hintikka adds

> All human limitations have to be abstracted from. The searcher in question will have to be thought of, if not as omnipresent, then at least 'omni-nimble', free of all those limitations of access we humans are subject to. (Ibid., p. 103.)

This caveat is motivated by the desire that the semantics deliver the classically correct truth conditions for the quantified sentences. Consider the sentence 'All *F*s are *G*', and suppose that it is false, but only because some inaccessible *F*s are not *G*: all the accessible *F*s are *G*. In running through Hintikka's semantic rules, we learn that for 'All *F*s are *G*' to be true, it has to be true that there is nothing we can find or choose which is not *G*. (Here I am assuming the version in which Nature is not personalized, and in which universally quantified matrices are rewritten as negated existential quantification of the negation of the given matrix: see *Logic, Language–Games and Information*, p. 101.) Without the imagined property of being 'omni-nimble', that could be true, and yet the universal quantification 'All *F*s are *G*' false. Now since we are not in fact omni-nimble, as Dummett has repeatedly and convincingly insisted, any account of the quantifiers which mentions that property will have to say what features of our thought give it the same truth conditions as the thoughts and utterances of the imagined beings who do have it. (Even if Hintikka were not to accept Dummett's point, there remains an internal difficulty for his semantics. If we were omni-nimble, we could travel faster than light. But the sentence 'Everything travels no faster than light' is actually true: how can Hintikka's semantics acknowledge that it is true? We could also make the point with 'No one is omni-nimble'.)

[27] If we adopt the Revised Account, we will want to say that the sense in which we cannot find an object of a particular kind when a universal quantification is true, where this abstracts from all human limitations, is itself to be explained by appeal to the existence or non-existence of a place with an object of the given kind located at it—rather than conversely. It remains, of course, a question for further work how we can so much as have the conception of inaccessible places and times, such as those outside our present and our ancestors' light cones: I plan to discuss this elsewhere.

temporal relation T to t': if the operation, applied to any time already in the domain, gives any value at all, that value is also in the domain. Again, the concept of the relevant temporal relations T is indefinitely extensible. In some other domains, because of special features of the range of objects in question, we do not need to appeal to indefinite extensibility in the determination of the range: we know that all natural numbers, for instance, will be captured by the ancestral of the successor function applied to 0. So we can say that one who judges 'All natural numbers are G' is committed to all instances of 'If n is $sss \ldots s0$, then n is G', where the number of applications of the successor function 's' is any natural number; any other commitments of the judgement are derivative from this family of commitments. The use of the phrase 'any natural number' in the first half of the preceding sentence is not within the scope of any attitudes attributed to the thinker: we use it from the outside, in describing his judgemental commitments.

The Revised Account allows a level of uniformity in the description of universal quantification over concrete objects and natural numbers. In particular, it does not make knowledge of what would constitute a proof of a content of the form 'All natural numbers are G' a prerequisite for grasp of such contents. In adopting the Revised Account, we take at face value the situation of someone who understands quantifiers over natural numbers, but who does not know how such contents would be proved—the situation of all of us before we discovered or learned inductive proofs. What we learn when this method of proof is taught is that certain premises guarantee the truth of a content previously grasped. Is the understanding of quantification over all natural numbers possessed by someone who does not know of inductive proof defective? We will not want to insist generally on conclusive means of establishing quantifications, since this is not to be had for a posteriori quantifications over concrete objects. Nor is knowledge of proof conditions required for understanding, or for establishing, complex contents in which universal quantifications are embedded. If the truth condition really is determined by the canonical commitments, a thinker who knows nothing of proof conditions in the arithmetical case may be able to appreciate that if his commitments in judging 'All Fs are G' and 'Fa' are fulfilled, so too will be the commitments he incurs in judging 'Ga'. This can establish for him the complex content 'If all Fs are G and a

is *F*, then *a* is *G*' without his knowing any proof conditions for the universal quantification.

The Revised Account has no natural extension to universal quantification over the real numbers, or over large totalities of sets. There may be, then, a more general account of universal quantification which is applicable over all domains whatsoever. The Revised Account is at best partial. But we can still hope that, for the areas with which it deals, the Revised Account would be a consequence of the more general account when taken together with the special features of these areas.

I will take the Revised Account as my official, though partial, elaboration of a neo-Ramseyan account of universal quantificational contents. It fits one of the general forms which I mentioned earlier, and to which I aimed to adhere: namely that the canonical commitments determine the classical truth condition, in the sense that those conditions for a given thought are all fulfilled if and only if the thought is true. In giving the neo-Ramseyan account, I have at no point made use of the idea of a human, or any idealized thinker, being able to recognize that the truth condition for a universally quantified thought obtains. Dummett has written

since ... from the supposition that the condition for the truth of a mathematical statement, as platonistically understood, obtains, it cannot in general be inferred that it is one which a human being need be supposed to be even capable of recognizing as obtaining, we cannot give substance to the conception of our having an implicit knowledge of what that condition is, since nothing that we do can amount to a manifestation of such knowledge.[28]

The neo-Ramseyan account suggests that the classical truth condition is manifested not by a thinker's actions when he recognizes the truth condition to obtain, but rather by his (manifestable) commitments when he judges the universal quantification: for those

---

[28] *Elements of Intuitionism* (Clarendon Press, Oxford, 1977), at p. 375. See also his *Frege: Philosophy of Language* (Duckworth, London, 1st edn., 1973), 465: 'On a realistic conception of meaning, an understanding of a sentence consists in a knowledge of what has to be the case for it to be true; and such knowledge must, in turn, consist in a model for what it would be to recognize the sentence as true by the most direct means.' It is the 'must' here which I am questioning.

commitments to be fulfilled, the classical truth condition has to obtain, albeit that it is not conclusively knowable that it does so. Dummett regards the classical truth conditions for universal quantifications as illegitimately projected from observational cases, where he holds that it is legitimate and correct to speak of a thinker's ability to recognize that the truth condition for a sentence obtains.[29] But according to the present account, the observational case itself displays the same structure as the neo-Ramseyan account of quantification. The thought 'That box is cubic' has the truth condition it does because the constitutive counterfactual commitments of the thinker—roughly that in suitable circumstances the box would be perceived as cubic from different angles—are fulfilled if and only if the box really does have the shape of a cube. When we reflect on the observational case, it appears that there is no need to appeal to a thinker's recognition of a truth condition as obtaining for there to be manifestation of grasp of a classical truth condition: and no possibility of so appealing either, when we reflect on the irregular quadrilaterals and the rest. On the neo-Ramseyan account, universal quantification is just another illustration of this general point. There are special features peculiar respectively to observational concepts and to quantifiers; and there are mistaken ways of defending the classical truth conditions, many of which have been criticized by Dummett; but there remains on the present theory of content a level at which, in respect of the relations between truth and evidence, observational and universal quantificational contents are structurally identical.

3. The general Conjecture we formulated at the start of this paper can be made more convincing only by the detailed investigation of many other problematic kinds of content. The model of a content p and its associated canonical grounds $G(p)$ or commitments $C(p)$ is in no way sacrosanct in carrying out this programme. It is plausible that something different will be needed where the concept in question is governed by inferential principles. It may also be that for some contents—perhaps contents about inaccessible places and times—we need to draw on truth conditions of contents for which we already have a plausible implementation of the programme; these

---

[29] 'What is a Theory of Meaning? (II)', especially p. 98 ff.

would then be cases to which the second clause of our initial Conjecture would apply. But this is all speculative and tentative. As for the general programme, I conclude with two remarks. First, the cases we have considered suggest there cannot be a sound *general* argument that acceptance conditions fail to determine realistic truth conditions. Second, I have not been doubting that the correctness of an attribution of a particular truth condition must be manifested in the attributee's thought and action. The position towards which I have been moving can be summarized thus: manifestationism without verificationism.

CHAPTER 8

DOES *PHILOSOPHICAL INVESTIGATIONS* I.258–60 SUGGEST A COGENT ARGUMENT AGAINST PRIVATE LANGUAGE?*

CRISPIN WRIGHT

1. What is a 'Private' Language?

As the notion is usually understood in the literature, a private language is one which, necessarily, only one person can understand. Wittgenstein's own remarks (I. 243, 256)[1] may encourage such an interpretation. But it is not quite right. Intuitively, two people share an understanding of a predicate if what qualifies an item to fall within its extension is the same for both of them. Accordingly, if I somehow invented a language apt for the description of material— sensations, or whatever—in principle accessible only to myself, someone else might nevertheless understand the language: he would do so if he associated with its various descriptions material of the same respective kinds as I associated with them. This is just the natural and familiar thought that, while the phenomenological qualia associated by each of us with the word 'pain' are unknowable by anyone else, and are regarded as playing a constitutive role in our

* © Crispin Wright 1986. This material originated in one section of a paper on Kripke's interpretation presented to the 7th International Wittgenstein Symposium at Kirchberg-am-Wechsel, Austria, in 1982, and grew under the stimulus of seminars given in 1983–4 and 1984–5 at the Universities of Pennsylvania, Glasgow, Cambridge, Durham, Lampeter, Leeds, and Edinburgh; and at a Wittgenstein 'Workshop' held in Paris under the auspices of the Collège International de Philosophie. I am grateful to those who participated, for many helpful comments and criticisms, especially R. Rockingham Gill, Hugh Mellor, James Ross, Flint Schier, Bob Sharpe, John Skorupski, and Scott Weinstein. I should particularly like to thank Warren Goldfarb for his work, at my request, on the problems of the Appendix. The proof of claim (d) is due, in all essentials, to him. Finally, let me thank Simon Blackburn, Peter Carruthers, O. R. Jones, and Leslie Stevenson for useful comments on an earlier draft.

[1] All references are to *Philosophical Investigations* unless otherwise stated.

respective understandings of 'pain', there may nevertheless *be* mutual understanding if, as it happens, our qualia are appropriately similar. Only, if at all, in the case of proper names for which knowledge of reference is held necessary for understanding would the inaccessibility of my material to others be an essential bar to shared grasp.

A successful polemic against private language is meant, *inter alia*, to refute this picture of the meaning of sensation vocabulary. Since the picture does not entail that each of our idiolects of sensation is private in the standard sense,[2] we need to qualify somewhat the usual terms of the discussion. Private language had better be, not a language which necessarily only one person can understand, but a language which, necessarily, no two people can have adequate reason to believe they share. If your pain-quale is inaccessible to me and constitutive of your understanding of 'pain', what (uncontroversially) follows is not that your understanding cannot coincide with mine but only that I cannot have adequate reason to think that it does.

It merits remark that the inaccessibility, to others, of a speaker's material would not be the only possible source of private language (in the qualified sense). For the condition presented above as sufficient for shared understanding is also necessary: even if we are speaking of material accessible to everybody, shared understanding of an expression requires, in addition, that our uses of it be informed by the same conception of what qualifies an item to fall within its extension. So evidence of shared understanding has to involve evidence of a certain community of intention: evidence that we intend to let our respective uses of the expression be answerable to the same constraints. Now, a familiar sceptical line of reasoning aims to generate doubt whether a third party can ever have satisfactory evidence for the content of another's intention. If that were so, it would follow that intentions are, by their very nature, things which no two people can reasonably believe they share; so *all* language would be private, whether concerned with a publicly accessible subject matter or not.

The scepticism in question trades on the apparent first/third-person asymmetry in our knowledge of intention. *My* intentions (to

---

[2] As Edward Craig notes ('Privacy and Rule Following', in Jeremy Butterfield (ed.), *Language, Mind and Logic*, (CUP, Cambridge, 1986), this blocks any interpretation of Wittgenstein's argument which would build directly upon the impossibility of *consensus* in the description of private material.

prescind from consideration of the unconscious) are immediately, that is non-inferentially, available to me, and my beliefs about them are authoritative. For *your* intentions, on the other hand, I have only the evidence of what you say and do. What you say, however, is of no evidential use to me until it is interpreted; that is, until I have arrived at grounded hypotheses concerning the intentions which inform (your use of the ingredients in) your utterances. So your linguistic behaviour, it appears, can justify me in attributing a certain intention to you only if I assume knowledge of others of your intentions. Presumably, therefore, the *ultimate* basis for my beliefs about your intentions must lie in your non-linguistic and uninterpreted linguistic behaviour. And now it appears that this 'basis' must inevitably be hopelessly crude: that no end of alternative construals of your intentions, beliefs, and desires will be reconcilable with it. So, in outline, runs the sceptical argument: the prototype of the refinements respectively developed by Quine, in his writings on meaning and translation, and by Kripke, in his exegesis of Wittgenstein.

2. The Significance of the Issue

The philosophical consequences of the impossibility of private language will remain profound. First, solipsism will be an untenable position. Solipsism holds that no subject can have adequate reason to believe in the existence of any consciousness besides his own. It follows that no subject can have adequate reason to believe that he shares a language with another—since that would require belief in the *existence* of the other. From the standpoint of solipsism, language is essentially private; if there can be no such language, the solipsist is deprived of the medium in which to conduct his solipsistic dialectic. A demonstration of the impossibility of private language will therefore be a demonstration that there is error in any philosophy of mind, or epistemology, which has the consequence that the existence of another consciousness is at best a groundless assumption.

Second, a remodelling will be called for of the natural pre-philosophical conception, touched on above, of the kind of meaning possessed by our talk of sensations and other mental states. We tend to view the understanding each of us has of a word like 'pain' as possessing both a public and a subjective component. The public component is conceived as graspable by one incapable of feeling pain: it is constituted by our shared concept of what pain-behaviour is and of the consequences, personal and social, of someone's being in pain. The subjective component, in contrast, is fixed by the character of painful experience; only one who can suffer pain can imbue his understanding of the word with such a component, and the component is, in the nature of the case, idiosyncratic. Now, the niche here granted to a public component may be held to obviate any implication that the language of sensation, and of the passions generally, is already, for each of us, a private language. But if the felt quality of my experience has *some* part to play in determining the content of the relevant parts of my vocabulary, and if it is accepted that this quality can be known only by myself, it must follow, it seems, that we cannot have reason to think that we *fully* understand each other's talk of sensations, and so on. Besides, if it is coherent to grant that material in principle accessible only to me contributes at all towards determining what I mean, what obstacle can there be to the fiction of a language in which it makes the *sole* contribution—a full-fledged private language in just the sense we are concerned with? The pre-philosophical conception, even if it escapes the outcome that the language of sensations is already, for each of us, private, must at least, it appears, be committed to the *possibility* of a private language. Accordingly, a demonstration of its impossibility will be a demonstration that this conception cannot contain the germ of a satisfactory philosophical understanding of the language of mind.

The issue is potentially of significance in at least one other important respect, connected with the sceptical argument adumbrated above. The first/third-person asymmetry which we are tempted to find in the epistemology of intention is no less tempting, of course, in the case of a speaker's meaning; what *I* mean by an expression is available to me directly and with special surety, whereas the meaning *you* assign to that expression is, for me, a theoretical construct, earned by inference, and as precarious as any (strictly) unverifiable hypothesis. Once speaker's meaning is so conceived, we can hardly avoid thinking of a communal language as itself a theoretical postulate; something which, if it exists at all, is constituted by the overlapping of first-person transparent idiolects, but whose existence can be at best a good conjecture. Now, if the sceptical argument succeeds, 'good conjecture' has to be replaced by 'assumption'; and communal languages, if any exist, will have to be constituted by overlappings of private languages. So if the sort of sceptical argument adumbrated is sound or, more generally, if the first/third-person asymmetrical view destabilizes, under one form of pressure or another, to a point where only unjustifiable conjecture is available to a third person, then a demonstration of the impossibility of private language will accomplish a proof that the intuitive asymmetry is already a misconception; that no priority can coherently be accorded to the notion of an idiolect, conceived as first-person transparent, in an account of what a *communal* language is.[3]

The issue, then, really is a pivotal one in general epistemology, in the philosophy of mind, and in the philosophy of language. Not that I think that many are under any illusion about that. But a reminder may be salutary, when so much of the literature concentrates on its success or failure, of how deep the roots of significance of Wittgenstein's argument penetrate. And we need to be clear, as the above, I hope, makes it clear, that this depth is in no way compromised by the marginal re-interpretation of 'private language' with which I am going to work.

3. *Constraints on a Cogent Argument against Private Language*

A genuinely cogent argument against private language will have to observe a number of special constraints.

First, whatever the detail of the argument, it had better not have the additional strength sufficient to make trouble for Robinson Crusoe. A private language is to be a language which no two people can *in principle* have adequate reason to believe they share: if the argument seems to show that merely *practical* obstacles—like desert island isolation—defeat the possibility of language, then, even if we can find no fault in it, it will fail of cogency because seeming to prove too much. A cogent argument should be effective in the moulding of reasonable people's opinions. So no argument which generates a *paradox*, however seemingly watertight, can be cogent in the sense we require. To suppose that a solitary individual, even if isolated from birth, could not invent and utilize consistently (or as nearly consistently as need be) a system of notation could only be defensible, it

---

[3] Such a result would not have to be the death warrant of programmes—the most famous is H. P. Grice's—in which the notion of individual speaker's meaning is assigned priority. But it would require such programmes so to construe individual speakers' meanings as to build in third-person availability from the outset.

seems, if it could be shown that *any* sort of rule-following was impossible for such an individual. And that seems preposterous: there is no limit to the kinds of behaviour in which such an individual might engage which would be utterly inexplicable unless construed as involving purpose, insight, and the mastery of rules. (A nice example of Michael Dummett's: suppose Robinson finds a Rubik's Cube washed up on the beach, and learns to solve it. . . .)

A second constraint is similar but more immediate: 'going public', as it were, must make all the difference. There are two ways in which this constraint might be violated. First, a seemingly genuine problem might be disclosed in private language which, however, would remain even after sufficient alteration in the content of its vocabulary to enable a number of speakers reasonably to believe that they had the language in common. Obviously, whatever independent interest the problem might then possess, it could not provide the basis of a specific argument against private language. And the same holds, secondly, if, although going public would solve a specific difficulty disclosed with private language, some relevantly *analogous* difficulty could plausibly be argued to beset language in general. A cogent argument against private language must leave communal language alone. Abstractly so presented, the point might seem hardly worth stating. But it has been violated by a number of interpretations of Wittgenstein, favoured both by sympathizers and critics; and it should anyway alert us to the risk attending the reading of Wittgenstein in this context as any sort of epistemological *sceptic*, despite the temptations posed by passages like I. 265.

A third desideratum, if not quite a constraint, is that the argument should be effective against two quite different opponents. The usual antagonist, for most commentators, has been *Cartesianism* about sensations: a standpoint according to which not merely are sensations private to a subject, but they constitute necessarily self-intimating material—no aspect of whose character can pass unnoticed—about which the subject's opinions have an error-proof authority. Now, no doubt the privacy of sensation has some connection, in Cartesian thinking, with its putatively self-intimating and indefeasibly certain character. But that there is at any rate no entailment is evident in the possibility of a weaker standpoint—that of the *Fallibilist*—according to which the subject may be sincerely mistaken, or fall prey to oversight, in the description of his sensations, or other psychological material, its privacy notwithstanding. The

Cartesian conception encourages us to think of our sensations as events played out on a stage to which necessarily we alone are witness, but there is no reason why such a picture has to involve the idea that our witness has to be all-seeing and error-proof. Yet the Fallibilist standpoint—well represented in recent literature[4]—is as much committed to the possibility of private language: if you are privy, albeit fallibly, to events and processes of a kind of which you and I can never be *jointly* aware, even in principle, there is no means whereby I can make the sort of comparison between our respective linguistic behaviour necessary if I am to arrive at reason to think that we share an understanding of the language which we use to describe that material. Something worthy of the title of a demonstration of the impossibility of private language ought, therefore, to be effective against this weaker position. An argument of less general bearing, trading upon the additional features present in Cartesianism proper, might still be of some interest. But it would necessitate no more than repair to the Cartesian philosophy of mind; it would not extract the root. And it could not have the wider sort of philosophical significance outlined in section 2.

4. Three Interpretations of I.258–60

It is worth quoting in full G. E. M. Anscombe's translation of the passage with which we are especially concerned:

258. Let us imagine the following case. I want to keep a diary about the recurrence of a certain sensation. To this end I associate it with the sign '*S*' and write this sign in the calendar for every day on which I have the sensation.—I will remark first of all that a definition of the sign cannot be formulated.—But still I can give myself a kind of ostensive definition—how? Can I point to the sensation? Not in the ordinary sense. But I speak, or write the sign down, and at the same time I concentrate my attention on the sensation—and so, as it were, point to it inwardly.—But what is this ceremony for? For that is all it seems to be! A definition surely serves to establish the meaning of a sign.—Well, that is done precisely by the concentrating of my attention; for in this way I impress on myself the connection between the sign and the sensation.—But 'I impress it on myself' can only mean: This process brings it about that I remember the connection *right* in the future. But in the

---

[4] See, for instance, Ross Harrison, *On What There Must Be* (Clarendon Press, Oxford, 1974), Chapters 3 and 6; and Simon Blackburn, 'The Individual Strikes Back', *Synthese*, lviii (1984), 281–301.

present case I have no criterion of correctness. One would like to say: whatever is going to seem right to me is right. And that only means that here we can't talk about 'right'.

259. Are the rules of the private language *impressions* of rules?—The balance on which impressions are weighed is not the *impression* of a balance.

260. 'Well, I *believe* that this is the sensation *S* again'.—Perhaps you *believe* that you believe it! . . .

The principal question is: what is the thought at the end of I.258? Why should it follow, if 'whatever is going to seem right to me is right', that the very notion of the *correctness* of the private linguist's would-be descriptions is emptied of content? Wittgenstein's transition has, indeed, the appearance of simple question-begging against the Cartesian; for if infallible authority, about any subject matter, were ever a possibility, then—trivially—whatever seemed right to the authority would be right. The Cartesian conception is exactly that each of us is such an authority for the character of his own sensations. A reader could be forgiven the impression that Wittgenstein has done nothing to disclose a specific fault in that conception of *sensation*; his reservation, whatever it is, would apply, it seems, to any such putative cognitive authority. And, whether one intuitively suspects the coherence of the idea of such authority or not, it does seem unclear what exactly the reservation is.

It will be useful to consider a number of interpretations which contrast with the one I want eventually to recommend. There is, to begin with, the possibility of reading the passage along the following, broadly verificationist lines. Meaning is an essentially normative notion: if an action—like making a noise, or marking down a symbol—is to be credited with meaning, there has accordingly to be sense in the distinction between situations in which tokens of that action accord with this meaning and situations in which they do not. This is as much as to say that, from the point of view of a subject, trying to keep his actions in accordance with the meaning, there must be sense in the distinction between what seems right to him and what is right. For someone of verificationist sympathies, however, there has to be doubt about the *content* of a distinction which no one can possibly be in a position to exploit: a distinction, that is, between states of affairs which, in the nature of the case, cannot be verified to obtain independently of each other. For the verificationist, then, there is, in the case of putatively private language, doubt about the sense of a distinction which *has* to make sense if the notion of meaning, and with it that of language, is to have any proper application.

The spirit of this train of thought could, of course, be formulated and refined in various ways. It is notable, in particular, that its purpose would be as well served by the slogan 'Meaning is Use' as by explicit versions of the verification principle. For it is exactly the lack of any contrastive *uses* for 'seems right to me' and 'is right' which Wittgenstein seems to be presenting as undermining any contrast in their content. I myself would not regard the presence of verificationist premisses as importing any error of substance. Indeed, I had better declare now that the interpretation I shall eventually recommend is not guaranteed to disturb the privacy of a theorist who is *sufficiently* resolute and comprehensive in his fidelity to the verification-transcendent. Nevertheless, the rather *direct* play which the kind of argument sketched makes with a quite general principle about meaning has to be associated with costs in point of pure cogency. The point is simply the unlikelihood that purely theoretical argument can provide absolutely compelling support for such a general principle: however well grounded it may seem, in the abstract, to be, consequences of a sufficiently *outré* character will generate suspicion. Anyone who wishes to base far-reaching metaphysical conclusions on (an analogue of) the verification principle had better recognize the substantial body of philosophical opinion which is prepared to find others of the known consequences of the principle to be sufficiently implausible to discredit its use as a tool of persuasion.

The answer provided by this first interpretation to our title question is, in effect: yes, provided there is a cogent argument for the verification principle, or for the principle that differences in meaning have to correspond to differences in use. What, I am suggesting, is doubtful is whether we have any conception of what it would be for argument in support of a principle of such generality to be *cogent* if 'intuitions' about the plausibility or implausibility of consequences are not allowed to come into play; and doubtful, in consequence, whether something as controversial as the present question can be resolved by an argument which relies directly on a general principle of this sort.

A second, quite natural interpretation finds Wittgenstein's thought to be that the private linguist has no basis for trust in his own judgement, no effective controls on his own competence to practise the system of concepts which he believes his private language to encode. Now this is, I believe, a point that Wittgenstein is keen to have recognized; it may plausibly be read into I.265 and seems to be exactly the thrust of

> Always get rid of the idea of the private object in this way: assume that it constantly changes, but that you do not notice the change because your memory constantly deceives you (II, xi, p. 207).

It is, from the inner perspective of the private linguist, all the same whether his ongoing practice keeps accord with the original, putatively definitive use of '*S*', or whether his memory of the kind of sensation he wished to mark lets him down repeatedly and in diverse ways, so that his use of '*S*' is actually quite chaotic. And there is, of course, no *other* perspective to be had. But what exactly does the point show? That the Cartesian conception of the inner, characterized above, is itself unstable under sceptical attack. Wittgenstein is urging on the Cartesian the realization that there is a difference between a guaranteed *fit* between impressions and fact and the mere inability to distinguish them. Once it is insisted that there really is to be such a thing as a *correct* description, in the private language, of the subject's occurrent sensation, whose correctness is settled by the character of that sensation and the original private ostensive definition, there is absolutely no basis for an opinion about the reliability or otherwise of the subject's impression—so scepticism seems to be the only rational standpoint.

The point is well taken. But, whatever Wittgenstein's intention, it is plain that it is effective only against the Cartesian and does not tell against the possibility of private language as such. The Fallibilist counter will be to acknowledge that, ultimately, there is no decisive riposte to sceptical doubt about his private linguistic competence, but then to enquire how exactly 'going public' would get around the difficulty. For one thing, the subject will still need to rely upon his own memory, and other faculties, if he is to make effective use of others' judgements as a check on his own, since ultimately he must judge for himself what their judgements are and whether they accord or conflict with his.[5] For another, no sooner do we admit—as we

---

[5] A point first made, I believe, by A. J. Ayer in the symposium with Rush Rhees, 'Can there be a Private Language?', *Aristotelian Society Supp. Vol.* xxviii (1954), 251–85; see p. 256.

are inclined to do—that correctness is never *constituted* by a community-wide consensus than we leave scope for a similar kind of sceptical doubt about the shared judgements of the speakers of a public language: if coincidence between correctness and communal consensus is a matter of the proper functioning of individuals' faculties, it is difficult to see what could obstruct the possibility of sceptical query, of one or another familiar sort, about whether, in any particular case or range of cases, such proper functioning had taken place. If, on the other hand, there proved to be some sort of *conceptual* connection between correctness and the considered verdict of a whole linguistic community, that might well exempt the community from forms of sceptical doubt to which the private linguist is vulnerable; but it would be a conclusion for which we still await the supporting argument—which would have to embrace considerations quite outwith the scope of the interpretation we are presently considering. If this interpretation were correct, indeed, the verdict would have to be that, as a purported demonstration of the impossibility of private language, I.258–261 falls foul of *each* of the three constraints outlined above.

There is evidence, however, that Wittgenstein may have wished a would-be believer in the possibility of private language to ponder what is apparently a deeper-reaching sceptical doubt.[6] A little earlier (I.237) he writes

Imagine someone using a line as a rule in the following way: He holds a pair of compasses, and carries one of its points along the line that is the 'rule', while the other one draws the line that follows the rule. And while he moves along the ruling line he alters the opening of the compasses, apparently with great precision, looking at the rule the whole time as if it determined what he did. And watching him we see no kind of regularity in this opening and shutting of the compasses. We cannot learn his way of following the line from it. Here perhaps one really would say: 'The original seems to *intimate* to him which way he is to go. But it is not a rule.'

The quotation reminds us that there is a difference between following a rule and acting under a sense of constraint; it is even possible, as a result of hypnosis or in the throes of who-knows-what sort of

---

[6] This line is briefly canvassed, if I read him correctly, in Leslie Stevenson's *The Metaphysics of Experience* (Clarendon Press, Oxford, 1982), 45–6.

manic episode, to have the impression that you are rule-following, that your performance is guided by a concept, when that is not the case. The practice of the private language is to be, at least, a rule-governed practice. What reason, then, can the private linguist offer *himself* for thinking that he genuinely has such a practice, that his performance is not to be compared to that of the lunatic with a pair of compasses?

This train of thought is in one way more, and in another less sceptical than that which we have just discarded. It is more sceptical because what is in doubt is not the *reliability* of the judgements of the private linguist but whether he is so much as making judgements at all; at issue is not what grounds there are to think that the private linguist is competent to follow certain rules but what grounds there are to think that there are any appropriate rules in the offing. But the train of thought is, at least arguably, also less sceptical inasmuch as it does not seem to need recourse to doubt about the subject's memory. Under the second interpretation, we were to imagine that changes in the type of sensation which the subject was willing to describe as '*S*' are compensated for by changes in his memory of the kind of sensation which he originally so baptized; but the delusion, whatever exactly its nature, suffered by the lunatic with the compasses need not involve, it seems, his misremembering anything. This asymmetry holds out the promise that the interpretation may serve better than its predecessor. Challenged to produce a reason for thinking that he is using '*S*' correctly, the private linguist will naturally refer to his memories of his previous practice; the challenge, if it is to continue, must then assume the form of a demand for reason to rely on those memories. But, challenged to give himself reason to think that he is so much as following rules at all, it is not clear that the private linguist has even the beginnings of a reply. If the lunatic need be under no *further* illusion about his previous conduct and experience, a debate (with his doctor, say) about whether he really is rule-following will have to involve considerations of a quite different kind. And now what could such debate pivot around except the capacity of the lunatic to explain, or of others to interpret, either the specific rule which he believes himself to be following or, at least, the *kind* of rule it might be—perhaps one too complex for others to follow, for example—and what was at stake for him in his pursuit of it? The emergent suggestion is, accordingly, that nothing counts as giving yourself, or anyone else, reason to take certain episodes of your behaviour as genuine cases of rule-following which does not consist in supplying reason for thinking that it could reasonably be so interpreted *by others*.

This seems a promising outline, whose detail it may well be possible to fill in convincingly. If so, the private linguist does confront a distinctive difficulty: he cannot give himself even the weakest reason for thinking that he has a rule-governed practice. Robinson Crusoe, in contrast, need confront no such difficulty; at least, it is not an *immediate* consequence of his social isolation that nothing in the course of his experience, as he interacts with his desert island environment, can give him reason to think that others would reasonably regard him as rule-following if appropriately placed to attempt to interpret his behaviour. Naturally, he may have no defence against a *sceptical* doubt on the point; but the challenge to the private linguist, under this third interpretation of the argument, is not to produce sceptic-proof reason to think that he is rule-following, but merely to show that he is in no way disadvantaged by comparison with Robinson or the individual in the community. Since it seems clear, in addition, that it is merely privacy, rather than the assumption of any sort of Cartesian certitude, which gives rise to the difficulty, we appear to have the germ of an argument which, if successfully developed, might succeed in observing all the outlined constraints.

However, second thoughts are less encouraging. Even if we anticipate a completely convincing demonstration that the range of reasons to believe a subject to be rule-following is restricted in the way suggested, two major sources of dissatisfaction remain. First, accepting that no one can have even the weakest reason for supposing that the private linguist has a rule-governed practice, transition to the conclusion that it cannot be *true* that he does would seem to require mediation by some general form of verificationism, so that the cogency of the argument confronts the same impediment as afflicted the first interpretation. Second, whatever the extent of one's sympathies with verificationism, the fact is that there is a large class of propositions whose acceptance is normal among us, and whose non-acceptance, in very many cases, would be unthinkable, for which we nevertheless can supply no solid reason. Examples like 'There exist other consciousnesses besides my own', 'The world did not come into being five minutes ago', 'There are material bodies' all have the feature that they are *beyond* evidential support: that unless they are presupposed, nothing counts as support for the sort of more specific claims from which they may be inferred. Simon Blackburn[7] makes a case for supposing that a similar groundlessness ultimately belongs to the belief that we share communal language; if that is so, the third interpretation does not, after all, fully satisfy the second of our earlier constraints. But whether Blackburn is right in detail matters less than the reflection that we do not in general wish to equate groundlessness with unacceptability (or, if we do, it is only human irrationality which explains why scepticism is not a dominant ideology). Accordingly, the groundlessness of the private linguist's belief that he has a rule-governed practice would not be *eo ipso* a criticism of that belief; it would remain to be shown that it is not a belief to which he is perfectly entitled, a framework belief, as it were, comparable in its own sphere to our belief in the existence of other minds or of material bodies.

Each of the three interpretations, even if not providing something fully cogent, nevertheless affords a useful and instructive version of the argument. Collectively, they suggest that a defender of private language had better be anti-verificationist, anti-Cartesian, and a proponent of the propriety of groundless belief. It immediately occurs to one to wonder whether this is a consistent set of characteristics: whether, in particular, an anti-verificationist can make a decent fist of explaining our entitlement to beliefs which, on his construal, are associated with transcendent truth-conditions for whose obtaining we can, in the nature of the case, have absolutely no evidence. One possible way of completing the demolition of private language would be to show that there is indeed an irresoluble tension here. Another would be to show that the province of legitimate but groundless belief cannot extend to the case in point. And a third would be, of course, further research into the semantic presuppositions of verificationism. In each of these various ways, then, the issue is very open. However I do not think that we have yet considered the most persuasive version of Wittgenstein's train of thought, a version which, although textual evidence can be found in support of each of the interpretations so far considered, arguably best fits the actual letter of I.258–61. Before we do so, let me briefly explain why I believe the interpretation which takes centre stage in Saul Kripke's *Wittgen-*

---

[7] Loc. cit., pp. 291 and following.

stein on Rules and Private Language[8] ultimately affords no cogent argument against the possibility of private language.

5. *Kripke's Interpretation*

A wide class of long-standing philosophical disputes pivots on the question whether the statements of some problematic region of discourse—ethics, aesthetics, theoretical science, and pure mathematics are the most immediate examples—should be regarded as having a *genuinely factual* subject matter, or whether—as argued for example by certain forms of ethical prescriptivism, and by scientific instrumentalism—their grammatical form contrives to mask the fact that their role is not that of fact-stating at all.

There are a variety of ways in which an anti-factualist standpoint might be supported. One way—essentially Hume's strategy with statements about causation—would be to argue that a preferred epistemology recognizes no means for our attaining any adequate conception of the putative species of fact. Thus there is, for Hume, within the means provided by his preferred empiricist epistemology, no way of attaining any satisfactory idea of the *necessitation* which the causal relation is supposed to involve; the way is then open—or so Hume believes—to regard that component as marking, rather, the projection of an attitude which human beings naturally take up towards tried and tested regularities. A second approach would be to attempt to establish a topic-neutral account of ways in which the distinction between fact-stating and non-fact-stating declarative sentences emerges in their uses, and then apply that account to the problematic class in question. The difficulty with this way of proceeding, of course, is that the general topic-neutral account has not merely to isolate marks of a distinction which we already perfectly understand but must, in addition, go some way towards legitimating the distinction.

There is, however, a rather ingenious third strategy. The leading idea is that any genuine species of fact ought to be knowable by an appropriately endowed subject. Accordingly, if we can specify what powers a subject would have to have in order to be in a position to know a fact of some putative species, and if it then emerges that even

---

[8] Blackwell, Oxford, 1982.

such a subject could make no such defensible knowledge claim (could provide no compelling reason for preferring one such claim to another incompatible with it), it must follow that there cannot be any such facts in the first place. It is this third strategy which informs the Sceptical Argument which Kripke finds at the heart of Wittgenstein's discussion of following a rule in I.185–242. The conclusion of the argument, as Kripke interprets it, is that all talk of meaning and understanding ceases to qualify as factual, so that there are no objective truths about, for example, what particular expressions mean, or how subjects understand them, or what specific uses accord with their meanings.

An argument against private language now emerges under the aegis of a non-factualist reconstrual of this region of discourse. It is this reconstrual which Kripke, following the Humean model, calls a Sceptical Solution. Sentences like 'Jones means addition by "plus"' and 'If Jones means addition by "plus", he will answer "259" when asked "What is 132 + 127?"' may still, according to the Sceptical Solution, possess a determinate use even if divested of objective truth conditions. And the respective uses which they have are, roughly, to ratify Jones's membership of the class of speakers whose uses of 'plus' are generally reliable, and to express a test for membership in that class which the speaker believes would be ratified by the responses of those already accredited with membership. The suggestion, in general, is that once we prescind from the idea that talk of meaning and understanding is apt to convey substantial matters of fact and look instead to an account of the role and purposes which such talk plays in our lives, we find that there is invariably a reference, explicit or implicit, to the linguistic practices of a speech *community*. Kripke's interpretation of the private language argument would then draw the conclusion that such a reference is essential to the legitimate use of those concepts, and that they can accordingly have no proper application to the activities of a would-be private linguist.

The foregoing is just the barest outline of Kripke's interpretation: it can convey little of the excitement and fertility of Kripke's book to someone unfamiliar with it. But it will serve to indicate various points at which, in my judgement, Kripke's version of the private language argument fails of cogency. To begin with, the whole package can succeed—obviously—only if the Sceptical Argument succeeds, and it is open to serious question whether it does so; I have, however, already had occasion to try to indicate places where the Sceptical Argument seems to me to go astray, and I have no space to elaborate on that discussion here.[9] There are, however, two slightly less obvious points. First, even if the success of the Sceptical Argument were assumed, much more would need to be done to explain why the Sceptical Solution is not just an optional extra. Hume *could* quite consistently have drawn the conclusion that we should simply drop the notion of causation as a piece of discredited mythology. Kripke writes as though a parallel option was not available in the case of meaning, since it would involve us in the 'incredible and self-defeating conclusion that all language is meaningless'.[10] But that cannot be the right way of formulating the conclusion of the Sceptical Argument, since it involves, in effect, descriptive use of the very notion whose grip on reality the Sceptical Argument aims to dislodge. It is rather as if we construed the conclusion of Hume's argument as being that all regular associations between events are *coincidental*, when the point is rather that nothing in the world—if the argument is sound—corresponds to our distinction between causal and coincidental regularity. The conclusion of the Sceptical Argument must—at least if it is to be a factual claim—be something expressible without recourse to any notion cognate to that of meaning; so it cannot be the 'incredible and self-defeating' conclusion described by Kripke.

Quite how it should be formulated is a question which we can leave to be pondered by proponents of the argument. For present purposes it suffices merely to note that it is at least not obvious that the conclusion has to take a self-defeating form; and that what would be called for would presumably be something akin to the Quinean programme for an account of language, and language-related institutions, in which the traditional notion of meaning plays no part. It is accordingly an *assumption* that the Sceptical Solution is so much as called for, and any conclusion about private language, drawn in the manner indicated, can so far at best be provisional. The argument needs a back-up demonstration either that no Quinean

---

[9] See 'Kripke's Account of the Argument against Private Language', *Journal of Philosophy*, lxxxi (1984), 759–78. For additional criticism of the way Kripke involves the community in the Sceptical Solution, see Warren Goldfarb's critical study of Kripke's book, in the same journal, lxxxii (1985), 471–88.

[10] Kripke, loc. cit., p. 71.

account of language can be satisfactory or that such an account would independently be inhospitable to private language.

It is in any case open to question whether the Sceptical Solution is so much as coherent. The problem is that the notion of meaning is platitudinously connected with that of truth: whether an utterance expresses a truth is a function only of its content and the state of the world in relevant respects; and the content of the utterance is, in turn, a function of the meanings of its constituents, the way in which they are therein put together, and the context. So if there were no facts about meaning, it would appear to follow—by the compelling principle that non-factuality among the parameters in a question must divest the question of factuality too—that there can be no facts about an utterance's truth value either. Such an outcome would call into question the very possibility of explaining what exactly it is that the non-factualist about a given region of discourse intends to hold.

There is no doubt a great deal of scope for further exploration of the implications of and possibilities for Kripke's interpretation. But perhaps enough has been said to justify the claim that, whatever else such exploration might teach us, it is unlikely to disclose the cogent argument which we seek.

6. *The Recommended Interpretation*

The verificationist interpretation appealed, in effect, to the idea that the independence of the requirements of a rule from what anyone takes them to be is a precondition of genuine rule-following; so that the need for a distinction between what seems right to the private linguist and what really is right is a simple consequence of the consideration that private language, like all language, is to be a rule-governed practice. But the trouble is that exactly this platitudinous-seeming conception of the autonomy of rules is one of the things which is under scrutiny in the discussion of rule-following in the *Investigations* and *Remarks on the Foundations of Mathematics*. A typical passage (RFM IV.48):

Then might it not be said that the *rules* lead this way, even if no-one went it? For that is what one would like to say—and here we see the mathematical machine, which, driven by the rules themselves, obeys only mathematical laws and not physical ones. I want to say: that the working of the mathematical machine is only the *picture* of the working of a machine. The rule does not do work, for whatever happens according to the rule is an interpretation of the rule.

I do not believe that Wittgenstein intended to question the *correctness* of the platitudinous conception: his intention was rather to expose certain misunderstandings of it to which he believed we are prone. But we would need to be sure, it seems, exactly how matters stand with the autonomy of rules before the earlier verificationist interpretation of the private language argument could be considered cogent, even if the correctness of some appropriate form of verificationism were assumed. Fortunately, we can bypass the issue. There is a different, somewhat more subtle route to the perception that a 'seems right'/'is right' distinction is prerequisite for the private linguist's enterprise, which there is some textual evidence Wittgenstein may have had in mind.

The suggestive passage is the exchange in I.260 quoted above:

'Well, I *believe* that this is the sensation *S* again.'—Perhaps you *believe* that you believe it!. . .

Wittgenstein's response to his interlocutor has no point unless he thinks that he—the interlocutor—may believe that he has such a belief yet be wrong. But in what circumstances can a second-order belief—a belief about one's beliefs—be incorrect? The sort of cases that most immediately spring to mind would involve the conception that the true character of one's (first-order) beliefs can be veiled in the sort of way that notions like self-deception, or the psychoanalytic idea of the unconscious, standardly presuppose. But that sort of example is not to our purpose. A quite different possibility—the one which, I suggest, Wittgenstein is getting at—is that *X*'s belief that he believes that *P* is false because there is *no such thing as* the belief that *P*. That will be the situation whenever the clause apparently specifying the propositional content of the supposed first-order belief, although prima facie apt for that role, actually fails to have the appropriate kind of content. A genuine belief is an attitude to the type of state of affairs described by the clause which specifies the content of the belief, namely the conviction that it is realized. So if there simply is no such thing as that type of state of affairs (which is not, of course, the same issue as whether there exists a particular state of affairs of that type), no more can there be any such belief. Accordingly, if the clause purportedly supplying the content of the belief belongs to a family of declarative sentences which correspond to no genuine matters of fact, it cannot be used to specify the content of a possible belief. (You can no more believe something which is not apt to be genuinely true or false than you can wonder what is the answer to something which is not really a question.)

On this interpretation, then, Wittgenstein's suggestion is that the existence of a genuine distinction between what seems right to the private linguist and what is right is necessary if the private language is to be apt for the making of *genuine statements*. And so there would be a point of affinity with Kripke's discussion. Only Wittgenstein's point would not be that talk of meaning and understanding *in general* lacks a factual subject matter, but that the 'sentences' of a private language cannot qualify as having a factual subject matter unless the 'seems right'/'is right' distinction can be made good for them—which, he has suggested in I.258, it cannot.[11]

Argument is now needed for two claims: first, that there is indeed the connection between the 'seems right'/'is right' distinction and factuality which the interpretation demands; and second, that the distinction eludes the resources of the private linguist.

The grounds for the first claim are relatively straightforward. What, more exactly, is at issue is whether the sentences of a given family are apt for the expression of fact only if:

(a) X believes what 'P' expresses

and

(b)   What 'P' expresses is true

have an appropriately contrasting content where 'P' is any of (appropriately many of)[12] the sentences in question. Now, it is in the nature of facts to stand to us in various cognitive relations—like

---

[11] What will follow, if Wittgenstein is correct, is not, strictly, that private language is impossible, but that it cannot provide a medium for the formulation of genuine statements, commands, questions, wishes, the framing of hypotheses, or any kind of speech act which presupposes the availability in the language of the means for depicting genuine states of affairs. It is a further question whether anything so impoverished as to lack all these expresive resources could qualify as a language (perhaps a private language apt only for the expression of expletives would still be a possibility). However since all the lines of thought which attract, or pressure, towards the possibility of private language involve regarding it as a medium for expression of knowledge, there is no comfort for anyone in such a possibility—if possibility it be.

[12] There are very delicate questions here concerning what, if any, notion of a *family* of sentences would sustain the validity of the principle that if some members of a family are factual, all are; and whether every member of such a family should be required to admit the (a)/(b) contrast; and who X may be. Presentation of the argument which follows does not require us to engage them—though a supporter of the Blackburn/Harrison strategy (see below) would have a definite interest in doing so.

being known, overlooked, reasonably supposed, and so on. A realist (contrast: verificationist) may press us to countenance in addition a class of facts which are cognitively inaccessible, about which neither knowledge nor reasonable opinion can be achieved. Whatever the merit of that thought, it at least suggests an argument by dilemma. If '*P*' is apt for the expression of fact, then there must at least be sense in the idea of a subject standing in one of the various possible cognitive relations to facts which are relevant to the appraisal of '*P*'. So if—going along with the realist—all such facts are inaccessible, *X* can only be ignorant of them, and any belief he has about the status of '*P*' can have no bearing on the likelihood of its truth. If, on the other hand, certain relevant such facts are accessible, the cognitive processes involved in their investigation must nevertheless be *fallible*, and hence any opinions formed by *X* as a result of such investigation can be at best a fallible guide to the likelihood of the truth of '*P*'. Either way, there will be no entailment from (a) to (b); either way, then, there has to be an appropriate contrast in their content.

An immediate afterthought is that this reasoning begs the question against the Cartesian. The Cartesian conception is exactly that a subject's sensations, for instance, constitute a domain which is transparent to him, about which his judgements cannot be mistaken; so if '*P*' and the other sentences in the family are apt for the description of such a domain, the entailment from (a) to (b) must go through. Admittedly, we have already recorded a doubt, in discussion of the second interpretation above of Wittgenstein's argument, whether the Cartesian account can defend itself against scepticism. But that would not exonerate the present interpretation from the charge of question-begging. It would be better to show that the Cartesian is committed to upholding a contrast in content between (a) and (b) for a different reason.

Well, that can be shown quite easily. For the Cartesian claim is precisely that *X* possesses certain *guarantees* when it comes to judgement concerning the character of, for example, his own sensations which he does not possess elsewhere. This claim has to be understood as comparable to the claim, for example, that the arithmetical functions, x^2 and $8(x-1)-4$, although divergent in value generally, necessarily coincide in value when $x=6$. There is no way of understanding what the Cartesian believes is guaranteed to *X* unless we take it that the sentence forming operators, '*X* believes what——expresses' and 'What——expresses is true' have their standard senses. Any substitution, within their gaps, of a sentence with a factual subject matter about which X has no Cartesian authority will reveal, by the argument just run through, that those senses are different. Hence the Cartesian has to grant that there will be some sort of difference of sense in the sentences which result respectively from substitution of a sentence about whose subject matter X *does* have Cartesian authority, notwithstanding the mutual entailment which he then wishes to claim.

So much, then, for the first claim. The second claim is that such an 'appropriately contrasting content' cannot be given to (a) and (b) if 'P' is a sentence of a putative private language. But what exactly should count as the existence of the appropriate kind of contrast? The Cartesian at least is in no position to advert to a difference in the *truth conditions* of sentences corresponding as (a) and (b).[13] And a moment's reflection discloses that the obvious thought—namely that (a) and (b) differ in content merely because the sentence-forming operators which they respectively involve are different—is merely question-begging. For that consideration suffices for them to differ in content only if 'P' expresses an argument appropriate for those operators to be applied to, that is, expresses a thought apt to be believed or true—the very point at issue.[14] So how should matters proceed?

The least that is required, it seems, is that the *information* conveyed by (a) should differ from that conveyed by (b). And it is plausible that, for a large class of examples, two items of information differ just in case there can be such a thing as reasonably regarding oneself as possessing one without the other. It is in exactly this sense that the informational content of two logically equivalent sentences may diverge, since unawareness of a logical equivalence need not be unreasonable. So let us propose as a general, though perhaps not exceptionless, principle that items of information coincide for a subject just in case to have reason to accept either, in a sense which need not involve closure under logical implication, involves, for him, hav-

---

[13] How far the Fallibilist, on the other hand, might get with a purely truth-conditional construal of the (a)/(b) contrast is a question for section 10.

[14] I do not mean to deny that 'X believes what "P" expresses' and 'What "P" expresses is true' have different meanings even if 'P' is not so apt, or is not a declarative sentence at all. But the Cartesian requires, in addition, that they be capable of simultaneous *truth*. It is that which the 'argument' from difference of composition cannot, unsupplemented, give him.

ing reason to accept both. Now there ought, presumably, to be no objection to supposing, of any particular belief held for good reason, that the subject is aware that he has reason for that particular belief. (That is: if there is no conceptual difficulty in the idea of a particular subject having reason for a particular belief, it cannot *introduce* a difficulty to suppose that he is aware of the fact.) It follows that—unless they are to be exceptions for the principle—we are entitled to regard (a) and (b) as conveying different items of information only if someone could have reason to believe one but not the other and could be aware of the fact. The argument will now be that when '*P*' is, putatively, a sentence of a language which no two people can reasonably believe they share, that is not a possibility.

It will suffice to consider four cases. Letting '*A*' range over believing subjects, we have

(i) *A* is aware of possessing both reason to believe (a) and reason to doubt (b);

(ii) *A* is aware of possessing both reason to doubt (a) and reason to believe (b);

(iii) *A* is aware of possessing both reason to believe (a) and no reason to believe (b);

(iv) *A* is aware of possessing both reason to believe (b) and no reason to believe (a).

Our question is whether any of (i)–(iv) represents a possible conscious state of information either for an *A* who is some *Y* other than *X*, or for *X* himself. But no *Y* distinct from *X* can, it appears, enjoy any of the four states. Consider states (ii) and (iv). Both involve *Y*'s possession of reason to believe that '*P*' expresses a truth. But he cannot have reason to think that he knows *what* truth it expresses since, by hypothesis, '*P*' is a sentence of a language private to *X*, a language which no one could have reason to think he shares with *X*. So the only ground *Y* could have for supposing '*P*' true would be *X*'s authority on the matter—which contradicts the supposition that *Y* has reason to doubt (a), or at least no reason to believe it, which (ii) and (iv) respectively involve.

State (i) involves *Y*'s possession of reason to doubt that '*P*' expresses a truth despite accepting that *X* believes that it does: that would require either that *Y* has some independent purchase on what

'*P*' says—contrary to hypothesis—or, at least, that he has reason to
think that some third party does who does not share *X*'s view and in
whom *Y* places greater trust. But what reason could *Y* have for
thinking that *X* and the third party share an understanding of '*P*'
when the hypothesis of privacy dictates that the third party could
have no such reason?

Y's enjoyment of state (iii) might seem less problematic. If, after
all, *Y* has no conception of the meaning of '*P*', he can have no reason
to think either that *X* is, or that he is not, more likely than not to be
reliable about the sort of subject matter with which it deals. Hence
he has no reason to regard grounds for thinking that *X* believes '*P*'
to express a truth as tending to support (b). But one trouble with this
thought is that it illicitly equates the supposition that the sense of '*P*'
is private to *X*—that is, that it is impossible for *Y* to have reason to
think that he shares an understanding of '*P*' with *X*—with its being
impossible for *Y* to have *any* conception of the kind of subject matter that '*P*' deals with. That is not an equation which can be
endorsed by the defender of the possibility of private language about
the psychological. It is, for example, supposed to be consistent with
my recognition that I can know neither the specific character of your
sensations nor (in full) the meaning of the language in which you describe them that I can nevertheless apply the concept of sensation to
you and hence have a general idea of the kind of thing which, when
you give voice to the character of your sensations, you seek to describe. Generally, if one may at least suppose that '*P*', as used by *X*,
concerns some aspect or other of *X*'s psychological state, then one is
bound to take reason for (a) as supporting (b); and note that the
point is not dependent on crediting *X* with Cartesian authority for
his psychological states—it is enough that he be any sort of (fallible)
authority about them, that his opinions about them count for something.

In section 2 I noted a different kind of pressure for admitting private language, exerted by sceptical predations on the communicabi-
lity of intention in general and hence of idiolectic semantic rules in
particular. If the possibility, indeed the universality of private
language were granted for that sort of reason, there would not, presumably, be the sort of difficulty with (iii) just described. But there is
a different, prospectively insuperable difficulty, connected with an
aspect of the holistically interlocking character of psychological concepts. Without attempting detailed argument, it is at least highly

plausible that it is only on the hypothesis of a subject's possession of certain intentions that his linguistic or non-linguistic behaviour can be regarded as expressive of a certain belief. The relevant sort of example is familiar: dashing out into a street full of traffic may evince the belief that there is space to cross safely to the other side, if we assume, say, that the subject intends to make an appointment in fifteen minutes' time; but the same action may also evince the belief that there is no such space, if we assume the subject's intention to be suicide. The point, then, is that if we really took seriously the idea that all intention is inscrutable from a third person's point of view, we should surely be committed to saying the same about belief; and case (iii) would be precluded not because reason to believe (a) would give Y reason to believe (b) but because he could not have reason to believe (a) in any case.

Let us try matters from X's own point of view. We can immediately discount (i) and (ii). If X were to enjoy the state of information described by (ii) he would be in a position to claim ' "P" is true but I do not believe it'—precisely Moore's 'Paradox'—and state of information (i) would put him in a position to claim the equally paradoxical obverse: 'It is not the case that "P" is true but I do believe it'. Whatever the correct analysis of utterances of this bizarre sort, it is clear that they are not apt for the expression of self-consciously held reasonable belief and so do not correspond to possible states of information in the sense which concerns us. Further, it is not clear that the distinction between (iv) and (ii) can now be upheld: at any rate, if it can, it is because it is possible for X to be aware that he has no adequate reason for supposing that he has a particular belief without thereby acquiring reason to think that he lacks it. No doubt there is scope for further discussion of the matter, and it would be unwise to be dogmatic that the separation cannot be affected in certain sorts of (psychoanalytical) case. But it seems a dangerously nice distinction on which to rest a defence of private language.

A further point about (iv) emerges when we consider (iii). What the latter seems to describe is a state of information which X would occupy if he found himself smitten, as it were, with a belief for whose truth he recognized he had no adequate ground. Isn't that a possibility? Well—again—not if the subject matter of the belief is such as to render X's very possession of it a ground for supposing it to be true; so not if the private language is to have a psychological subject matter about which a Cartesian, or weaker authority is claimed. But a more general consideration is that, independently of the subject matter of '*P*', (ii) does not describe a state of information which a *rational X* can achieve for arbitrary '*P*'. No doubt restriction would be necessary on the thesis that a rational subject believes only what he has reason to believe. But this had better be true in general. The result is that a proponent of private language ought to regard *X*'s idiolect as containing the resources for expression of a wide class of statements for which (iii) can represent, for *X*, a possible state of information only if *X* is imperfectly rational. The same point applies to (iv). But the possibility of (iii) or (iv) for an imperfectly rational *X* had better not be the *only* thing that a proponent of private language can oppose to the claim that the needed contrast cannot be made between the content of (a) and (b); otherwise the conclusion will stand that a private language could not be employed by a perfectly rational subject—an interesting enough conclusion, and quite sufficient seriously to damage any philosophical thesis about language, or mind, which demanded the possibility of private language.

7. *Does This Interpretation Meet the Constraints on Cogency?*

So much by way of outline is the interpretation of I.258–60 which I wish to recommend. I am not claiming that Wittgenstein had exactly these thoughts but then mysteriously chose to put no more than a do-it-yourself kit on paper. What I claim for this interpretation is that it elaborates the *kind* of doubt which Wittgenstein's text seems to be urging us to have about private language, and that it promises a cogency missing from the other lines of interpretation considered. One thing necessary, in order to make good the latter claim, is to consider how the interpretation fares in relation to the constraints listed earlier, which is the task of this section. Then, in the next two sections, I shall review two lines of objection which force interesting further extensions of the argument.

First, the Crusoe constraint. Let '*P*' be any statement, of whatever subject matter, in Crusoe's invented language. It would appear, taking Crusoe as *X*, that he is as badly placed to draw a distinction between (a) and (b) as the private linguist, and for exactly the same reasons: none of (i)–(iv) represents a state of information which he can achieve if he is entirely rational. It is also plausible that, so long as Crusoe remains isolated on his desert island and no one else has the slightest idea of what, if anything, any of his utterances means, no third party *Y* can achieve any of the states of information (i)–(iv) for the reasons described above. (I say 'plausible' because at least one of the considerations relevant to the discussion of private language, namely sceptical pressure towards third-person inscrutability of intention, would not be relevant.) Accordingly, let us suppose that Crusoe's isolation *de facto* prevents anyone else from arriving at any of the states of information whose possibility is demanded by a distinction in content between (a) and (b). We can even suppose Crusoe's isolation to be permanent and unalterable. Still, the difficulty about concluding that the argument, if sustained, defeats Crusoe's language too is that we do not ordinarily suppose that it suffices for a distinction to be unreal that nobody is *in fact* going to be able to make any use of it. The crucial matter is, putting it crudely, whether we know *what it would be, as rational subjects, to have occasion to make use of the distinction.* No doubt clarification is desirable of what exactly such knowledge should be held to consist in. But, whatever the truth about that, it is surely highly questionable a priori whether there can be such a thing as knowing what, counterfactually, it *would be* to be in a certain state of information if that state of information *necessarily* cannot be achieved. The thought governing the whole argument was that (a) and (b) possess an appropriately contrasting content only if the information which they convey is different; which it is only if there *could be* such a thing as having one item of information without the other. Any reader who found the principle plausible will not have supposed that the 'could' was meant to be constrained by contingent obstacles to investigation; but if it is not constrained by conceptual obstacles, it is doubtful whether it can mean anything at all.

There were two aspects to the second constraint, that 'going public' must remove the difficulty. First, the precise difficulty besetting the private linguist must disappear; and second, there must be no analogous difficulty for public language. Now, the precise difficulty is that, when X is taken to be the private linguist, neither he nor anyone else can attach appropriately contrasting informational content to (a) and (b). But 'going public' means: bringing it about that 'P' has sufficient public content to enable others, at least in favourable circumstances, to form a well-founded opinion about its truth value independent of X's opinion. That ought to make space for (iv). Of course X may still be invested with authority about the truth value of 'P'. But the possibility of independent assessment is likely to involve that that authority is, if only in special circumstances, defeasible—which is to say that there ought to be space for some or all of (i)–(iii). In any case, whether or not the feasibility of (i)–(iv) follows from the very publicity of the meaning of '*P*', the important point is that there is never any significant obstacle to establishing the (a)/(b) distinction for the statements of a public language. What counts as enjoying one of the states of information, (i)–(iv), varies depending on the subject matter of '*P*'; but there is in general no difficulty in explaining what it would be to enjoy one of those states of information *vis à vis* some third party *X*.

Whether the second aspect of the 'going public' constraint—the demand that there be no analogous difficulty for a public language—is satisfied may seem less straightforward. Suppose we take *X* as the entire linguistic community. Then may not the argument for the case *A* = *X* proceed more or less as before? Analogues of Moore's Paradox and its obverse may as well be formulated using 'we' rather than 'I'; and it is presumably legitimate to hypothesize that the community is collectively rational, so that at least the final consideration urged against the possibility of (iii) and (iv) in the relevant part of the earlier discussion can survive. As for the situation from the point of view of *Y* distinct from *X*, the fact is that there is, by hypothesis, no such *Y* who understands the language. So the argument can proceed much as before with, perhaps, only the additional consideration, for the case of (iii), that confrontation with a solid communal consensus about the truth of a sentence would have to provide an observer with *some* reason to suppose that sentence true even if he had not the slightest idea what it meant.

The thought is, in effect, that the argument outlined has no special bearing on private language but may be run for any entire linguistic community, whether of one or many members. It is a nice question what the proper response to the argument would be if that were so. But if we were right to conclude that the Crusoe constraint is satisfied, it cannot be so. And, in fact, the relevant consideration here is the same: the existence of contingent barriers to anyone's achieving one of (i)–(iv) provides no decisive basis for the conclusion that no one understands *what it would be* to achieve one of those states of information. The community will no doubt have a conception of the circumstances in which it would subsequently be forced to judge that such a consensus about the truth of '*P*' *had been* mistaken. So we know *now* what it would be for there to be a *Y* who was in a position to make that judgement about us: such a *Y* would be an additional member of the linguistic community who had adequate reason for supposing that the circumstances had indeed induced mass error. There is, by hypothesis, no such Y, but there could be—just as there could be a translator of Crusoe's language. Accordingly, there can be no special difficulty with this aspect of the second constraint if it was right to conclude that the argument satisfies the Crusoe constraint.

The third constraint, conceived for the special case of the psychological private language on which Wittgenstein himself concentrates, was that the argument should be effective against both Cartesian and Fallibilist opposition. It will suffice to remind the reader that, by and large, the argument proceeds without special assumption concerning the subject matter of the private language or the authority, if any, about the truth value of his utterances supposedly possessed by the private linguist; and that at both points where such authority is presented as contributing towards the difficulties, it is of no consequence whether it is thought of as Cartesian or fallible.

Arguably, then, all three constraints are satisfied. Since he can make out no (a)/(b) contrast—either truth-conditionally; or by appeal to difference of composition; or by appeal to difference of informational content, in accordance with the principle of section 6—and since the reasons for demanding the contrast seem absolutely compelling, we discharge the Cartesian from further punishment at this point. But the Fallibilist is not yet done for.

8. *The Return of the Community*

One important line of objection to the argument is suggested by the thought, three paragraphs above, that even a community-wide consensus may legitimately be regarded as mistaken *at another time*. Moore's Paradox and its variant depend upon present-tense formulation: there is nothing bizarre about for example '"P" was true but I did not believe it'. But nothing in the original argument, that (a) and (b) must possess contrasting content if 'P' is to count as apt for the expression of fact, seems to require the present-tense formulations which (a) and (b) actually assumed—the fallibility of our cognitive powers would be as well reflected by a contrast in the content of corresponding past-tense formulations. Such reformulation would not, to be sure, affect the course taken by the argument for the case $A = Y$, distinct from X. The objection, rather, will be that the discussion of the case $A = X$ was at best incomplete: we have simply not considered, in particular, whether the private linguist could get in position to pass principled *retrospective* verdicts of ignorance or error on himself. Should it emerge that he can, the argument would be met head-on: it would be possible to grant its claims about what is necessary for factuality, while contending that the thought which Wittgenstein expressed by 'Whatever is going to seem right to me is right' in I.258 is just mistaken.

The question, then, is whether X, the private linguist, can himself assign an appropriately contrasting content to:

(a)* X believed what 'P' expressed

and

(b)* What 'P' expressed was true.

Let the private language be one for the recording of sensation types; and let P be 'This sensation is S'. No doubt it may happen that X is afflicted with a sensation which, at first, he wishes to record as an occurrence of sensation S but which, as it continues, comes to seem to him significantly different. He may then want to say with respect to some recent past time that (a)* is true but (b)* is not. Now that, so far, is not good enough. With what right does X propose to regard his former impression of the sensation as having been mistaken, rather than view the sensation itself as having subtly changed from an instance of type S to something different? If the latter were the correct account, both (a)* and (b)* should be allowed to stand. Hence there can be, for X, such a thing as a state of information warranting assertion of (a)* but denial of (b)*—a state of information of type (i) with respect to (a)* and (b)*—only when he has equipped himself with a criterion for marking off the irrelevant kind of case when it is the sensation itself which has undergone subtle change. But it is utterly unclear what form such a criterion might take: all X has to go on, it appears, is his own conscious phenomenology; and phenomenologically there simply *is not* any difference—things will seem the same 'on the inside' whichever of the two descriptions is supposed to be accurate.

The point is vivid in the case of sensation, but in fact it is of general bearing. More needs to be done by a proponent of private language, whatever the envisaged subject matter, than simply to invoke the possibility that the private linguist might find himself inclined to correct a former judgement. We considered two ostensibly contrasting accounts of the situation in respect of sensation *S*. We could in fact have considered three, the third being that it is *X*'s inclination at the later time not to regard his then-occurring sensation as being of type *S* which is astray. So: on the basis of what principle should *X* give his present descriptive inclination priority over the previous one? This question must arise even if, for whatever reason, the subject matter of the private language is not conceived of as giving rise to the possibility of the kind of gradual transformation which would allow both of *X*'s descriptions to stand. What needs to be shown by someone who would have us believe that a retrospective analogue of (i) is accessible to the private linguist is that a situation may arise in which it is *rational* to accept both (a)* and the negation of (b)*; that has not been accomplished if the contrasting uses envisaged for (a)* and (b)* are based on nothing more substantial than the subject's arbitrarily giving priority to his present over his previous descriptive inclinations.

There is, as far as I am aware, only one line of thought extant in the literature which promises a reply. This is Simon Blackburn:

> ... in the usual scenario, the correctness or incorrectness of the private linguist's classification is given no consequence at all. It has no use. He writes in his diary, and so far as we are told, forgets it. So when Wittgenstein imagines a use made of the report (e.g. to indicate the rise of the manometer) he immediately hypothesises a public use. He thereby skips the intermediate case where the classification is given a putative private use. It fits into a project—a practice or technique—of ordering the expectation of the occurrence of sensation, with an aim at prediction, explanation, systematisation, or simple maximising of desirable sensations. To someone engaged on this project, the attitude that 'whatever seems right is right' is ludicrous. System soon enforces recognition of fallibility.[15]

Blackburn does not elaborate, but it is not difficult to imagine the kind of thing he could have in mind. The essential idea is to let the private linguist become a *theorist*, concerned not just with the recording of sensations, say, but with anticipation of their future character and the disclosure of patterns of occurrence among them. And the thought is that, once he embarks on this theoretical project, the routine constraints on all scientific theorizing (of comprehensiveness,

---

[15] Blackburn, loc. cit., pp. 299–300. Compare Ross Harrison, loc. cit., p. 161. And see Ralph Walker's *Kant* (Routledge and Kegan Paul, London, 1978), 115, for a terse gesture at the same idea.

predictiveness, simplicity, and so on) will supply a framework in terms of which it may be rational, on occasion, to discount former, or even present, descriptive inclinations.

Let us construct a simple example. Suppose the private linguist is afflicted, as it seems to him, with three distinct sensation types which within any instance of some specified period—one hour, say—invariably comply with the following two hypotheses:

H_1: if no instance of S_1 occurs, then an instance of S_2 occurs:
H_2: if an instance of S_3 occurs, then no instance of S_2 occurs.

Imagine now an occasion on which the private linguist sets himself to record the occurrence of his sensations over an instance of the specified period. We can list the various possibilities in the form of a truth table:

	S_1	S_2	S_3
1*	T	T	T
2	T	T	F
3	T	F	T
4	T	F	F
5*	F	T	T
6	F	T	F
7*	F	F	T
8*	F	F	F

Line 1, for instance, is to be taken, in the obvious way, as expressing the possibility than an instance of each of the three types of sensation occurs during the specified period. The reader will note that the possibilities expressed at lines 1, 5, 7, and 8 are at variance with the two hypotheses, while the remaining four possibilities are consistent with them. Now, the general point is that although, ultimately, theory must be the slave of observation, a theory can fare sufficiently well over a sufficient period of time to make it rational to discount a prima facie discordant set of data. H_1 and H_2 may together constitute a repeatedly corroborated, long-standing little theory; or they may represent the output, for these three sensation types, of a well-entrenched theory of wider content. Either way, it can be rational for the private linguist, if at the end of the specified period he finds that his record is of one of the four types at variance with the theory, to look askance at his 'observations' rather than at the theory.

Let his policy in such circumstances be the commendable one of making the simplest adjustment to his findings consistent with retention of his faith in the theory and in his own powers to, by and large, record his sensations properly. And now ask, what, if that is his policy, ought he to say in each of the four possible cases of discordance? The answers are interesting. Clearly he will not make two adjustments if one will do. But if he has recorded occurrences of all three sensation types, that is, we are concerned with line 1, there are two possibilities open, namely rejecting that an instance of S_2 occurred, so transforming the data into line 3, and rejecting that an instance of S_3 occurred, so transforming the data into line 2. And *two* choices is one too many. The objection to which the introduction of theory was a response was precisely that the private linguist had no principled basis for according priority to a present preferred description over a former one. But, in the situation envisaged, a preference for his verdict about S_2 over that about S_3 or vice versa is open to just the same reproach. The lesson is that the objection is met only when there is some *uniquely* best way to resolve the inconsistency between theory and data; so long as there are choices, the decision among which is arbitrary, the invocation of theory has, in the present context, no point.

Matters are no better with line 8, when it seems to the private linguist as though no sensation of any of the three relevant kinds has occurred; either of the suppositions that S_2, or S_3, did in fact occur (unnoticed?) transforms the data into an acceptable set, and no non-arbitrary basis for a choice between them presents itself. But it is different with line 5: here re-assessment of the verdict about S_3 represents the best, indeed the only suitable transformation. So it would appear that this theory does indeed provide for the possibility of a state of information in which the private linguist may reasonably deem the statement that an instance of S_3 occurred to be mistaken: the state of information is that constituted by the grounds for the theory itself and his other recorded data. A similarly favourable case is presented by line 7 for the statement that no instance of S_1 occurred. The Blackburn/Harrison idea is accordingly a plausible one: equip the private linguist with well-entrenched theoretical beliefs and he may very well get into situations in which he may rationally discount verdicts which he would otherwise have endorsed and may indeed have endorsed for a time. Have we got private language off the ground?

It certainly is not as easy as that. Remember, to begin with, that the establishment of an appropriate distinction between (a) and (b) (or (a)* and (b)*) is only a necessary condition for qualification of a class of statements as factual. Suppose you found it possible, for example, to draw up an integrated system of moral principles in such a way as to coincide with the pattern of your untutored moral responses and to predict new ones. You might then have a theoretical basis, in just the sort of way envisaged, for describing certain of your moral judgements about particular situations as involving error or ignorance. But no non-factualist about morals need be dismayed by the prospect of such system; he will hold that it is one thing to talk as if moral judgements have a factual subject matter and another thing for them really to do so (though it would remain a decisive point in his favour if we could not so much as establish the practice of talking as if they did). We do not at present have an account of conditions both necessary *and* sufficient for a class of statements to qualify as genuinely factual; a proof of the possibility of private language would have to appeal to such an account.

Still, in fairness, Wittgenstein's claim was that a necessary condition could not be met. And Blackburn has at least suggested how it might be. But cause for dissatisfaction with the sort of theoretical scenario depicted emerges in any case, once we reflect on what further conditions are necessary for factuality. One compelling principle—(*T*)—is that a class of statements can qualify as factual only if every truth-functional compound of them does so; hence in particular the negation of any factual statement must itself be factual. But the theory described does nothing to establish the possibility of contrasting uses for (a)/(a)* and (b)/(b)* when *P* is taken as 'No sensation of type S_3 occurred'. So what the theory does achieve for 'A sensation of type S_3 occurred' is not enough.

In addition, the theory goes no way at all towards establishing the (a)/(a)*–(b)/(b)* contrast for either 'A sensation of type S_2 occurred' or its negation. A proponent of the Blackburn/Harrison strategy is, I suggest, going to be hard-pressed to explain why that sort of omission does not set up a kind of 'rotten apple' effect. There are two reasons for anticipating such an effect. The first, somewhat intricate, involves appeal to the principle—(*U*)—noted above in discussion of Kripke, that if the acceptability—to use a neutral term—of a statement is a function of that of others, some of which are deemed not to be genuinely factual, then the original statement may not be regarded as genuinely factual either. The theory described, when well established, puts X in position to deny the appearance of acceptability of 'An instance of S_3 occurred' when and only when 'No instance of S_1 occurred' and 'An instance of S_2 occurred' are both acceptable with respect to the relevant period. Accordingly, if the latter does not qualify as factual, then—by (U)—neither, when asserted on that basis, does the conjunction of (a)* and the negation of (b)* with 'A sensation of type S_3 occurred' substituted for 'P'. Hence—by the principle (T)—not both its conjuncts qualify as factual. Since it is completely unclear what ground sympathetic to a proponent of Blackburn could be given for regarding the first conjunct as failing in factuality, the trouble, it seems, would have to lie with the second: the statement, 'It is not the case that what "A sensation of type S_3 occurred" expressed was true'. And if that is not a factual statement, it ought to be permissible to say the same about 'What "It is not the case that a sensation of type S_3 occurred" expressed was true' and hence about the statement mentioned therein.[16] A further application of the principle (T) then gives the result that 'A sensation of type S_3 occurred' does not qualify as factual after all.

The second reason for anticipating a 'rotten apple' effect concerns whether the presence of statements in the situation of 'A sensation of type S_2 occurred' in the example described leaves open any possibility of a coherent account of the private linguist's methodology. No problem, of course, if all the ingredients in the private linguist's record of his observations may be regarded as factual: in that case the three observations represented by line 5, for instance, are straightforwardly *inconsistent* with the theory, retention of which will therefore demand some reappraisal of them. But it is not clear whether it is legitimate to invoke the notion of consistency in this kind of way if certain of the ingredients in a putatively inconsistent set are not genuine statements. I do not mean to dispute, of course, that perfectly respectable notions of consistency and inconsistency are applicable outwith the domain of genuine statements—to commands, for instance, and rules, as well as to moral judgements (if they are indeed

---

[16] The two principles implicit in this transition are:

    (a) ⌜Not: what 'P' expresses/ed is/was true⌝ is factual iff ⌜What 'Not: P' expresses/ed is/was true⌝ is factual;

and (b) ⌜What 'P' expresses/ed is/was true⌝ is factual iff ⌜P⌝ is factual.

thought to be a doubtful case). The fact remains that the notion of consistency has its *primary* place when we are concerned with genuine statements. It is applied elsewhere, I suggest, only in a derivative sense. (Commands, for example, are inconsistent when and only when those corresponding statements are, which articulate the conditions under which the commands are complied with.) In any event, anyone who wants to apply the notions of consistency and inconsistency outwith the domain of genuine statements, and to sustain their ordinary connections with the notion of rationality, owes an account of what exactly inconsistency among the relevant sentences amounts to and why it is to be avoided. It is quite unobvious how such an account should proceed in the present case; certainly, nothing like the story appropriate for the case of commands can be appropriate here.

The foregoing remarks are premised on the assumption that unless the theory provides for the possibility, with respect to each particular 'observation' statement, of a state of information in which some sort of (a)/(a)*–(b)/(b)* contrast may be drawn, no sense has yet been attached to the contrast in that particular case. But someone may be inclined to question this assumption. In discussion of the Crusoe and publicity constraints above, it was contended that it suffices, in order for (a) and (b) to contrast in content, that we possess a clear account of what it *would be* to enjoy any of the states of information (i)–(iv); and that it is not required that any of those states of information *actually* be attainable. Now, cannot the private linguist claim to have such an account for each of the statements which he wishes to regard as a possible report of his sensations? For he would be in a position to make the appropriate contrast, in each such case, just when he happened to be impelled towards a theory which furnished a line in the truth table standing to that statement as line 5 stands to 'A sensation of type S_3 occurred' in our example. There is thus, it may be contended, no need to aspire to some *single* theory which can provide the needed contrast in every case; it is enough, for each putative report of sensation, to be hospitable towards the possibility of *some* theory's providing a basis for its correction.

This point, if sustained, would certainly be convenient for the private linguist. It would mean that he did not *actually* have to engage in any theorizing at all! It would be enough to indicate that he was 'hospitable' to the possibility of sometime attempting to integrate his 'reports' within the framework of a theory; and that if the theory then proved to supply a criterion for his self-attribution of ignorance, or error, concerning the status of some particular such report, then—no matter which it might be—he would be willing to reappraise it. But this implication should make us wary. If we deem that the occurrence of no *actual* attempt at theorizing, or only of an unsuccessful attempt, is quite compatible with the existence of all the requisite distinctions, so long as the private linguist acknowledges that the drawing of each of them could be appropriate under theoretical pressure, we would seem committed to the view that his 'observation' statements may already be credited with a meaning which will be more or less invariant across the various theory-inclusive systems of beliefs in which they may come to be embedded. If that commitment seems untroublesome, we shall do well to remember how difficult it has proved to sustain the corresponding claim about the content of reports of observation in the context of our ordinary scientific theories (and, indeed, to sustain so much as the claim that there is a well-defined class of 'observation statements' at all).

There is a second, more fundamental point. A theory ought not to require the truth of any particular observation statement *unconditionally*. Naturally, depending on whether a particular observation statement is supposed to be true or false, a theory may enjoin a differential assessment of other such statements; but *both* the union of the theory with any single observation statement *and* its union with the negation ought to express coherent possibilities. We have not pressed the Fallibilist for an account of the *sources* of possible error in the private linguist's reports of his sensations; but such an account is owing, and it is hard to see how a satisfactory story could avoid sanctioning the possibility that error might take place, in any particular case, *whatever* theory, if any, the subject held about the dependable patterns of occurrence among his sensations. So much is demanded by the analogy with observation and ordinary empirical theorizing which the Blackburn/Harrison proposal imposes. If, accordingly, it is on the intelligibility of error that the supporter of private language wishes to base the needed (a)/(a)*–(b)/(b)* contrast, it is perfectly fair to insist that he explain how the private linguist might achieve a state of information of type (i) compatibly with a reasonable confidence in whatever theory he had arrived at.

To relate the point to the example above. A satisfactory explanation of what it is for the private linguist to have been in error about

'A sensation of type S_2 occurred' ought to represent it as a possibility consistent with the truth of his belief in H_1 and H_2. The conjunction of 'X erroneously believed "A sensation of type S_2 is occurring"' with H_1 and H_2 ought therefore to represent a conceivable, self-consistent item of information—differing, for instance, from the information represented by the result of replacing 'erroneously' by 'erroneously but excusably'. But, so long as we stay with the principle about information content which has governed the discussion to this point—that two items of information differ only if there could be such a thing as having one without the other[17]—no way presents itself for giving sense to that sort of contrast. There is, simply, no prospect of an account of what it would be for X to have just the theoretical information incorporated in H and H_2 plus reason to think that his prior acceptance of 'A sensation of type S_2 is occurring' was mistaken.

Let us see where we have got to. I have argued for two theses. *Thesis A* affirms that the private linguist can satisfactorily draw the (a)/(a)*–(b)/(b)* contrast for a particular S_k only if he can draw that contrast both for *every* such statement which, he conceives, may contribute with S_k to a body of evidence for or against his theory, and for *the negations* of all such statements. The grounds for this thesis are the principle (T), the argument for the 'rotten apple' effect, and the doubt about the capacity of the private linguist to justify the play he will need to make with the notion of consistency unless the thesis is respected. *Thesis B* affirms that if—which is the private linguist's situation—*only* theory can assist in the drawing of these contrasts, then they are drawn satisfactorily only if drawn within the framework of a *single* theory. In particular, it is not good enough merely to advert to the possibility of different theories which might repair the omissions of whatever theory the private linguist happens to respect. The grounds for this thesis are two. First, the private linguist needs to suppose that the 'omitted' cases *already* enjoy the content which they would possess when harnessed to a theory which

---

[17] Of course, this principle may be called into question; and it will be the task of the next section to review how. But what seemed interesting about the Blackburn/Harrison proposal was exactly that it promised the private linguist the prospect of drawing the requisite sorts of distinction in *operational* terms, compatibly with the requirements of our governing principle. (The invocation of theory would be pointless if that principle were no longer accepted, since the enjoyment of an appropriately contrasting content by instances of (a)* and (b)* would no longer have to answer to the possibility of states of information of type (i)–(iv).)

actually drew the (a)/(a)*–(b)/(b)* contrast for them—otherwise he will run afoul of the 'rotten apple' and consistency points; and he holds out a substantial hostage to fortune if he undertakes to defend that supposition against the familiar difficulties which beset the notion of the continuity of 'observational' contents through theoretical change. Second, it is part of our ordinary concept of observational error that it may occur whatever theory we hold. Accordingly the private linguist has not attained a satisfactory conception of what it is to be in error about, for example, the occurrence of an instance of S_2, if he does not understand what it would be both for that to be so and for his current theory to be correct. The operationalism implicit in the Blackburn/Harrison response—that the 'seems right'/'is right' distinction should be one the private linguist can actually draw—entails, accordingly, that reason to suspect obervational error—error in the appraisal of some S_k or its negation—should always be attainable compatibly, at least when taken in isolation, with *whatever* theory the subject is inclined to endorse. (Or, if it does not, it has suddenly turned suspiciously eclectic.) Of course there is no difficulty in meeting this condition when, as is usual, the criteria for observational error are, at least in part, of a largely nontheoretical sort—discord with others' reports, poor lighting, mislaid spectacles, and so on. But in the present case such criteria *have* to be theoretically generated.

Putting theses *A* and *B* together, we arrive at the intriguing result that Blackburn's and Harrison's strategy can be both pointful and successful for the private linguist only if his theory can indeed do for *each* member of the relevant class of 'observation statements' and their negations what the theory in the example does for 'A sensation of type S_3 occurred'. Could there be such a theory, and what would it look like?

Consider the total set of rows of Ts and Fs which specify all possible truth value assignments to the ingredient variables in a formula in *n* variables of classical sentential logic—let us call this structure of Ts and Fs the *assignment block*. Let us say that one row is an *n*-transform of another just in case the first results from the second by changing the assignment to exactly *n* of the variables. Then the theory in the example does what it does for 'A sensation of type S_3 occurred' because the relevant assignment block contains a row—line 5—which falsifies the theory as a whole, assigns T to S_3, has a 1-transform which verifies the theory as a whole and is achieved by changing just the assignment of T to S_3, and has no other

1-transform which verifies the theory as a whole. All that is the formal reflection of the point that the findings which line 5 represents are inconsistent with the theory but can be restored to consistency with it by a reappraisal which is *uniquely* least disturbing of them. The upshot is that if the private linguist wishes to bring what strike him as different sensation types under theoretical rein, and satisfactorily to meet what I am presenting as Wittgenstein's argument in the Blackburn/Harrison way, his 'theory' had better take a form whereby its output for the n relevant types of 'observational statement' corresponds to a classical truth function, ϕ, in n variables with the following features:

For each variable v_i there are rows in the assignment block, $V_j(v_1 \ldots v_n)$ and $V_k(v_1 \ldots v_n)$, such that:

$V_j(v_i) = T$;	$V_k(v_i) = F$
V_j falsifies $\phi(v_1 \ldots v_n)$;	V_k falsifies $\phi(v_1 \ldots v_n)$
$V_j^*(v_1 \ldots v_n)$, differing from $V_j(v_1 \ldots v_n)$ only in the assignment to v_i, verifies $\phi(v_i \ldots v_n)$;	$V_k^*(v_1 \ldots v_n)$, differing from $V_k(v_1 \ldots v_n)$ only in the assignment to v_i, verifies $\phi(v_1 \ldots v_n)$
There is no other 1-transform of $V_j(v_1 \ldots v_n)$ which verifies $\phi(v_1 \ldots v_n)$;	There is no other 1-transform of $V_k(v_1 \ldots v_n)$ which verifies $\phi(v_1 \ldots v_n)$

We now need to do some formal work whose details I relegate to an Appendix. But here are some pertinent results. If $n = 2$, there are no theories of the requisite sort. If $n = 3$ or 4, all the theories of the requisite sort correspond to truth functions which are verified only by a pair of complementary rows in the assignment block; for example, by [TTF] and [FFT]—lines 2 and 7 in the assignment block for H_1 and H_2 above—which would correspond to the theory:

H_3: a sensation of type S_1 occurs if and only if a sensation of type S_2 occurs; and

H_4: a sensation of type S_2 occurs if and only if a sensation of type S_3 does not occur.

Indeed one way to arrive at a suitable theory, irrespective of the size of n, is simply to write up the chain of biconditionals which correspond to any single row in the assignment block in the manner in which $\{H_3,H_4\}$ corresponds to line 2 in the three-variable assignment block tabulated earlier. But this is not the only way of finding a suitable theory if n is greater than or equal to 5. For example, the function in 5 variables which is verified at each of [TTFFT], [FFFTT], and [FTTTF] but nowhere else corresponds to a suitable theory for a language of 5 sensation types; as does that which is verified at each of [TTTTT], [TTFFF], [FFFTT], and [FFTFF], but nowhere else. (The alert reader will spot that the crucial consideration is that each designated row be at least a 3-transform of all the others, and that the designated rows collectively comprise assignments of both T and F to each variable.)

The resulting situation is somewhat peculiar. The feeling that a private language, in particular a private language of sensation, is possible is quite indifferent to the degree of complexity and variety of the material to be described. But if the private linguist happens to have only two sensation types, or if only two out of a larger number of types by which he is afflicted prove to be theoretically tractable, the Blackburn/Harrison strategy is no good to him. And if his inner world is richer, and a threefold or larger variety within it does seem to prove amenable to theoretical regimentation, the chances that his experience will suggest a theory falling within the range of those which deliver all that has been argued to be necessary are signally slim. There are, for example, half as many distinct biconditionally constituted theories, of the sort illustrated, in n types of 'observation statement' as there are rows in the assignment block; so the ratio of the number of such theories to all possible theories, where each possible theory corresponds to a distinct truth function in n variables, is $2^{n-1}/2^{2^n}$. Since the biconditionally constituted theories are the only suitable theories when $n=3$ or 4, this gives the would-be private linguist a one in 64 chance of meeting Wittgenstein's objection if his theory deals in three sensation types, and a one in 8,192 chance if it deals in four! Even the most determined soliloquist ought to be dismayed by such odds. The reader will anticipate that matters get worse as n increases, and so indeed they do. In particular, the limiting frequency of suitable theories among all possible theories tends to zero as n tends to infinity. (For proof, see the Appendix.)

I conclude that the Blackburn/Harrison objection can at most oblige some refinement of Wittgenstein's claim; it does not, in the end, qualify its force. The argument proposed a necessary condition for a class of statements to qualify as genuinely factual and suggested that private language could not meet it. Not so, said Blackburn, provided the language embeds an appropriate theory. And thus far, except for the case $n = 2$, he is entirely right. But we have seen that Wittgenstein's objection can be amplified in such a way that only possession by the private linguist of a very special sort of theory can put him in position satisfactorily to respond to it in the Blackburn/Harrison way. The result is that although we find in favour of the *bare possibility* of private language—or, more accurately, of surmounting the barrier to it adverted to in I.258—enough has been done to undermine the *motivation* of each of the foreseeable species of believer in private language distinguished in section 1. One who believes in the essential privacy of large parts of his mental life will surely want to suppose that his capacity to record its character in terms no one else can have reason to think he understands would be *in no way contingent* on the particular form of the patterns, if any, of concomitance which the various event types display, but would depend only on the adequate functioning of his faculties. One who succumbs to sceptical pressure towards the third-person inscrutability of intention, or to solipsism, will want to say the same. The extra element of contingency might be tolerated if it was associated with high probability; but quite the reverse is true. Blackburn's objection forces a concession which offers absolutely no comfort to Wittgenstein's traditional antagonists.

It remains to draw a further moral. It is a fact that we actually possess an 'operational' grasp of the notions of error and ignorance for statements of every sort, including everything we might incline to regard as a report of observation. One implication of the preceding is that it is wildly unlikely that this could be so unless this grasp owed more to our membership in a language community in which we have faith in others' judgements than to our engagement in theory-building. This is one crucial difference which a community, actual or potential, makes: only by reference to a (potential) community of speakers of his language can a subject guarantee himself any reasonable likelihood of globally applicable, operational notions of ignorance and error.

9. Drawing the 'Seems Right'/'Is Right' Distinction Non-operationally

I warned in section 4 that the interpretation to be recommended would not entirely distance itself from verificationism. Such verificationism as it involves is implicit in the erstwhile governing principle that (at least for a very large class of cases, including relevant instances of (a)/(a)* and (b)/(b)*) statements may be regarded as differing in their informational content only if there could be such a thing as having reason to believe one without the other. For the principle leaves no space for the possibility (as some will see it) of grasping that the informational content of a pair of statements differs although there can be no such thing as having even the weakest reason to accept *either*.

Anyone who was not already dissatisfied with the governing principle when it was introduced but now dislikes its Wittgensteinian consequences should probably have a bad conscience about dramatizing this verificationist aspect. But, in any case, the belief in the possibility that verification-transcendent statements may differ in informational content is not to the purpose for a supporter of private language, since he will not wish to maintain that there is no such thing as having either piece of information conveyed by statements of types (a)/(a)* and (b)/(b)*. Prima facie, then, the verificationist aspect of the governing principle plays no part in the argument.

The reply should be that the principle actually imports verificationist cargo in two places. It entails, as noted, that the informational content of a pair of statements can be contrasted only if there can be reason to believe one of them: but it also entails that if possession of reason to believe either involves reason to believe both, we cannot attain *distinct* conceptions of their informational content, that is, understand them as depicting different states of affairs. And that is tantamount to the assumption that the meaning of a statement cannot be determined by truth conditions over and above the possible grounds for believing it. Since (prescinding from presently irrelevant considerations about conversational practice) grounds for belief and grounds for assertion coincide, the assumption is, in effect, that the contrast between (a)/(a)* and (b)/(b)* has to be drawn by reference to conditions of warranted assertion; that it cannot coherently be allowed that their assertion conditions might coincide while the *truth conditions* diverged, with the latter divergence supplying the requisite contrast in content.

It would be natural to suppose that this reflection takes the private language issue up into the general dispute between realists and anti-realists in the theory of meaning, which has recently increasingly resembled a dialogue of the deaf. It is true of course that if we were to decide—for example for the sort of reason developed by Dummett—against the realist conception of truth, then that would be that. But I do not think that this is the best way to look at the matter. Rather, suppose we find *against* verificationism in general; that is, we satisfy ourselves that there are at least some areas of discourse for which the sort of idea of truth which the verificationist complains about can be made intelligible and is suitable to serve as the basis of a truth-conditional conception of meaning. Still, the victory over verificationism has to be gained piecemeal: persuading ourselves that the verificationist has no cogent *general* point would still leave open the task, for any particular class of statements where realism is our antecedent conviction, of showing that we have indeed attained the kind of conception of truth which the verificationist believes we cannot attain. Even someone who is persuaded that there are no compelling general arguments for verificationism ought not to find it simply *obvious* that the private linguist can intelligibly draw the needed contrasts in the sort of truth-conditional way proposed. It demands a special idea of truth, which has to be earned.

I continue to concentrate on the example of sensation (though the considerations which follow will generalize). The notion which has to be earned is that the private linguist may simply mistake how he ought to describe an occurrent sensation without its being in any way possible for him, then or later, to acquire evidence of the mistake. One consequence of admitting this idea is that he divests himself of any worthwhile reason for supposing that this situation is not *frequently* realized. When the idea of mistake is bound to (at least a high probability of) detectability, it is possible to get some purchase on the question of how error-prone a particular subject is. But to suppose that any mistake made by the private linguist is going to be undetectable entails that he has absolutely no basis for any view about the frequency of his errors. And that in turn entails that he has no entitlement to regard any of his opinions as likely to be correct.

So one who favours this pre-emptive way with the line of reasoning developed in the preceding section immediately pays a significant price: he surrenders not merely Cartesian authority but even the weaker authority which the Fallibilist is likely to want to claim for his descriptions of those of his mental states which he conceives as private. Ironically enough, he thereby places himself in position to meet the demand which his strategy was designed to avoid: the demand that he give *operational* content to the (a) and (b) contrast. For he now has reason to say that states of information of type (iii) are available, the fact of his believing 'P' to be true invariably providing absolutely no reason for supposing it to be so. Of course he is no closer than before to explaining how he could perfectly *rationally* enjoy such a state of information, since he has no evident defence against the thought that to allow himself to have any beliefs at all with the relevant sort of subject matter is a kind of passive irrationality. But, in any case, the availability of states of information of type (iii) is no longer to the dialectical purpose: the distinction demanded by Wittgenstein's argument has already been drawn if the private linguist can indeed attain so deeply realist a conception of the truth conditions of his private 'statements'. The question remains whether he can.

There are a number of reasons for doubting it, even if we forgo invocation of the general considerations about concept-acquisition and concept-display on which Dummett, for instance, builds a global anti-realist case. One important line of attack would pivot on whether it is permissible to think of meaning as possessing the strong objectivity which this defence of private language demands: the objectivity implicit in the idea that the meaning of a statement can be settled by a presumably finite set of behavioural and intellectual episodes in such a way as to determine truth value (with appropriate assistance from the world) quite independently of any actual or possible response from those whose understanding might naturally be held to constitute the meaning of the statement. An opposing conception would be that the responses of those who understand it stand to the meaning of a statement rather as someone's behaviour stands to his character: there is conceptual space for a failure of fit—acting out a character, misuse of the statement—but the relationship is somehow, at bottom, still a constitutive one. If anything like this latter conception is right, the meaning of the private linguist's statements could not possibly sustain the utterly fortuitous connections with his preferred uses of them which the realist defence of private language demands. A strong case can, I believe, be made for this conception without invoking anything which should be regarded as question-begging anti-realist presupposition.[18] But it would take us too far afield to review it here.

There are, however, two rather more specialized lines of thought. Both contend, in different ways, that the realist defence puts the ordinary idea of *intention* under intolerable strain. First, the realist owes an account of the precise mechanism which, quite independently—as we have seen—of the private linguist's beliefs, determines the truth values of his statements. What makes it the case that, say, 'A sensation of type S_2 is occurring' is true, when it is true, independently of the private linguist's view? The answer has to be: resemblance between the occurrent sensation and those of its predecessors whose association with the label 'S_2' established its meaning. But what determines what kind, or degree, of resemblance is *good enough*—qualifies the sensation as a member of the relevant class? Pain, for example, can vary in duration, in intensity, and in a host of other qualitative ways. What is going to settle how far an S_2 sensation may vary, and in what parameters, before it is disqualified? The issue has to turn on the subject's intentions on the baptismal occasions: the resemblance is close enough when it is the kind of resemblance that the subject intended. But the concept of intention has a breadth far in excess of the concept of thought: I need not have explicitly entertained a detailed scenario comprising a specific course of action in specific background circumstances before it can be true to say of me that I intended that that course of action should take place in those circumstances. It is unclear how it would be possible for the concept of intention to have this breadth if we did not take a subject's actual responses as criterial for the character of his former intentions. Suppose now, however, that the private linguist has a sensation which—if you think you understand what it means to say so—is strictly qualitatively unlike any of the baptismal cases, but which he has no hesitation in describing as a further instance of S_2. The realist defence is committed, as we have seen, to the view that there can be no better reason for regarding this response as correct than as incorrect—committed, therefore, to surrender of the ordin-

---

[18] Cf. my 'Rule-following, Meaning and Constructivism', in C. Travis (ed.), *Meaning and Interpretation* (Blackwell, Oxford, 1986).

ary criterial connection just noted. So what is to be regarded as establishing the *content* of the intention which settles whether or not this particular response is correct?

It is very unclear that the materials are to hand for a satisfactory reply. Suppose the private linguist did not envisage this precise case (again, assume we know what it is to envisage a *precise* case). Then, when we are forced to regard the character of his present response as irrelevant, it is baffling what could give the intention the requisite determinacy, could make it true, or not, that the occurrent sensation should be described as an instance of S_2. Suppose instead, more conveniently, that the private linguist did envisage the precise case. Then the question is whether that can be true indefinitely often; whether, in other words, his intention could have had the *general* content necessary in order to establish a meaning, that is, a rule. Is it possible to envisage indefinitely many 'precise cases'? The requisite rule would have taken a form, I suppose, something like:

> Whenever a situation occurs exactly like this one, 'A sensation of type S_2 is occurring' is true.

But that is open to the simple-minded reproach that a situation 'exactly like this one' is never going to occur again: something is bound to be different. The rule needs some notion of *relevant* similarity. But now the class of 'relevantly similar' situations has got to be indefinitely various, since its members may vary indefinitely in the putatively irrelevant respects. So the question recurs: what can make it true that each of these was intended to count as a case of relevant similarity when all that is available to fix the content of the original intention is the explicit thoughts which the subject entertained at the time, and when only a proper subclass of these situations can have been so explicitly thought about?

The foregoing is, of course, strongly reminiscent of Kripke's Sceptical Argument. But it would be wrong to conclude that it presents a real difficulty for the would-be private linguist only if Kripke's sceptic argues cogently. For there is a difference. Kripke's sceptic gulls his interlocutor into accepting that the content of his previous intentions has to be recoverable—if it is determinate at all—from his previous thoughts and behaviour. The possibility is thereby passed over that the subject be granted non-inferential recall of previous intentions, that it be analytic of the concept of intention that people are, by and large, authoritative about their own intentions past and present. The *special* problem to which the realist defence of private language is vulnerable is that, by transcendentalizing the notion of mistake and hence that of the subject's reliability, it abrogates the right to call on this aspect of the concept of intention and thereby—I suggest—leaves Kripke's sceptic with a clear run on goal.

The second way in which the realist defence places the concept of intention under strain is perhaps more immediate. Meaning, it is again platitudinous to say, is normative: it is because statements have meaning that there is such a thing as correct, or incorrect, use of them. This is a platitude which the truth-conditional conception of meaning, like any other, must respect. The story will be, presumably, that the making of a statement is basically correct when its truth conditions are realized (though it may be criticizable on all sorts of other grounds); and is basically incorrect when its truth conditions are not realized (though it may then be excusable on all sorts of grounds). But this story respects the normativity of meaning only if the making of statements just when their truth conditions are realized constitutes a feasible policy. And it is important to realize that its feasibility is not guaranteed if one merely accepts—which of course an anti-realist would not in certain controversial cases—that there is such a thing as the truth conditions of the statement being realized or not. It is necessary, additionally, that there can be such a thing as *aiming* at making or assenting to a statement only when its truth conditions are realized. It is about that that there is a doubt in the present case.

The trouble, once again, flows from the consequence of the realist's defence that the private linguist's believing 'A sensation of type S_2 is occurring' is no longer even the weakest ground for supposing it true. The truth of an 'observation statement' in the private language has become utterly dissociated from any practical criterion. Can the private linguist still aim at making such statements only when they are true—is there any such thing as having that intention? The question, in effect, is whether there can be such a thing as aiming at a transcendent target: a target such that there is no criterion for saying of any particular shot whether it hits, or is likely to hit, or not, and hitting or missing which can have no consequences for the course of your own or another's future experience.

To sample the flavour of the difficulty, try the following thought experiment. Suppose you are confronted with a pair of sealed boxes, one empty and the other containing an Egyptian scarab. The scarab will vaporize instantaneously and without trace if the seal on its box is disturbed. And there is no exterior sign—no difference in weight, or rattle, and so on—to betray which box is which.[19] Suppose finally that the craftsman who originally made and sealed the boxes is dead and has left no record to help you, although it is quite certain that one and only one of the boxes does contain a scarab. And now suppose you are invited to pick the box with the scarab in by placing your finger on top of it. Can you so much as *try* to do so? What exactly will distinguish your performance from a response to the invitation to pick the empty box, or just to pick a box? Not, at any rate, the exact form taken by your behaviour; that will be consistent with its being a response to any one of the three invitations. Nor the fact that it is a response to one in particular of the invitations, since—if each of the three aims really is possible—it ought to be possible, out of contrariness, to aim, say, at the scarab when invited to pick the empty box. So the distinguishing feature or features have to be *interior*—what are they?

If the circumstances were different, the distinction could emerge in your response to the discovery that your chosen box did, or did not, contain the scarab—disappointment, self-satisfaction, relief, indifference, and so on. So could it not, in the circumstances described, be true of you when you make your choice that if it *were* possible to uncover the scarab and if it *were* in your chosen box, then your response *would* be one of relief, for example? Perhaps. But making the sought-for difference reside in the truth or falsity of such counterfactual conditionals doesn't make it any clearer how it is supposed to be apparent *to you* which intention you have; the problem merely shifts to that of explaining how you can tell which among such counterfactuals are true of you. And there would, in any case, be a strong suspicion of circularity about an attempted counterfactual analysis of the relevant differences, since it would have to be stipulated that the counterfactual circumstances be ones in which your intentions had *remained the same.* But most serious of all: the obstacles for the detection of the beetle are at best causal; whereas the realist defence of private language makes it a *conceptual* truth that there is no detecting the truth value of the private linguist's 'observation statements'.

---

[19] The empty box is lined with a quantity of the same volatile material sufficient to equalize the weights.

Once that is recognized, it ought to seem quite unclear what is being said if it is claimed to be true of the private linguist for instance that if he *were* to get an independent check on the truth value of 'a sensation of type S_2 is occurring', he would be gratified, or whatever.

10. Conclusion

The net effect of the foregoing is to confront a proponent of the possibility of private language with a dilemma. One way or another he has to draw the 'seems right'/'is right' contrast. If he accepts the need to do so operationally, by reference to practical criteria, our finding was that he will be able to do so in a satisfactory way only in very special, at best unlikely circumstances; and that an element of contingency will thereby intrude into his central claim which is quite foreign to his original conviction. If, on the other hand, he claims the distinction need not be operational but may be drawn purely truth-conditionally, he commits himself to the unwelcome consequence that the private linguist can have no satisfactory basis for his belief in his general competence to practise the private language; and this, besides involving a substantial hostage to fortune in his commitment to a highly objective notion of meaning, generates special difficulties in explaining what constitutes the truth of a statement in the private language and what constitutes the private linguist's aiming at the truth. The answer which all this suggests to the title question is therefore: 'Probably'. The ball, anyway, is in the opposition's court.

APPENDIX*

On the number of classical truth functions in n variables which are congenial to the Blackburn/Harrison purpose.

I

The assignment block (cf. p. 247) consists of 2^n distinct n-fold rows of Ts and Fs. Let us say that one such row is an m-transform of another just in case they differ in exactly m places, $1 \leqslant m \leqslant n$. A truth function, ϕ, in n variables

* This is not an exclusive for formal logicians. At least, I have *tried* to present the reasoning which follows in a way which should be intelligible to a logical, rather than logically expert, reader with a memory of school arithmetic that can at least be jogged, and a rudimentary grasp of elementary logic and set theory.

may be identified with that subset of these rows for which it yields the value T. Call the members of such a subset, ϕ, the ϕ-selected rows. Our question is this:

> How many subsets are there, as a function of n, with the feature that for each variable there is *both* a ϕ-unselected row where that variable is assigned T, which has a ϕ-selected 1-transform involving change in just that assignment, and which has no other ϕ-selected 1-transform, *and* a ϕ-unselected row where that variable is assigned F, which likewise has a ϕ-selected 1-transform involving change in just that assignment, and which has no other ϕ-selected 1-transform?

I can at present provide no general answer to this question; nor even a proof that the ratio of the number of such *congenial* subsets over 2^{2^n}—the number of all possible classical truth functions (theories) in n variables—is strictly decreasing as n increases. But, where $\lambda(n)$ is the number of such congenial subsets, we can justify the following claims:

(a) for $n=2$, $\lambda(n)=0$;

(b) for $n=3$, $\dfrac{\lambda(n)}{2^{2^n}} = \dfrac{1}{64}$;

(c) for $n=4$, $\dfrac{\lambda(n)}{2^{2^n}} = \dfrac{1}{8192}$;

(d) for n in general, $\displaystyle\lim_{n\to\infty} \dfrac{\lambda(n)}{2^{2^n}} = 0$.

I conjecture that $\dfrac{\lambda(n)}{2^{2^n}}$ is strictly decreasing as n increases. And I suggest that the *philosophical* import of Claim (d) is the same as that of the truth of this conjecture.

II: Claims (a), (b), and (c)

It will be apparent that any congenial subset will contain more than one row, selected from opposite halves of the assignment block (given the usual conventions for listing the Ts and Fs). More generally, the selected rows must collectively involve assignments of both T and F to each of the n variables. Each selected row is associated with n 1-transforms. Let us say that an unselected row is *useful* with respect to a variable or the negation of a variable, just in case it is a 1-transform of a selected row in which that variable is assigned F/T and of no other selected row. So: we have to select rows in such a way as to generate at least $2n$ useful unselected rows, each useful in a different respect. (I shall say that a selected row gives a *decision* with respect to a variable or its negation just in case some unselected 1-transform of it is useful with respect to that variable or its negation.)

Case (a), $n = 2$:

ϕ must generate at least $2n$, $= 4$, useful unselected rows. But the assignment block contains only 4 rows. So there is no such ϕ; whence Claim (a).

Case (b), $n = 3$:

ϕ must generate at least $2n$, $= 6$, useful unselected rows. The assignment block contains only 8 rows. Hence ϕ must contain at least and at most 2 rows, which—since they must together involve assignments of both T and F to each of the 3 variables—must be *complementary* (where rows a_i and a_j in the n-variable assignment block are complementary just in case they are n-transforms).

So

$$\frac{\lambda(3)}{2^{2^3}} = \frac{2^{3-1}}{2^{2^3}} = \frac{1}{64}.$$

Case (c), $n = 4$:

Note the following three points. First, each ϕ-selected row is potentially associated with 4 useful rows. This potential is frustrated, however, if ϕ contains rows which are 2-transforms of each other, for then some of their 1-transforms will coincide, so will not be useful. If, for example, ϕ contains [TFTT] and [TTFT], we lose the potentially useful rows [TFFT] and [TTTT] since they are each 1-transforms of both those rows. More generally, a pair of selected 2-transforms can be associated with only 4, rather than 8, useful rows; and these 4 can be useful in only 2 respects—[FFTT] and [FTFT], for example, are both still useful when ϕ is as above; but they are useful in the *same* respect, namely with respect to the negation of the first variable.

Second, there is no point in ϕ's containing rows which are 1-transforms of each other since the useful rows associated with them will be useful in the same three respects—determined by the asignments of Ts and Fs shared by the selected rows—and no useful rows will be associated with them with respect to the variable over whose assignment they differ, nor with respect to its negation. So: if ϕ is congenial and contains a pair of 1-transforms, there is a congenial ϕ which omits one member of the pair. *Lemma*: if there are no k-fold congenial sets not involving 1-transforms, there are no $k+1$-fold congenial sets which do involve 1-transforms. So we can, for the moment, disregard the possibility of selecting 1-transforms.

Third, if ϕ contains (at least) three rows, no two of which are 1-transforms, then it must contain at least one pair of 2-transforms.*

* *Proof*: let a_i, a_j, a_k be three distinct rows no two of which are 1-transforms. Suppose, for reductio, that no two are 2-transforms either. So a_i is a 3- or 4-transform of a_j, and a_j is a 3- or 4-transform of a_k. If a_i is a 4-transform of a_j, then $a_i = a_k$, contrary to hypothesis, if a_k is a 4-transform of a_j; and a_i is a 1-transform of a_k, contrary to hypo-

Consequences: (i) No ϕ, not involving 1-transforms, containing exactly *three* rows can be congenial. *Proof*: since at least two must be 2-transforms, their associated useful rows can be so in only the same two respects, as noted above. The third row can generate at most four more associated useful rows—so we finish with only, at most, six decisions out of the eight we need.

(ii) No ϕ, not involving 1-transforms, containing exactly *four* rows can be congenial. While a fully explicit proof would be a bit involved, the reason, basically, is that any such ϕ includes four 3-fold subsets, each of which must contain at least one pair of 2-transforms. There are then two possibilities. *Either* ϕ includes two *disjoint* pairs of 2-transforms—in which case we get at most four decisions out of the eight we need. *Or* ϕ includes a *transitive triple* of 2-transforms—a_i a 2-transform of a_j; a_j a 2-transform of a_k; and a_i a 2-transform of a_k—which, as the reader may verify, can collectively contribute only a *single* decision so that, given that the fourth selection can contribute at most a further four, ϕ can yield at most five decisions out of the eight we need.

I leave it to the reader to verify that as ϕ increases to five, six, seven, or eight rows, the proliferation of disjoint pairs, and/or of transitive triples, of 2-transforms invariably results in fewer than the requisite eight decisions. As with $n = 3$, the only congenial sets for $n = 4$ are pairs of complementary rows. So

$$\frac{\lambda(4)}{2^{2^4}} = \frac{2^{4-1}}{2^{2^4}} = \frac{1}{2^{13}} = \frac{1}{8192}.$$

It is not true, however, even for $n = 5$, that every congenial ϕ consists in a pair of complementary rows. For example, [TTFFT, FFFTT, FTTTF] is a congenial *three*fold ϕ and [TTTTT, TTFFF, FFFTT, FFTFF] a congenial *four*-fold ϕ (each selected row being at least a 3-transform of all the others). So the natural conjecture, that

$$\frac{\lambda(n)}{2^{2^n}} = \frac{1}{2^{(2^n - n) + 1}}.$$

is false.

III: Claim (d)

Strategy of proof:
First some further definitions. Let $\tau_i a$ be the 1-transform of row a which differs from it in the ith place. (Let $\tau_o a = a$.) Let an r-tuple $[a_1, \ldots, a_r]$ of rows

---

thesis, if a_k is a 3-transform of a_j. So a_i must be a 3-transform of a_j. Likewise a_j must be a 3-transform of a_k. But then, if $a_i \neq a_k$, they must be 2-transforms, since a_k must differ from a_j both in that assignment which a_j and a_i have in common and in two over which they differ.

from the assignment block be *F-good*, respectively *T-good*, iff the ith place of a_i is F, respectively T. Let such an r-tuple *fit* a particular subset (truth function) ϕ iff, for each a_i, $\tau_i a_i \varepsilon \phi$ but neither a_i itself nor any other 1-transform of $a_i \varepsilon \phi$.

Plainly, where n is the number of variables with which we are concerned, ϕ is congenial iff it is fitted both by a T-good n-tuple and by an F-good n-tuple. (For the constituents of the two n-tuples will thereby comprise $2n$ useful rows, each useful in a different respect.)

Let S be the set of all rows in the 2^n-fold assignment block. And let $Y(a_1, \ldots, a_r)$ be the set consisting of some $a_1, \ldots, a_r, \varepsilon S$, and all their 1-transforms. Let an r-tuple $[a_1, \ldots, a_r]$ be *independent* if $a_1, \ldots, a_r$ are all distinct and none is a 1- or 2-transform of any other. And let an $(r+1)$-tuple $[a_1, \ldots, a_r, a_{r+1}]$ be *barely dependent* if $[a_1, \ldots, a_r]$ is independent but a_{r+1} is a 1- or 2-transform of at least one of $a_1, \ldots, a_r$.

Finally let $m = \dfrac{n}{2}$ if n is even, $\dfrac{n+1}{2}$ if n is odd. Let C be the set of subsets, ϕ, of S such that some independent F-good m-tuple fits ϕ. And, for each $r \geqslant 1$, $\leqslant m$, let D_r be the set of subsets, ϕ, of S such that some barely dependent F-good $(r+1)$-tuple fits ϕ.

The proof of claim (d) hinges on the observation that if ϕ is congenial, then $\phi \varepsilon \{C \cup D_1 \cup D_2 \cup \ldots \cup D_{m-1}\}$.

Proof: if ϕ is congenial, it is fitted by an F-good n-tuple $[a_1, \ldots, a_n]$. Let $[a_1, \ldots, a_m]$ be the first m terms of $[a_1, \ldots, a_n]$. If $[a_1, \ldots, a_m]$ is independent, then $\phi \varepsilon C$. If $[a_1, \ldots, a_m]$ is not independent, let $[a_1, \ldots, a_i]$ be its longest independent initial segment (which might just be a_1). In that case $[a_1, \ldots, a_i, a_{i+1}]$ is a barely dependent F-good $(i+1)$-tuple which fits ϕ; so $\phi \varepsilon D_i$.

Accordingly the number, $\lambda(n)$, of congenial such subsets, ϕ, is less than or equal to the cardinality of the union of $C, D_1, D_2, \ldots, D_{m-1}$; which is in turn less than or equal to the sum of the cardinalities of $C, D_1, D_2, \ldots, D_{m-1}$. The proof now proceeds by estimation of upper bounds on the cardinality of these sets. We establish

Lemma A:

$\overline{\overline{C}} \leqslant 2^{2^n - n}$, for arbitrary n, and

Lemma B:

$$\overline{\overline{D_1}} + \overline{\overline{D_2}} + \ldots . \overline{\overline{\overline{D_{m-1}}}} \leqslant 2^{2^n - \left(\frac{n}{2} + 1\right)},$$

provided that $n \geqslant 32$.

It follows that, for $n \geqslant 32$,

$$\lambda(n) \leqslant 2^{2^n - n} + 2^{2^n - \left(\frac{n}{2} + 1\right)}.$$

Since, for $n > 2$, $2^n - n < 2^n - \left(\dfrac{n}{2} + 1\right)$, we may infer that

$$\lambda(n) < 2 \times 2^{2^n - \left(\frac{n}{2} + 1\right)}, \; = 2^{2^n - n/2}, \; = 2^{2^n} \times 2^{-n/2}, \; = 2^{2^n} \times \frac{1}{2^{n/2}}, \; = \frac{2^{2^n}}{2^{n/2}}.$$

Hence, dividing each side by 2^{2^n}, we have

$$\frac{\lambda(n)}{2^{2^n}} < \frac{1}{2^{n/2}}, \text{ for } n \geqslant 32.$$

Whence, since $\lim\limits_{n \to \infty} \dfrac{1}{2^{n/2}} = 0$, Claim (d) follows.

Let us therefore establish the two lemmas.

Proof of Lemma A

We prove three sublemmas:

   Lemma A1: if $a_1, \ldots, a_r$ are any rows in S, the number of subsets ϕ such that $[a_1, \ldots, a_r]$ fits ϕ is less than or equal to $2^{\overline{\overline{S - Y(a_1, \ldots, a_r)}}}$, that is, 2 to the power of the number of rows in S which are distinct from $a_1, \ldots, a_r$ and are not 1-transforms of them; which is the number of sets of such rows.
   Proof. If $[a_1, \ldots, a_r]$ fits ϕ, then the only members of $Y(a_1, \ldots, a_r)$ which are members of ϕ are each $\tau_i a_i$, $1 \leqslant i \leqslant r$. Hence if $[a_1, \ldots, a_r]$ fits distinct ϕ and ϕ', then the membership of ϕ and ϕ' must be the same as far as $a_1, \ldots, a_r$ and their 1-transforms are concerned. Hence ϕ and ϕ' must differ by virtue of one, or both, containing k-transforms, $k \geqslant 2$, of some of $a_1, \ldots, a_r$ which the other does not. So the number of distinct such sets cannot be greater than the number of sets of such k-transforms of $a_1, \ldots, a_r$, $= 2^{\overline{\overline{S - Y(a_1, \ldots, a_r)}}}$.

   Lemma A2: if $[a_1, \ldots, a_r]$ is independent, then

$$Y(a_1, \ldots, a_r) = r \times (n + 1).$$

   Proof. Clearly $Y(a_p) = n + 1$; that is the set consisting of a_p and all its 1-transforms is an $(n+1)$-fold set. So it suffices to reflect that, since each element of $a_1, \ldots, a_r$ is at least a 3-transform of every other, they have no 1-transforms in common.

   Lemma A3: for each r, there are at most $2^{r \times (n-1)}$ independent F-good r-tuples.
   Proof. For each i, there are 2^{n-1} rows with F in the ith place. Hence there are $(2^{n-1} \times 2^{n-1} \times 2^{n-1} \times \ldots r$ times$)$ ways of selecting an F-good r-tuple, so $2^{r \times (n-1)}$ F-good r-tuples altogether.

By Lemma $A1$, the number of subsets, ϕ, such that a particular (independent) $[a_1, \ldots, a_m]$ fits ϕ is less than or equal to

$$2^{2^n - \overline{\overline{Y(a_1, \ldots, a_m)}}}.$$

By Lemma $A2$, if $[a_1, \ldots, a_m]$ is independent, then

$$\overline{\overline{Y(a_1, \ldots, a_m)}} = m \times (n+1).$$

So the number of subsets fitted by a particular independent $[a_1, \ldots, a_m]$ is less than or equal to

$$2^{2^n - (m \times (n+1))}.$$

Since, by Lemma $A3$, there are at most $2^{m \times (n-1)}$ independent F-good m-tuples, the number of subsets fitted by some independent F-good m-tuple or other, $= \overline{\overline{C}}$, can be at most

$$2^{2^n - (m \times (n+1))} \times 2^{m \times (n-1)},$$
$$= 2^{2^n - mn - m + mn - m} = 2^{2^n - 2m}.$$

Since $2m \geqslant n$,

$$\overline{\overline{C}} \leqslant 2^{2^n - n}, \text{ Q.E.D.}$$

Proof of Lemma B

We prove two further sublemmas:

Lemma B1: if $[a_1, \ldots, a_{r+1}]$ is barely dependent, then

$$\overline{\overline{Y(a_1, \ldots, a_{r+1})}} \geqslant (r \times (n+1)) + (n + 1 - 2r).$$

Proof. By Lemma $A2$, $\overline{\overline{Y(a_1, \ldots, a_r)}} = r \times (n+1)$. And $\overline{\overline{Y(a_{r+1})}}$, of course, is $n+1$. So Lemma $B1$ holds provided $Y(a_{r+1})$ does not contain *more* than $2r$ members which are also members of $Y(a_1, \ldots, a_r)$. Suppose, for reductio, that there are more than $2r$ such. Then (*) there must be some a_p in $[a_1, \ldots, a_r]$ such that $Y(a_p)$ and $Y(a_{r+1})$ have at least three members in common. Now a_p and a_{r+1} cannot be k-transforms, for any $k \geqslant 3$, or $Y(a_p) \cap Y(a_{r+1})$ would be empty. But they are distinct, by the definition of 'barely dependent'. Hence there are two cases:

Case (a): a_p and a_{r+1} are 1-transforms. Then $Y(a_p) \cap Y(a_{r+1}) = \{a_p, a_{r+1}\}$, contrary to (*).

Case (b): a_p and a_{r+1} are 2-transforms, differing in the ith and jth places. Then $Y(a_p) \cap Y(a_{r+1}) = \{\tau_i a_p, \tau_j a_p\}$, again contrary to (*).

Lemma B2: for each r there are at most

$$\frac{r \times n \times (n+1)}{2} \times 2^{r \times (n-1)} \text{ barely dependent F-good } (r+1)\text{-tuples.}$$

Proof. Each such $(r+1)$-tuple is constituted by an initial independent F-good r-tuple, plus a 1- or 2-transform of one of the first r elements. By

Lemma $A3$, those first r elements may be chosen in at most $2^{r \times (n-1)}$ ways. Now, any a, εS, has n 1-transforms and $(n-1+n-2+ \ldots +1)$ 2-transforms; so $\dfrac{(n+1) \times n}{2}$ 1- and 2-transforms. Hence, given that the first r elements have been chosen, the $r+1^{st}$ may be chosen in at most

$$\frac{r \times n \times (n+1)}{2} \text{ ways.}$$

(Of course, some of these choices will not be consistent with F-goodness. But remember that we are estimating an *upper* bound.) Thus the total number of ways of choosing the first r, plus the $r+1^{st}$ element, will not exceed

$$\frac{r \times n \times (n+1)}{2} \times 2^{r \times (n-1)}.$$

Now $\overline{\overline{D_r}}$, = the number of subsets, ϕ, of S which are fitted by some barely dependent F-good $(r+1)$-tuple, will not exceed the product of the maximum number of subsets fitted by a particular $(r+1)$-tuple and the maximum number of barely dependent F-good $(r+1)$-tuples.

By Lemma $A1$ and $B1$, the first is less than or equal to
$$2^{2^n - ((r \times (n+1)) + (n+1-2r))}.$$

By Lemma $B2$, the second is $\dfrac{r \times n \times (n+1)}{2} \times 2^{r \times (n-1)}$.

So $\overline{\overline{D_r}} \leqslant \dfrac{r \times n \times (n+1)}{2} \times 2^{r \times (n-1)} \times 2^{2^n - ((r \times (n+1)) + (n+1-2r))}$

which is

$$\frac{r \times n \times (n+1)}{2} \times 2^{rn - r + 2^n - ((rn+r)+(n+1-2r))},$$

i.e. " $\times 2^{rn-r+2^n-rn-r-n-1+2r}$,

i.e. " $\times 2^{2^n-(n+1)}$.

Hence $\overline{\overline{D_1}} + \ldots + \overline{\overline{D_{m-1}}} \leqslant$

$$\frac{n \times (n+1)}{2} \times 2^{2^n-(n+1)} \times [1+2+ \ldots +m-1],$$

$$=\frac{n \times (n+1)}{2} \times 2^{2^n-(n+1)} \times \frac{(m-1) \times m}{2},$$

$$=\frac{n \times (n+1) \times (m-1) \times m}{4} \times 2^{2^n-(n+1)}.$$

Let $\alpha = \dfrac{n \times (n+1) \times (m-1) \times m}{4}$, and $\quad \beta = 2^n - (n+1)$,

and $\quad k = \bar{\bar{D}}_1 + \ldots + \bar{\bar{D}}_{r-1}$.

So we have shown that $k \leqslant \alpha \times 2^\beta$.

Now an interesting arithmetical fact: for values of $n \geqslant 32$, and only for such values,

$$\alpha \times \frac{1}{2^{n/2}} \leqslant 1.$$

So $\alpha \leqslant 2^{n/2}$.

So $k \leqslant 2^{n/2} \times 2^\beta, \quad = 2^{\beta + n/2}, \quad = 2^{2^n - (n+1) + n/2},$

$= 2^{2^n - (n/2 + 1)}$, which is Lemma *B*.

Q.E.D.

CHAPTER 9

TRANSCENDENTAL ANTHROPOLOGY*

JONATHAN LEAR

1. Even a sympathetic reader of Wittgenstein's later philosophy must, I think, conclude that it represents an unfinished work. The *Philosophical Investigations*, as Wittgenstein himself says, 'is really only an album': discrete paragraphs are juxtaposed and the reader is left to extract an argument, or a point of view. This was not the result of a deliberate attempt at aphorism—to be a latter day Heraclitus—but of what Wittgenstein called failure 'to weld my results together' into a continuous whole.[1] Biographically speaking, there may be many reasons for this failure. But from a philosophical point of view the interesting question is whether this failure had to occur because Wittgenstein was pursuing disparate strands of thought which cannot coherently be reconciled. The two strands in greatest conflict are what I shall call his *anthropological* and his *transcendental* approaches to philosophy.

Language, for Wittgenstein, is one of the many activities in which men engage; and if it is to be understood, it must be seen as embedded in the context of men living their lives. A 'language-game' is not merely a language, but a 'whole, consisting of the language *and the actions into which it is woven*'.[2] And 'the term "language-game" is meant to bring into prominence the fact that the *speaking* of a language is part of an activity, or of a form of life.'[3] This would suggest that the proper study of language requires that one take an

* © Jonathan Lear 1986. I would like to thank the National Endowment for the Humanities for a Fellowship for Independent Study and Research, during which this paper was written. A draft of this paper was delivered to the Institut für Philosophie, Freie Universität, Berlin, and I would like to thank the participants for their comments. John McDowell, Philip Pettit, Timothy Smiley, and Bernard Williams read a draft of this paper and offered valuable comments.

[1] Ludwig Wittgenstein, *Philosophical Investigations* (hereafter *PI*) (Blackwell, Oxford, 1968), p. vii.
[2] Ibid. I.7.
[3] Ibid. I.23.

anthropological stance: one views a language in the context of the customs, institutions, practices of a community. It is one of the myriad ways in which a group of people interact with each other, with their environment, with themselves.

The anthropological stance would seem to encourage a naturalistic outlook: 'What we are supplying', says Wittgenstein at one point, 'are really remarks on the natural history of human beings; we are not contributing curiosities, however, but observations which no one has doubted, but which have escaped remark only because they are always before our eyes.'[4] Moreover, the anthropological stance is all-embracing. Even philosophical problems are formulated in language, and thus their meaning depends on the customs and practices in which language is used.

. . . if the words 'language', 'experience', 'world' have a use, it must be as humble a one as that of the words 'table', 'lamp', 'door'.[5]

When philosophers use a word—'knowledge', 'being', 'object', 'I', 'proposition', 'name'—and try to grasp the *essence* of the thing, one must always ask oneself: is the word ever actually used in this way in the language-game which is its original home? What *we* do is bring words back from their metaphysical to their everyday use.[6]

When I talk about language (words, sentences etc.) I must speak the language of every day.[7]

One might think: if philosophy speaks of the use of 'philosophy' there must be a second-order philosophy. But it is not so: it is, rather, like the case of orthography, which deals with the word 'orthography' among others without then being second-order.[8]

Philosophy, as it has traditionally been practised, has been an attempt to step outside our customs and practices in the hope of gaining a non-local perspective on how things really are. Wittgenstein's critique of traditional philosophy is not confined to pointing out the futility of this hope. Our striving for the philosophical perspective is itself subjected to the anthropologist's gaze. Going after the absolute truth is one of the things we think we do, and the true meaning of the activity can only be understood as such. *Everything* we do, according

---

[4] Ibid. I.415.
[5] Ibid. I.97.
[6] Ibid. I.116.
[7] Ibid. I.120.
[8] Ibid. I.121.

to Wittgenstein, is only more material for the anthropological stance.

But if there is no getting outside of the language-game, from what perspective can one take up the anthropological stance? The answer is easy when we are investigating a primitive language-game: the perspective is our own.[9] It becomes more difficult when we are investigating ourselves. On the one hand, it seems that we must give the very same answer—namely, that the perspective is our own. Yet it is not obvious how this could be the answer: the observation of another tribe's primitive activity and the acquisition of self-understanding would seem to require the exercise of different abilities. An even greater problem, though, is to show how Wittgenstein's apparent naturalism can live peaceably with the transcendental strain in his thought.[10]

A transcendental inquiry, according to Kant, was an a priori investigation into how concepts apply to objects.[11] And an object (*Objekt*), for Kant, was anything of which a concept could be predicated in a judgement.[12] If we substitute 'non-empirical' for 'a priori', then Wittgenstein's investigation of rule-following can plausibly be considered a transcendental inquiry. First, a concept for Kant has no life outside of the judgements in which it is used. And the function of a concept is to unify disparate representations under it. A rule for Wittgenstein has no life outside the actual contexts in which it is used. And we may think of the actual instances of following a rule as the 'particulars' which are unified under the 'universal' rule. A rule is a 'one over many'. And a judgement in which a concept is applied to an object is a special case of rule-following. Second, although we are to consider our rule-following procedures in the context of our customs and practices, the result of the investigation is not meant to be an empirical explanation of our ability to follow rules, but non-empirical insight into how we go on.[13]

[9] Cf. for example ibid. I.2.

[10] I began to discuss this issue in 'The Disappearing "We"', *Aristotelian Society Supplementary Volume*, lviii (1984), 219–42. See also my 'Leaving the World Alone', *Journal of Philosophy*, lxxix (1982), 382–403.

[11] Immanuel Kant, *Kritik der reinen Vernunft* (hereafter *KdrV*), Akademie-Textausgabe (De Gruyter, Berlin, 1968), B25. Cf. *Critique of Pure Reason* (hereafter *CPR*), translated by Norman Kemp Smith (Macmillan, London, 1929).

[12] See H. E. Allison's helpful discussion of the difference between *Objekt* and *Gegenstand* in the Transcendental Deduction: *Kant's Transcendental Idealism* (Yale University Press, New Haven, 1983), esp. Chapter 7.

[13] Cf. for example *PI* I.109, 126.

It is commonly thought that Wittgenstein's later philosophy could not be seen as a transcendental inquiry, not merely because he insists upon the anthropological stance, but because there is no room for the Kantian distinction between the world of appearance and the world as it is in itself. For one cannot filter out the mind's contribution to experience and consider it independently. There is thus no room for the concept of the world as it is independently of that contribution. But that there is no room for this transcendental distinction does not imply that there is no room for transcendental philosophy. One might be able to take a transcendental stance with respect to ordinary activities like speaking a language.

In contemporary discussion, the phrase 'transcendental investigation' is often used to describe an inquiry into the necessary structure of the mind, of the world, or of both. This is not how Kant defined the term; though it is a plausible extension of his usage, since, for him, an a priori inquiry into the application of concepts to objects would ultimately yield necessary truths about the formal structure imposed by mind. But I am suggesting an alternative. I suggest that we go back to Kant's definition and loosen it: so that a non-empirical inquiry into rule-following counts as a transcendental investigation. Wittgenstein's later philosophy can then be seen as a transcendental inquiry even though it displays no interest in necessary structures.

The most interesting question about Wittgenstein's later philosophy is, I think, how one can adopt the anthropological stance and the transcendental stance simultaneously.[14] The anthropological stance would seem to pull one in the direction of an empirical explanation of how we go on. Succumbing to this pull, however, would violate the stricture that philosophy should have no such concern. And it would threaten Wittgenstein's repeated demand that philosophical reflection should leave our practices and customs intact.[15] For if philosophy were to bequeath us an empirical explanation of how we go on, it would seem to be open to us to decide that certain features of the explanans were unsatisfactory and ought to be changed. Even if the explanation itself explained why we couldn't alter our condition—like for instance an anthropology that explained why it is psychologically impossible for us not to believe in

[14] See Bernard Williams, 'Wittgenstein and Idealism', in his *Moral Luck* (CUP, Cambridge, 1982).

[15] *PI* I.124, 133; and see my 'Leaving the World Alone', op. cit.

God—this feature alone could not be sufficient to transform anthropology into philosophy. What we are looking for is a philosophical understanding of why philosophy should be non-revisionary, not a psychological one.

Here a comparison with Kant might be helpful. When Kant argued that even basic laws of logic or arithmetic could ultimately not be understood independently of the activities of a judging mind, that was not supposed to undermine them. A transcendental consideration which revealed these laws to depend on a subjective contribution of mind was intended to provide insight into why, from an empirical perspective, these laws were genuinely objective and necessary. Kant attempted a remarkable juggling act: to preserve a full-blooded sense of objectivity, but give a philosophical account which revealed it as dependent upon mind. Whether or not Kant was successful, there is at least a serious attempt at a radical philosophical analysis which reflectively reinforces rather than undermines the beliefs we had before we engaged in philosophical inquiry. Is there any effort in Wittgenstein to show why his investigations should not be reflectively destabilizing? Why should we not come to view the law of non-contradiction as merely one of the deeply held tribal beliefs of our tribe? If, however, the anthropological stance would seem to pull us toward empirical explanations and relativism, the requirements of a transcendental investigation would seem to pull us away from any kind of anthropological insight.

2. The interest in the relation between a transcendental and an empirical inquiry spreads beyond a problem internal to Wittgenstein's philosophy. Ever since Hegel's critique of Critical Philosophy, it has been clear that Kant's attempt at a purely formal philosophy was a failure.[16] The a priori and the a posteriori, the transcendental and the empirical, the formal and the material cannot be kept as distinct as Kant thought they could. Yet in the wake of this realization it remains unclear what to do about it. The danger, on one side, is that philosophy will collapse into the purely empirical: concern itself solely with methodological problems in the empirical sciences. On the other side, the danger is that philosophy

---

[16] See for example G. W. F. Hegel, *Encyclopaedia of the Philosophical Sciences*, vol. I sections 40–60, translated by W. Wallace (Clarendon Press, Oxford, 1975); and Robert Pippin, *Kant's Theory of Form* (Yale University Press, New Haven, 1982).

will become vacuous by remaining a purely a priori inquiry. Studying the relation between the transcendental and anthropological
strains in Wittgenstein's later philosophy provides a way of focusing
on a central problem in the history of post-Kantian philosophy.

In Wittgenstein's mature thought the transcendental and the
anthropological appear to be intended to form a coherent whole. Indeed, the anthropological is invoked in the service of the transcendental. If we are to gain reflective, non-empirical insight into how
concepts apply to objects, we must become aware of how we go on.
Clearly, Wittgenstein is trying to gain deeper insight into the application of concepts to objects than is afforded by such conditions as
'x satisfies "is one metre long" if and only if x is one metre long'.
Nor would it help to give a more informative condition, for example,
'if and only if x is the same length as the standard metre rod in Paris'.
He believes a deeper insight is available than could be given by any
empirical account of the correct application conditions for a concept
to an object. And this insight becomes available to us by reflectively
considering how we use the concept: how the concept is 'woven into'
our customs, practices, and institutions. Transcendental insight
seems to require the anthropological stance. Yet why are we not then
simply substituting one type of empirical explanation for another? If
we have to consider our interests, projects, and desires before we can
fully appreciate the basis for the application of a concept to an object, is not Wittgenstein just offering a very different sort of empirical
account? If so, then isn't he vulnerable to this objection: 'If the moon
has a circumference of n metres, then the circumference would have
been such whether or not human life had ever existed; and whether
or not human beings had ever devised the metric system of measurement'? One would like to be able to treat this objection analogously
to the response Kant would make to the claim that there would have
been physical objects even if there had been no observers. As an
empirical claim the 'objection' may be true, but it is not then an objection. For Kant is not making a rival claim; he is investigating the
transcendental content of all such claims. There would have been
physical objects even if there had been no observers: but what it is to
be an object can only be fully understood by reference to the synthetic activities of a discursive intelligence.[17] The question is
whether an analogous response is open to Wittgenstein.

[17] *KdrV*/*CPR* B129–38.

One leaves the arena of empirical explanations on a *via negativa*: by a process of elimination one discovers that the obvious forms of empirical explanation could not possibly answer the question that is being asked. A purely physical account cannot explain language-mastery. If we treat the person as a complex physical machine—say, a computer that is programmed in the course of language-training—we leave out of account what it is about his behaviour that makes it the speaking of a language. Language-speaking is permeated with norms: there are ways one ought and ought not to behave if one is to speak a language. And these *oughts*, Wittgenstein believes, cannot be derived from the *is* of a physically based disposition to respond.[18] That I am disposed to call this object 'red' may be physically explicable, but my physical programming (if there be such) could explain neither why my calling it 'red' is correct nor why my utterance is an actual predication and not a meaningless vocalization.

Nor is a mental explanation possible. We discover, first, that our actions are *ultimately unconditioned* in the sense that whatever reasons we might have invoked as explaining our actions give out. Ultimately we just act.

. . . But how does he know where and how to look up the word 'red' and what he is to do with the word 'five'?—Well, I assume he *acts* as I have described. Explanations come to an end somewhere.[19]

. . . if a person has not yet got the *concepts*, I shall teach him to use the words by means of *examples* and by *practice*.—And when I do this I do not communicate to him less than I know myself.[20]

How can he know how he is to continue the pattern by himself—whatever instruction you give him?—Well, how do I know?—If that means, 'Have I reasons?' the answer is: 'my reasons will soon give out. And then I shall act, without reasons'.[21]

'How am I to obey a rule?'—If this is not a question about causes, then it is about the justification for my following the rule in the way I do. If I have

---

[18] *PI* I.193–5. See Saul Kripke, *Wittgenstein on Rules and Private Language* (Blackwell, Oxford, 1982), 23–37.
[19] *PI* I.1.
[20] Ibid. I.208.
[21] Ibid. I.211.

exhausted the justifications I have reached bedrock, and my spade is turned. Then I am inclined to say: 'This is simply what I do.'[22]

When I obey a rule, I do not choose. I obey the rule *blindly*.[23]

Second, we discover that within the realm of the mental, at least on a certain familiar conception of that realm, our actions are *completely unconditioned* in the sense that nothing available to an individual's consciousness (as it is portrayed within this conception) could direct or explain language-mastery. No 'mental' item, such as an image, idea, formula, rule, can dictate how it itself is to be used, nor can it guide the use of its correlated linguistic expression.[24] But it is the use we make of an expression that seems to give it its life, its meaning. If the mental item floats free of the use we make of the expression, then it floats free of the meaning as well. (Of course, Wittgenstein's critique is not confined to pointing out the inefficacy of such items: the very idea of the mind as an individual's container of these special items, and correspondingly the idea of his consciousness as his special access to the contents of such a container, are under attack.)

There is thus no image, and more generally no 'mental' item of that kind, which guides language-use, and this activity cannot be explained by appeal to any such item. This does not imply that there is no substance to the grasping of a concept or the following of a rule; but whatever substance there is must be understood in terms of how a person acts and the context into which his actions are woven. 'There is', as Wittgenstein famously said, 'a way of grasping a rule which is *not* an *interpretation*, but which is exhibited in what we call "obeying the rule" and "going against it" in actual cases'. (*PI* I.201.) One can say that someone has grasped a rule, and even that his linguistic activity is faithful to it: but the rule he has grasped does not explain his activity; his activity gives substance to the claim that he has grasped the rule.

Precisely because mental items, on the conception under attack, cannot explain use, one must look to the use itself. And this use is communal. In this way the lack of mental explanation seems to force us to adopt the anthropological stance. 'Language' as a term can

---

[22] Ibid. I.217.
[23] Ibid. I.219.
[24] Ibid. I.139–41, 152–3.

easily suggest something fixed and frozen, something object-like. But, for Wittgenstein, language is not a thing we possess, in virtue of which we are able to engage in the activities of speaking a language; the myriad activities *are* the language. And it is in virtue of participating in these activities that we say that someone 'understands the language'.

The form of life in which a language is embedded is, for Wittgenstein, an activity. And it is constituted by the activities of a community of persons who share perceptions of salience, routes of interest, feelings of naturalness in following a rule.[25] These people are, let us say, *so minded*.[26] Consider, for example, measuring. It is obviously a contingent matter that we measure as we do: not merely that we use feet and metres, but that we go in for exact measurement. The interesting point, for Wittgenstein, is not that we measure as we do, but that what measuring is is to some extent determined by the ways we measure. These ways of measuring are expressive of our interests and purposes. To become reflectively aware of this, we may imaginatively present ourselves with people whose practices are expressive of other interests; for example, people who use flexible measuring rods to deal with each other flexibly, or a tribe who 'piled lumber in arbitrary, varying height and then sold it at a price proportionate to the area covered by the piles'.[27] To make it even prima facie plausible that these activities are alternative forms of *measuring*, we must surround the practices with a set of interests and concerns that give life to them. The point is not merely that it is contingent that we go in for exact measurements. For what it is for something to be an exact measurement is itself partially constituted by our practices.

There are several important aspects of this thought experiment which it is easy to overlook. First, this entire imaginative and reflective exercise is being conducted from our perspective. We are deciding what to countenance as an alternative form of measurement. Even when we try to come to grips with a form of other-mindedness, it is we who are trying to come to grips with it. Second, the result of the thought experiment is not that this other tribe is measuring correctly.

[25] See Stanley Cavell, 'The Availability of Wittgenstein's Later Philosophy', in *Must We Mean What We Say?* (CUP, Cambridge, 1976), 52.

[26] See 'Leaving the World Alone', op. cit.

[27] Ludwig Wittgenstein, *Remarks on the Foundations of Mathematics* (hereafter, *RFM*), (Blackwell, Oxford, 1967), I.5, 148–9, cf. 118.

They are not. Since what it is to measure correctly is partially constituted by our practices, in failing to conform to those practices, they fail to measure correctly. Ultimately, we must conclude that their practices do not constitute (any form of) correct measurement. (We might also conclude that they have no need for or interest in correct measurement, and that this alternative form of exchange was sufficient for their purposes.) So it is a mistake to conclude from the thought experiment that there is no fact of the matter as to who is measuring correctly, we or they. The tribal practices do bear a 'family resemblance' to measuring practices, and thus we can imaginatively entertain them, at least momentarily, as 'an alternative form of measuring'. But the point of the thought experiment for Wittgenstein is not to establish the existence of alternative forms of measurement, still less to prove that relativism is true with respect to incommensurable measurement systems. The point is to help us reflectively to grasp the fact that our own form of measuring—that is, measuring—is itself expressive of and partially constituted by our interests and practices. We find it easier to realize this about ourselves after we have imaginatively 'observed' a tribe whose practices are expressive of other interests.

So, if we wish to interpret the man who says 'If the moon has a circumference of n metres, the circumference would have been such whether or not human life had ever existed' as speaking truly, we must interpret him as presupposing our current practices. That is, we must interpret him as saying that the moon's circumference is not dependent on human decision (in the way that the circumference of the Berlin Wall is), and (given the practices of measuring we actually do employ) that circumference is n metres. So (a) given the truth of the antecedent, the conditional as a whole is true. But if we take the conditional as asking us to abstract completely from current measuring practices, then, for Wittgenstein, the conditional loses content. For (b) if we do not presuppose our present mindedness, we cannot assign a determinate truth value to the conditional. It would not be false (as it would be if, in those conditions, the moon were of circumference m (less than n) metres). The reason for (b) is: (c) if we do not presuppose our mindedness, we cannot assign determinate content to the antecedent. So the conditional fails not because it is impossible to determine the truth of the consequent, given the truth of the antecedent, but because the antecedent ceases to express a condition.

Although, as we have seen, there is a naturalistic strain in Wittgenstein's thought, he is pretty clear that the anthropological stance is not intended to yield a natural history. We imagine various tribal practices not to study them seriously but to cure our (natural) tendency toward conceptual platonism:

> . . . we are not doing natural science; nor yet natural history—since we can also invent fictitious natural history for our purposes.

> I am not saying: if such-and-such facts of nature were different people would have different concepts (in the sense of a hypothesis). But: if anyone believes that certain concepts are absolutely the correct ones, and that having different ones would mean not realizing something that we realize—then let him imagine certain very general facts of nature to be different from the ones we are used to, and the formation of concepts different from the usual ones will become intelligible to him.[28]

But even if we are ultimately concerned with ourselves and not with other tribes, why isn't Wittgenstein's account of measuring a piece of empirical anthropology? Why can we not explain measuring as the outcome of the interests we have? And why would this explanation not serve to explain the shifts in interests and concerns that might lead us to adopt other practices—to become other-minded?[29] Is there any room for a distinctively philosophical account of our practice?

3. One way of dealing with this puzzle, which I shall call the *split-level interpretation*, would be to maintain that there are two levels of discourse, the empirical level where one can offer a genuine explanation of our activities, and the philosophical level which provides a reflective account of what such an explanation consists in. Thus the empirical anthropologist's explanation of our practice of measuring—that we act in these ways for these reasons—need not be in conflict with the philosopher's claim that we obey rules *blindly*. The philosophical claim that we obey rules blindly is only intended to make clear what it is to act with reasons: for example, that it is not a matter of having reasons present to consciousness (in the philosophically loaded sense).

On this interpretation, the empirical and transcendental

---

[28] *PI* p. 230.
[29] Wittgenstein does recognize the possibility of shifts in interests and practices. See *On Certainty* (Blackwell, Oxford, 1979), §63.

anthropologists are not making rival claims; the latter is giving a reflective analysis of the former's explanation. For example, when I assume the role of *empirical* anthropologist—put on my pith helmet, hide behind a chair, and watch me cooking dinner—I see my behaviour as rule-governed. I am engaged in various actions, among them occasionally measuring out ingredients; and these actions have explanations in terms of intentions, reasons, and desires. Now after a certain amount of philosophical reflection, I am also supposed to see myself as acting blindly. The empirical anthropologist in me has seen me as acting for reasons, the philosopher in me asks, 'What is it for me to be doing such?'. In philosophical reflection I discover that there need be nothing 'in my mind' which guides my behaviour. I can be said to be following a rule if I have been initiated into the custom or practice, I am relatively alert, and my behaviour conforms to the rule. Thus if I pour out the required amount of flour, I am genuinely following a recipe, even if my thoughts are absorbed in this essay. And this rule-following behaviour is to be distinguished from the behaviour of a man who has never before encountered cooking or recipes but happens to pour out the same amount of flour. The latter man's behaviour, as Kant would say, has mere legality: it is in accordance with the rules, but it doesn't follow them. There is, on the split-level interpretation, no disagreement between philosopher and empirical anthropologist at the reflective level of explaining actions in terms of reasons, beliefs, and desires. If there is to be a disagreement, it would have to be at the *meta*-reflective level: over what it is to give such an explanation. The philosophical claim that we obey rules blindly would be a rival only to an equally meta-reflective claim: for example that acting for reasons can only consist in consciously experienced reasons causing the actions. On the split-level interpretation, Wittgenstein is not challenging the empirical anthropologist, he is challenging an alternative philosophical account of what it is for the empirical anthropologist to give an explanation.

The main problem with the split-level interpretation concerns the plausibility of there being two levels of discourse, one empirical, one philosophical, which are relatively unimpugned by each other's claims. Kant was able to introduce the distinction between an empirical and a transcendental consideration of a subject matter because, for him, our ability to think far outstrips the conditions of our sensible experience. Thus, Kant thought, we can *consider* an object both as it appears to a human knower and as it is in itself independent of the conditions of human knowledge. Our knowledge of the object is of course confined to objects only in so far as they satisfy the conditions of knowledge. Thus, for Kant, it is possible to say of an object both that it is real and that it is merely appearance without thereby making rival claims.

But how, for Wittgenstein, could there be any distinctively philosophical consideration of a subject matter which would leave an empirical consideration of that subject matter unaffected? The idea of a separate philosophical level of discourse would have been anathema to him: thus it is fairly clear that he, at least, would have been hostile to the split-level interpretation.

Wittgenstein's own reasons for this hostility are admittedly open to criticism, even from a Wittgensteinian perspective. Wittgenstein insisted that philosophers must 'speak the language of every day', for an expression could have no more meaning than the use that was made of it. But the important point for a Wittgensteinian should be that meaning remains responsible to use, not that meaning cannot outstrip everyday use. Wittgenstein was of course concerned to deny the possibility of a transcendent perspective from which one can view our form of life. But one can grant this and still insist that an expression may acquire meaning in philosophy which outstrips everyday use. Philosophy is an activity in which some of us engage, and very little of it these days is a search for a transcendent perspective. Since philosophy is an activity, words may acquire uses within this activity which differ from the 'everyday use', though perhaps the uses bear a family resemblance to each other. (Consider, for example, Wittgenstein's own use of 'language-game'.) A Wittgensteinian ought to be able to show how his claims are grounded in legitimate philosophical activity—to show that he is not simply trying to speak from God's perspective. He should not have to 'speak the language of every day'.

The problem with the split-level interpretation, then, is not that philosophical activity may not stretch everyday use. It is rather that there is no way to keep the distinction between the empirical and the philosophical stable. If there were a distinctive activity, philosophy, which bore no relation to the rest of our lives, then words might get special meanings within that activity which differed from the meanings they had in our ordinary lives. The uses would occur, and continue to occur, independently of each other. But philosophy is not so divorced from the rest of our lives. This may be unobvious if we restrict our attention to Wittgenstein's tribes, who are all unreflectively engaging in their activities. But remember: (a) the divide between the philosophical and the empirical is supposed to have the philosopher on one side _and the empirical anthropologist on the other_; (b) much of the everyday lives of the readers of this essay will include a fair amount of reflection. It is thus a mistake to assume that the difference between the empirical and philosophical can be assimilated to a difference in the level of reflective awareness involved. Kant could make such an assimilation because he believed that the empirical coincided with the phenomenal world from which one could step outside, if only in thought. But if we abandon the distinction between world of appearance and world as it is in itself, the distinction between empirical and transcendental becomes less easy to draw. At first, it does look like a distinction between levels of reflection. For in Wittgenstein's own philosophy the transcendental coincides with a reflective consideration of unreflective activities. However, the reason that reflective consideration can plausibly be called 'transcendental' is not simply that it is reflective, but that it purports to provide non-empirical insight. Prima facie, there is room for an alternative study which is equally reflective, but which offers empirical explanation instead. It is therefore too quick to assume that empirical anthropology must be a less reflective discipline than transcendental anthropology. Empirical anthropology may incorporate a tremendous amount of self-reflection and self-understanding. To remain empirical, it need only continue to offer explanations of the tribe it studies: explanations which may cover the anthropologists in the tribe who are doing the explaining.

There can, therefore, be no isolated and immune level of philosophical discourse; though not for the reasons usually advanced. Words may acquire a special meaning within philosophical activity. However, since our lives form a (perhaps webbed) whole, this use tends to work its way into 'ordinary use'. Further, philosophical activity is not the only reflective activity there is. In so far as the special use is the outcome of reflection, it may engage with the claims of other reflective enterprises, such as empirical anthropology.

In general, Wittgenstein's philosophy is limited by its lack of consideration of reflective activity. Indeed, for Wittgenstein to claim that philosophy should be non-revisionary, he must be violating one of his other taboos. He must be standing _outside_ the form of life in order to describe it. If we take the simple cases of tribal behaviour Wittgenstein actually considered—for example, selling piles of lumber—both the empirical and the transcendental anthropologist are on the outside looking in. (None of the people piling lumber is wondering how this activity could best be understood.) But now suppose the form of life encompasses us all. Then Wittgenstein must be seen as trying to get some members of 'the tribe' to revise their practices: '*We must do away with all explanation*'.

To whom is this injunction addressed? Who are the *we* who must do away with all explanation: we philosophers? we anthropologists? On the split-level interpretation, the injunction would be restricted to philosophers, and it might be understood in the following way. Within a practice there may be certain types of explanations which would *justify* various aspects of the practice in the sense of providing the reasons why the agents in the practice act as they do. For example, my flour-measuring activity may be explained by my interests in cooking, eating, and feeding others. These interests permeate the community; indeed, I have been taught the standard practices which manifest them. No doubt I would measure out flour differently if I belonged to a community which ate only raw food, had no cooking practices, but did on occasion pour out flour in order to predict the weather. Thus my reasons do provide an explanation of my flour-measuring activity, but both my flour-measuring activity and my reasons for it are 'internal' to the cooking practices. On the split-level interpretation, these 'internal' explanations are all right. And so are the causal explanations which try to isolate the empirical causes of a community's evolution. The injunction is only directed at the philosopher who wants to continue the justificatory process: to justify the justifications, to provide a justification of the form of life as a whole. It is the philosopher who must recognize that reasons soon give out, that justifications are soon exhausted, that 'what has to be accepted, the given, is—so one could say—*forms of life*'.[30]

There are two apparent virtues of this interpretation. First, we are not forced to interpret Wittgenstein as implausibly denying the common-sense belief that we can explain my flour-measuring activities in terms of my reasons and interests. Second, an otherwise mysterious (and potentially threatening) injunction is explained in terms of other aspects of Wittgenstein's philosophy with which we are (by

---

[30] *PI* p. 226.

now) familiar. For Wittgenstein, explanations by reasons do eventually give out, there are no justifications of forms of life; and it is
reassuring to read Wittgenstein's injunction as no more than a re-
iteration of those points.

However, the danger of interpreting the unfamiliar in terms of the
familiar is that we may forfeit insight into the genuinely unfamiliar.
Wittgenstein, as we have seen, was himself aware that the *Investigations* was an unfinished work. And a problem which is crying out
for attention (perhaps it is *left* crying because Wittgenstein was sceptical that one could give it adequate attention) is how we are to
understand reflective philosophical activity when it goes on within a
form of life. Wittgenstein's ambivalence to philosophy is, I believe,
encapsulated in the pros and cons of the split-level interpretation.
On the one hand, it does give a distinctively philosophical account of
why philosophers should do away with philosophical explanations.
Thus it respects Wittgenstein's oft-repeated demand that philosophy
should be non-revisionary (at least with respect to our non-philo-
sophical practices). On the other hand, there is no reason to suppose
that there is any distinctive and isolated realm of philosophical reflection.

If the split-level interpretation is to be rejected, if philosophy is
not a self-contained activity providing insight into our other activities which are themselves unaffected by philosophical reflection, then
the injunction that we must do away with all explanation begins to
look more puzzling. Even if we do come to this injunction via philosophical reflection, and even if the reflection is (as the split-level
interpretation says) that ultimately we act without reasons or justifications, one would expect that insight to ripple through various aspects of our (reflective) lives. This would suggest a *dialectical
interpretation* of Wittgenstein's injunction: after a certain process of
philosophical reflection—for example, working through the *Philosophical Investigations*—we come to adopt a different attitude to the
practice of explanation by reasons. This is not a specifically 'philosophical' attitude, nor is it confined solely to 'philosophical' explanations.

Let me give a perhaps fanciful example of how this might work.
Suppose we come to realize not merely that reasons must ultimately
peter out, but that the very practice of reason-giving presupposes
that this is not so. For example, suppose that the implicit telos of any
reason-giving is ultimately a structure which terminates in self-justi-

fying reasons. Then if we come to realize that reasons must simply give out, we ought also to realize that even in our most primitive reason-giving explanations, we were engaging in an activity which could not ultimately be legitimated. Philosophical reflection might then have some (destabilizing) effect on our ordinary reason-giving practices. The philosopher in the kitchen might then not merely refrain from trying to justify the cooking form of life, but come to believe that even 'within' that form of life the account he is inclined to give of his flour-measuring activity in terms of his explanations does not itself constitute an explanation. He might come to think that we (all of us who are inclined to cite reasons) must do away with all (reason-giving) explanations.

An outstanding problem for philosophy is to give an account of how philosophical reflection ripples through the rest of our lives. Unfortunately, we cannot turn to Wittgenstein for this account, since he confines himself to giving a reflective account of unreflective practices. Indeed, it is only because he concentrates on un-self-conscious practices that his demand that philosophy be non-revisionary seems the least bit plausible. Because he ignores reflective practices, Wittgenstein's own philosophical practice must be deficient in self-understanding.

4. Let us assume that the dialectical interpretation is correct: that as we work our way through the *Investigations*, the insights gained will not be specifically philosophical, but will permeate through our various reflective activities. How then might the anthropological and transcendental strains in Wittgenstein's thought form a coherent whole? In trying to answer this question, I do not claim to be uncovering the hidden truth of Wittgenstein's later philosophy. One of the ways in which the *Investigations* is an unfinished work is that it does not provide a definitive answer to this question.

Remember, first, that the distinction between the empirical and the transcendental is not a distinction of subject matter, but a distinction in the way that subject matter is considered.[31] A transcendental

---

[31] See Gerold Prauss, *Erscheinung bei Kant* (De Gruyter, Berlin, 1971); and *Kant und das Problem der Dinge an sich* (Bouvier Verlag H. Grundmann, Bonn, 1974); Henry Allison, *Kant's Transcendental Idealism*, op. cit.; 'Kant's Conception of the Transcendental Object', *Kant-Studien*, lix (1968); 'Things in Themselves, Noumena and Transcendental Objects', *Dialectica*, xxxii (1978).

consideration of what we are like is considering the very same people as an empirical inquiry into human nature, but it purports to yield some form of non-empirical insight. Second, it is important to realize that Wittgenstein does not confine us to reflecting solely on what can be gleaned from the anthropological stance. Although Wittgenstein is often labelled a behaviourist, he makes heavy use of the first-person access we have to our lives ('perspective' is the wrong word) to draw us to his philosophical outlook. For example,

. . . *while* I am being guided everything is quite simple, I notice nothing *special*; but afterwards, when I ask myself what it was that happened, it seems to have been something indescribable. *Afterwards* no description satisfies me. It's as if I couldn't believe that I merely looked, made such-and-such a face, and drew a line.—But don't I *remember* anything else? No; and yet I feel as if there must have been something else; in particular when I say 'guidance', 'influence', and other such words to myself. . . . 'For surely,' I tell myself, 'I was being *guided*.'—Only then does the idea of that ethereal, intangible influence arise.

When I look back on the experience I have the feeling that what is essential about it is an 'experience of being influenced', of a connexion—as opposed to any mere simultaneity of phenomena: but at the same time I should not be willing to call any experienced phenomenon the 'experience of being influenced'. (This contains the germ of the idea that the will is not a *phenomenon*.) I should like to say that I had experienced the '*because*', and yet I do not want to call any phenomenon the 'experience of the because'.

I should like to say: 'I experience the because'. Not because I remember such an experience, but because when I reflect on what I experience in such a case I look at it through the medium of the concept 'because' (or 'influence' or 'cause' or 'connexion').[32]

It is only because we can reflect on our own inner experience that we can come to a proper understanding of what really happens when we want to say we 'experience the because'. The non-observational access we have to our lives necessarily escapes the anthropologist's gaze. And it is only because we have such an access to our lives that Wittgenstein's observations about acting blindly or acting ultimately without reasons begin to seem plausible.

The outcome of Wittgenstein's investigation is, of course, not meant to be the empirical discovery that, as it happens, there is no mental item, present to consciousness (in that philosophically

---

[32] *PI* I.175–7.

loaded sense), which determines my rule-following behaviour. The outcome is supposed to be the philosophical realization that no such mental item *could possibly* explain or legitimate rule-following activity. But how can we get such a strong conclusion from consulting the quality of our inner life? Certainly the appeal to our inner life cannot be a step in a purely a priori argument. Where does the argumentative force of Wittgenstein's reflections come from? And what must we be like to be able to work our way through these philosophical reflections?

Although our consultation of inner experience is not a priori, it is a priori that we can make such a consultation. Kant, as is well known, argued that it must be possible for the 'I think' to accompany all my representations. This, Kant argued, was a transcendental condition of self-consciousness: indeed it was an analytic principle, defining what it is for something to be a representation of mine. It is important not to conflate pure apperception with an 'I think'. Immediately after introducing the analytic principle of apperception, Kant says:

> I call it *pure apperception*, because it is that self-consciousness which, *while generating the representation 'I think'*, . . . *cannot itself be accompanied by any further representation.*[33]

There must be an I which is distinct from any 'I think' that I actually think. (And not for the reason that it is an 'I think' which someone else thinks.) Each 'I think' that I actually think is itself a representation, and thus is subject to the possibility of having an 'I think' attached to it. This *permanent possibility* of reflective consciousness is original apperception: *that which generates* the representation 'I think'. Original apperception is a form of consciousness. It is not the 'I think' that is predicated of a given representation. Nor, since it is a *permanent* possibility, is it even an 'I think' which is predic*able* of a representation in the sense that *it* could actually be predicated. When I actually predicate an 'I think' of a representation *R*, I judge that the representation is mine. The judgement 'I think *R*' may represent a form of self-conscious awareness, but one must

---

[33] *KdrV/CPR* B132. Again, see Allison's helpful discussion of the Transcendental Deduction and apperception in *Kant's Transcendental Idealism*, op. cit., Chapters 7, 13. See also Pierre Lachieze-Rey, *L'idéalisme Kantien* (Librairie Philosophique J. Vrin, Paris, 1950).

recognize that this judgement is no more than a judgement that is occurring within the conscious life of a self-conscious being: it is one more representation. Of course, I can now step back from the reflective judgement and consider it—I can actually predicate the 'I think' of 'I think R'—but now I am treating the judgement 'I think R' as an object of predication. The activity of judging or predicating cannot be fully captured by any judgement.

However, there *is* a form of awareness of the predicating, which is distinct from the predication itself. It is an awareness which is required for the representation 'I think R' to be itself part of a larger single self-consciousness, which is distinct from *all* its representations. It is a consciousness which can simply accompany the activity of predicating. The 'I think' which I actually predicate thus serves mainly as a dialectical tool which leads me to recognize a form of self-awareness distinct from it. But then Kant should have given it a different name, if only to distinguish it from the genuinely predicable 'I think'. Let us call the original synthetic unity of apperception an 'I:'. (I use a colon to symbolize the idea that this is the consciousness which must be able to accompany each of my representations.) Kant should then be amended so as to claim that the 'I:' must be able to *accompany* all my representations, whereas the 'I think' must be *predicable* of all of them. Once I have recognized the distinct forms of apperception, I can kick away the 'I think': *any* predicating or judging I do—any activity of applying a concept to an object— may be accompanied by this awareness.

That I must be able to accompany my rule-following activity with consciousness is a *transcendental condition of subjectivity*. (By contrast, the realization that what it is like to be a bat is inaccessible to human consciousness is empirical, discovered by reflection on the differing neurophysiological constitutions of bats and humans.)[34] So the point is not merely that Wittgenstein makes appeal to a non-observational access we have to our lives; it is a transcendental condition of our subjectivity that we have this access. This condition has a dual in the first person plural. If the form of life is *constituted* by our rule-following activities, then the non-observational consciousness with which each of us can accompany our rule-following activities ought, a fortiori, also to provide a non-observational

---

[34] See Thomas Nagel, 'What is It Like To Be A Bat?', in his *Mortal Questions* (CUP, Cambridge, 1979).

consciousness of the form of life itself. That we (that is, each of us) must be able to accompany our rule-following activities with consciousness is a transcendental condition of *our* subjectivity.

If we are able to work through the *Investigations*, we must also be beings who can reflect on what our non-observational consciousness can accompany. And reflecting on what this non-observational consciousness does accompany, we realize that nothing in it could explain or legitimate rule-following: nothing in it could be that extra something which turns my behaviour into rule-following or guarantees that my rule-following is correct. Yet this consciousness accompanies activity which is partially constitutive of the form of life. For Wittgenstein, as we have seen, the activity of following a rule need not occur in the mind of an individual thinker: there is a way of grasping a rule which is exhibited in our customs, practices, in actual instances of obeying and disobeying it. Yet each of us can simply accompany our rule-following activities with consciousness, and reflection on what the 'I:' can accompany may alter the judgements we wish to make about them. I discover that I act blindly. And I have an access to my blind actions which is denied to the empirical anthropologist watching me (even when I am the anthropologist). I can go along with them. My actions may be accompanied by consciousness and that should be a consciousness of unconditioned activity. That is a form of awareness of my actions which does not consist in looking down on them. It is not a form of reflective consciousness, but its presence does give more material for reflective consciousness. For, tempted as I am to say that I 'experienced the because', I know at first hand that I didn't.

A concept for the later Wittgenstein is merely the ontological shadow of a predicate. And the life of a predicate consists in the use we are so minded as to make of it. Thus if I am a competent speaker of a language, the 'I:' which can accompany my use of a predicate ought to provide a consciousness of the unfolding of a concept. Ironically, though, what is so remarkable about the quality of this consciousness is that there is nothing remarkable about it. We are not in direct contact with the concept, still less with the Absolute Idea. The fact that my consciousness is of the unfolding of the concept is ultimately a fact not about my consciousness but about the location of my activity in a larger context of customs and practices. When I use an expression, I exercise my practical ability to participate in the practice, but I may have little reflective understanding of how the expression is used.[35] Therefore, Kant's analytic principle of apperception needs to be qualified. While making an assertion *R*, I may self-consciously think 'I think *R*', but the full content of that to which the 'I think' attaches may not be within my grasp. For Kant, the mind was completely aware of at least the representational content of its representations. But for Wittgenstein the content of the thought 'I think *R*' will depend on a context of use in which I can participate, to which I can practically commit myself, but of which I may lack reflective understanding.

Therefore, to work through Wittgenstein's philosophical dialectic, we must also be able to take up the anthropological stance: it is by considering our activities as embedded in the context of customs and practices that we come to see how they could be genuine cases of rule-following. Yet, even leaving aside for the moment the question of its coherence with transcendental inquiry, it is hard to see that the anthropological stance is even possible. When I take on the anthropological stance with respect to my cooking activities, I cannot genuinely be in the role of observer. The 'sideways-on perspective' is not a perspective, it is an imaginative fiction. The anthropological stance is confronted with a distinct transcendental condition of subjectivity: *I cannot stand in the relation of observer to myself.* And this condition has its dual in the first person plural: *we cannot stand as observers to ourselves.*

The anthropological stance would thus appear to be both necessary and impossible. In trying to grasp the content of an expression, we cast ourselves as anthropologists observing the context in which an expression is used. But on further reflection we discover that we could never be such anthropologists, nor could we genuinely take up such an observational stance. Does this imply that meaning is ineffable? Is it only God—who can look down from a completely detached vantage point and see the entire context of use—who is able to grasp the meaning of our meaningful activities? The answer to these questions is 'No'; but it is important to recognize the tacit presuppositions about meaning which might tempt us to answer affirmatively. If we think of ourselves along the lines of a Wittgensteinian tribe, we will implicitly assume that meaning is constituted by our *non*-self-conscious activities. As tribesmen, we grasp the meaning 'in a flash'—we require practical competence with an

[35] *PI* I.69, 208, 210.

expression, but we have little or no reflective understanding of the context in which our rule-following activities are set. It is only the observer, standing outside the practices, who will be able to survey the context and reflectively grasp the meaning of our activities. On this picture, there is a determinate meaning constituted by non-self-conscious activities and unaffected by self-conscious reflection, which is fully available only to a being who can fully survey the activities. Meaning is not like that. And neither are we. We are self-conscious, reflective beings, and the meaning of our activities does not determinately exist, waiting to be grasped by self-conscious reflection on the context of use: self-conscious reflection is partially constitutive of the context and thus of meaning. The context of an expression's use includes agents who are taking the anthropological stance with respect to that context, and the content of the expression is partially constituted by the self-conscious judgements of the self-appointed anthropologists as to what the expression means. Meaning is by its nature an unfinished business: it continues to be constituted by those self-conscious interpreters who seek to comprehend it by 'observing' the context in which it is used.

This would suggest that the anthropological stance is not what it pretends to be. It is not genuinely an observational stance, it is rather an artefact of philosophical inquiry: one in which we discover that nothing in an individual's consciousness could legitimate his rule-following activity and that one must 'look' to the community practices in which the activity is embedded. We take up the anthropological stance not when we actually go out and observe various tribes, but when, in philosophical reflection, we construct various tribal practices and imaginatively locate rule-following activity within them. Therefore, the answer to the question 'How is the anthropological stance possible?' also answers the question 'How do the anthropological and transcendental strains in Wittgenstein's thought cohere?'. For when we penetrate its deceptive self-presentation, we discover that the anthropological stance is not at war with transcendental inquiry, it is of a piece with it.

Wittgenstein made an analogy between philosophy and therapy, but he used the analogy to diminish both. Each is used to dissolve what turns out to be a pseudo-problem. I believe that there is a much richer use of the analogy. In psychotherapy the agent (it is misleading to call a person engaged in psychological exploration a 'patient') creates a representation of himself—his desires, beliefs, his anxieties and character—and of the context in which he is located—his parents' and friends' personalities, the environment of childhood, the institutions in which he now operates. The ultimate value of the therapeutic process, though, is not the creation of this artefact. Although the agent will become a better 'observer' of himself, the point of the therapy is not the observation of an accurately represented person, but non-observational insight into the person creating the representation.[36] And the creation of the artefact is partially constitutive of a change in the creator. It would be absurd to claim that psychotherapy should leave everything outside of the therapy as it is. Philosophers have often complained that psychoanalysis is not an empirical discipline, that it is not a 'science'. This seems to me a reason for hope, not disdain: for perhaps reflection on the therapeutic model will shed light on how to proceed philosophically in a way which is neither a methodology of the sciences nor a purely transcendental investigation.

If the analogy between psychotherapy and philosophy is to hold, then the anthropological stance must be seen as only a step along a philosophical dialectic that Wittgenstein did not complete: 'observing' the context in which rule-following activity is embedded will not yield the full meaning of that activity, nor is the anthropologist the philosopher's final role. Perhaps, though, Wittgenstein should have distinguished between the *We* and a *form of life* in much the same way that Kant should have distinguished the 'I:' from the 'I think'. 'Form of life' is a predicate which may be predicated of various objects. We may use the term narrowly and label disparate social groups alternative 'forms of life'; or we may use the term widely to mark the form of life which we all constitute. The problem is thus not that self-reference is impossible. We can refer to ourselves, though such self-reference is only one more act within the form of life. The problem is, rather, that what we are trying to gain insight into is not, strictly speaking, a form of life. The relation in which we stand to ourselves is similar to the relation in which I stand to myself. Just as when I try to become reflectively self-aware I end up with an 'I think' rather than an 'I:', it is characteristic of our position that when we try to become reflectively self-aware, we end up with a form of life. We should eventually come to appreciate that when we talk philosophically about 'our form of life' what we are trying to de-

---

[36] Here I am indebted to Richard Wollheim's fascinating discussion of psychotherapy in *The Thread of Life* (CUP, Cambridge, 1984).

scribe is not an object—and thus not a possible object of judgement. This, I believe, is the germination of the idea that the will is not a phenomenon. We are trying to gain non-observational insight into that which from a 'sideways-on' perspective is a form of life. The activity is manifested in all our rule-following activities, including all our judgements, but is not the object of any of them.

The anthropological and transcendental strains in Wittgenstein's thought are, then, coherent, but they do not form a coherent whole. The problem with Wittgenstein's later philosophy is not inconsistency but incompleteness. One unfinished task, I have argued, is to provide a critique of the anthropological stance: to expose its pretence of pure observer, to recognize that it is an artefact of philosophical inquiry, and to weave it into a richer conception of philosophical consciousness.

Let us speculatively consider one way to begin. The very idea of an explanation by reasons is intimately linked with the anthropological stance: such an explanation is that which the anthropological stance produces. In so far as the anthropological stance is unproblematically assumed, the notion of an explanation by reasons will seem inevitable and invulnerable; conversely, it is difficult to imagine how the anthropological stance could suffer a critique while the notion of explanation by reasons remained untouched. It has been plausibly argued that when we take the anthropological stance with respect to others, and try to construct an explanation of their actions on the basis of their beliefs and desires, we must, to a significant degree, assimilate them to ourselves.[37] That is, we attribute to them beliefs and desires we have, or, perhaps, beliefs and desires we think we would have if we were in their circumstances. Although our observation of others appears prima facie to be the purest case of observation, it turns out that the very possibility of making this observation depends on the possession of a vast amount of information which is not itself derived from the observation.

How is this information derived? How do we come to know what our own beliefs and desires are? I cannot now answer these questions in any detail, but it suffices for my present purposes to recognize that the answers are not straightforward. Our own beliefs and desires are not immediately transparent to consciousness, nor can we take a

---

[37] See Donald Davidson, *Inquiries into Truth and Interpretation* (Clarendon Press, Oxford, 1984), especially essays 9, 10, 13–16; *Essays on Actions and Events* (Clarendon Press, Oxford, 1980), especially essay 11.

purely observational stance with respect to ourselves. It seems that we must construct a representation of ourselves as against acting on beliefs and desires. In part this is done by reflecting on beliefs and desires which are relatively obvious to us; in part by imaginatively taking the anthropological stance with respect to ourselves. For example, when we construct an explanation by reasons of our measuring activities, it seems that we subject ourselves to our anthropological gaze. We see ourselves in our various measuring activities, and construct a teleological explanation of those activities in terms of our desires and beliefs.

This teleological conception is the *self as it appears to itself:* a representation we construct when we try to explain to ourselves who we are and what we are like. The *self as it is in itself* would be that which the representation is trying to represent: the human agent who embodies the beliefs and desires which the representation ascribes. Thus the self as it is in itself is not a Kantian noumenal agent, located outside space and time; it is an ordinary human being engaged in living his life. One of his projects may be the acquisition of self-understanding, and this will be pursued by the formulation of a conception of himself as an agent acting on beliefs and desires. Some people are more sensitive than others, and some self-conceptions will be more accurate than others. However, one outcome of the present inquiry is that every representation of the self, no matter how accurate, must fail to capture fully the self as it is in itself. That consciousness which must be able to accompany each of my representations cannot itself be adequately represented by any of them.

Switching to the first person plural, *form of life* is a reflective concept, used by philosophers and anthropologists when they try to construct a representation of us. It is We as We appear to ourselves. We take the anthropological stance and construct a conception of ourselves as acting in similar (ritualized) ways on the basis of shared interests, beliefs, and desires. But again some aspect of our subjectivity must be left out of this representation. Even if we represent ourselves as reflective thinkers trying to understand who we are, by the very nature of the anthropological stance we will end up with a form of life, not with what I have gestured at calling We. The Metaphysical Subject need not be conceived, as Kant thought, as lying outside the world, nor, as the early Wittgenstein thought, at its limit: it is we who live in the world. What we are confronted with is not the limit of the world, but the limit of the anthropological stance.

Now if it is We into whom we wish to gain insight, it would seem that we must do away with explanation. Perhaps, though, the injunction is too strong. We must do away with explanation in the sense that nothing that could be explained could possibly count as that into which we are trying to gain insight.

5. The central problem for post-Kantian philosophy has been to steer a course between the empirical and the transcendental. I am not in a position to state a general solution to the problem, but I would like to conclude this essay by giving one example which might show a middle course. In Wittgenstein's later philosophy the tension between the transcendental and the empirical manifests itself in the following dilemma. Who are we?[38] If, on the one hand, we are one group among others, then Wittgenstein's remarks about forms of life lacking justification would seem to encourage a slide toward relativism. If, on the other hand, the *We* encompasses us all, encompasses any being who might in the widest of senses count as one of us, then doesn't the first person plural lose its force? Are we not left with a bare Metaphysical Subject, that for which these truths are true? This is one instance of the more general dilemma: either contentful and (too) empirical (and probably false) or transcendental and vacuous. In this instance at least, I believe there is a middle course.

There are certain truths about us which, though they must be expressed anthropologically, are not confined to any particular form of life. Nor are they merely universal in the sense of occurring in all forms of life. Rather they try to express the conditions of being minded in any way at all. For example, the reflective philosophical claim that *what correct measurement is is itself dependent on our interests, desires, practices* is not supposed to be a local claim about what constitutes correct measurement around here. Nor is it a universal sociological claim about human groups. It is a philosophical claim about the constitutive conditions of a form of life.

Thus the motivation for radical relativism derives from evidence which, in fact, tilts in the opposite direction. The argument for relativism proceeds, roughly, as follows. First, through philosophical

---

[38] This dilemma is posed by Bernard Williams in 'Wittgenstein and Idealism', op. cit.

reflection one comes to see that the practice of measuring correctly is partially constituted by our interests, practices, customs, which are themselves contingent. That is, we move reflectively from:

This is correct measurement

to:

We are so minded as to believe: this is correct measurement.

Such insight does not undermine our measuring practices precisely because they are genuinely expressive of our interests, and these are not changed by reflection. Second, one *infers* that:

Were there an other-minded tribe, there would be no fact of the matter as to who was measuring correctly, we or they.

Third, one *infers* that this situation holds for all our beliefs and practices:

Were there an other-minded tribe—a group which did not share our beliefs, practices, interests—there would be no fact of the matter as to whether their beliefs or ours were true. All our true beliefs are really only true for us.

The relativist argues that we ought to infer, whenever we believe that *P*, that

Were there an other-minded tribe, it might be that not-*P* (for them).

That we cannot imagine what it would be like for it to be the case that not-*P*, the relativist contends, is no argument against the inference. It only shows that the belief that *P* is one of the beliefs to which we are very attached. To argue that there simply could not be a form of life, or a world, in which not-*P*, the relativist continues, is simply to assume a form of verificationism. We simply assume that for something to be a form of life, like-minded or other-minded, we must be able to recognize it as such, and anything we could recognize as a form of life would have to involve believing that *P*.

This argument for 'general relativity' is invalid, for both of the inferences are septic. As we have seen, we cannot conclude from the thought experiments that these other practices would be another form of correct measurement. So the first inference, to the relativity of incommensurable systems, is invalid. And the second inference, to general relativity, is also invalid. For although we can posit a tribe with practices which fill a roughly analogous role to our practices of measuring, this is because there is conceptual space for a tribe which manages with rough measurements. There is no space for tribes with alternatives to all our beliefs and practices.

One way to see this is to apply the relativist's argument to a reflective, philosophical belief. For example, the relativist wants to affirm that:

Were there an other-minded tribe, it might be that some other practice would be correct measurement (for them).

Since we are convinced of that, we may add the prefix 'We are so minded as to believe':

We are so minded as to believe: were there an other-minded tribe, it might be that some other practice would be correct measurement (for them).

Of course, this sentence is of the form 'We are so minded as to believe: P'. So if the relativist's argument were valid, one ought to be able to infer the relevant instance of 'Were there an other-minded tribe, then it might be that not-P (for them)':

Were there an other-minded tribe, it might not be the case (for them) that: were there an other-minded tribe, it might be that some other practice would be correct measurement (for them).

But the relativist cannot afford to allow this conclusion in any sense in which it would undermine the following:

Were there an other-minded tribe, it would (even so) *be the case* that: were there an other-minded tribe, it might be that some other practice would be correct measurement (for them).

(Here what follows the colon says how in the envisaged circumstances, at least according to the relativist, things would be *for us*, minded as we now are.) Variations of this argument are about as old as philosophy itself. If relativism is not to be self-refuting, the philosophical belief that our beliefs are relative must itself stand outside its own compass.

That the relativist's argument fails might at first suggest that the *We* shrinks to a bare formal subject. Eventually we reach truths that express basic conditions of being minded, and the *We* is just the subject for whom these truths are true. To show that this suggestion ought to be resisted, let us consider the most challenging case: basic logical laws.

That there must be agreement in judgements, says Wittgenstein, 'seems to abolish logic, but does not do so'.[39] Logic seems to be abolished because various pictures we have of logic do get abolished. First, there is the picture of logical laws guiding or determining the behaviour of the man making logical inferences: we see him 'operating a calculus according to definite rules'.[40] But if rule-following is unconditioned, this picture is transcendental illusion. The situation is in fact almost the reverse: the meaning of any abstract formulation of the law of non-contradiction—say, '*Not: P and not-P*'—depends in part on the fact that in actual cases we generally regard sufficient evidence that not-*P* to be grounds for withdrawing our assertion that *P*. Second, there is the picture of logic as providing the metaphysical structure of the world.[41] Man's desire to know the basis of everything empirical is, Kant argued, what leads him to metaphysics. And it is this very desire, according to Wittgenstein, which lends significance to logic: which inclines us to regard it as sublime.[42] The laws of logic do not delineate the metaphysical structure of the world; they tell one how one ought to behave in arguing, in setting out deductions, in asserting.[43]

Logic, however, is not abolished. Logic itself is the outcome of reflection on our practices of arguing rigorously, of asserting and denying. Philosophy's task, as Wittgenstein sees it, is to remind us of that fact. Logic does not point to a transcendent truth beyond the practices; it is a normative codification we have made of the practices themselves. That insight, however, does not disturb the reflective equilibrium of the codification itself.

One might say: the axis of reference of our examination must be rotated, but about the fixed point of our real need.[44]

Our real need is, I believe, the need to say something: to act within a shared form of life. Of course it is contingent that we are beings who

---

[39] *PI* I.242.
[40] Ibid. I.81.
[41] Ibid. I.89.
[42] Ibid. I.94, 89.
[43] Cf. ibid I.81, *RFM* V.40, 48.
[44] *PI* I.108.

have this need. But given that we are such beings, it is not contingent that we have this need. We are beings partially constituted by this need: without it we cease to be who we are to such an extent that it seems fair to say simply that we cease to be. The correct conclusion to draw then is not

If we were other-minded, we would not have this need

but

Having this need is a condition of our being minded at all.

The basic laws of logic are abstract formulations of how one should act to meet this need. There is nothing local about this need: logic provides an abstract formulation of rules which must generally be obeyed in actual cases if our activity is to be an expression of mindedness. We can continue to say 'our mindedness' if we want, but we ought to understand that we are not thereby restricting the claim. This is not verificationism, for no claim is being made that we (humans) must in principle be able to recognize every form of life. Perhaps there are Martians who speak a language in principle inaccessible to humans. The point is that if they are speaking a language, living a form of life, they too will be generally obeying the law of non-contradiction. We (humans) may not be able to recognize all of us, but in this broad context being minded in any way at all makes you one of us. So when, in philosophical reflection, we prefix 'We are so minded as to believe:' to the law of non-contradiction, that cannot legitimately be the first stage of an argument which restricts its validity to one tribe among others.

Has the *We* collapsed to a bare formal condition of thought? The outline of a Wittgensteinian answer should now be clear. The question looks as though it requires a positive answer if we conceive of logic as presenting the 'laws of thought). The *We* then collapses into the mere subject which obeys those laws. But this conception itself collapses when we recognize that the 'laws of thought' themselves have no content in abstraction from the myriad activities in which we engage. A rule depends for its content on what counts as obeying it and going against it in actual cases. Far from the *We* disappearing, it is only by keeping the *We* vivid that we can ensure any content for the laws of thought.

One should not, therefore, even for logic, adopt a redundancy theory of the 'We are so minded as to believe:'. Studying logic, we

come to assert the law of non-contradiction. In philosophical reflection, we prefix 'We are so minded as to believe:'. Yet even though we
recognize that in this context there is no possibility of being other-
minded, such an exercise does not simply lead us back to where we
started. First, as we have seen, certain pictures of logic to which we
are naturally inclined are dismissed as illusion. Second, a transcendental consideration of our subjectivity need not be totally removed
from empirical experience: it may enhance what we can learn from
it. There are, as I have said, two distinct forms of reflection on our
ordinary rule-following activities. We may reflect on the consciousness which may accompany our activities—and thus discover what is
really happening when we want to say we 'experience the because'—
or we may take the anthropological stance. Both of these reflective
stances are informed by the insight that the law of non-contradiction
is true. The first person, either singular or plural, which can accompany our activities is not a bare Metaphysical Subject, a limit of the
world.[45] It is we in our ordinary lives who can accompany our
activi-
ties with consciousness. It is only in these activities that the law of
non-contradiction has any life, so, reflecting on the consciousness
which can accompany them, we gain insight into what the law of
non-contradiction asserts. However, the law of non-contradiction is
also a statement, one more move in the language-game. And since it
makes a general claim about our statement-making activities, we
must also take up the anthropological stance both with respect to
these activities and with respect to the law itself, if we are to have a
reflective understanding of its content. Here it seems to me there is
room for a transcendental anthropology: a reflection on our ordinary activities that yields non-empirical insight into them.

---

[45] Cf. Manley Thompson, 'On A Priori Truth', *Journal of Philosophy*, lxxviii
(1981).

INDEX OF NAMES*

* The editors are grateful for the assistance of Christie Slade, and also Jean
Norman, in preparing this index.